WE ARE HERE

WE ARE HERE

Politics of Aboriginal Land Tenure

Edited by
EDWIN N. WILMSEN

UNIVERSITY OF CALIFORNIA PRESS
Berkeley   Los Angeles   London

University of California Press
Berkeley and Los Angeles, California

University of California Press, Ltd.
London, England

Copyright © 1989 by The Regents of the University of California

LIBRARY OF CONGRESS
Library of Congress Cataloging-in-Publication Data

We are here: politics of aboriginal land tenure/edited by Edwin N. Wilmsen.
    p.   cm.
  Bibliography: p.
  Includes index.
  ISBN 0–520–06300–7
  1. Native races.   2. Land tenure.   3. Land tenure (Primitive law)
I. Wilmsen, Edwin N.
GN449.3.W4   1989
333.3′089011—dc19   88–17500   CIP

Printed in the United States of America

1 2 3 4 5 6 7 8 9

Contents

Preface

The adjective 'aboriginal' that appears in the title of this volume and in the essays within is used in its original meaning as found in the *Oxford English Dictionary* (*OED*): "1. First or earliest as far as history or science gives record . . . 3B. An original inhabitant of any land, now usually as distinguished from subsequent European colonists." This word is enshrined as a proper noun, Aborigine, applied to the indigenous peoples of Australia; as a result, it has come to be identified restrictively by the public, as well as by anthropologists, with those peoples and that continent. But, as the OED indicates, the term has a far wider reference. Indeed, that wider reference has a venerable philosophical and legal history in Europe. Furthermore, certain terms that are indigenous to regions examined in this book and that have become entrenched in anthropological literature have a similar fundamental meaning. *San* is derived from the Nama root 'sa'; the various Sotho-Tswana/Nguni forms of Basarwa, applied to "Bushmen," share the Proto-Bantu root '*-rwa'. Both roots have as one of their glosses "aboriginal, those who came before." We use 'aboriginal' in this wider sense.

That the peoples to whom we apply this term were, or were called, foragers (hunter-gatherers) when first encountered by Europeans (who most often thought of and referred to them as savages) is no accident. Peoples who foraged for all or a substantial part of their livelihood were conceived to be the dregs of humankind in the Age of Expansion and its colonial consolidation. Subsequently, after a period of agreement with this assessment, anthropologists found them to be not the dregs but the distillation of human essence. In both metaphors, however, they are sediment—at the bottom of the barrel. (One never hears of Japanese (who have their own, Ainu, aborigines) or Aztec or Ashanti aboriginals, although they, too, were first and earliest in their lands as far as history and science gave record at the time Europeans arrived.) Such an assessment of forager status—whether as dreg or distillate—has nothing to do, philosophically, with ways of making a living but is a categorization of peoples thought of as being in a different state of nature. This has had profound repercussions for the way in which the thus stigmatized peoples were integrated—rather, dis-integrated—into colonial enclaves and, later, their nation-state successors. Those repercussions and current efforts to rectify them are the subject of this book.

Claims by aboriginal peoples to land and its products in former colonies that are now developed industrial nations governed by peoples of predominantly European origin (e.g., Australia and Canada) are, of necessity, argued in terms of legal systems introduced by Europeans and subsequently institutionalized in those nations. In such claims, evidence from the recent prehistory of these aboriginal peoples, and from the history of their colonial encounters, may be admissible as evidence but not as structural components of arguments for inherent aboriginal land rights. Until very recently in these cases, aboriginal property relations and their adjudication in precolonial—as well as in colonial and even current—times were of only secondary consequence at best. It is this fact, perhaps, that has conditioned many anthropologists from Western countries to view aboriginal relations to land in normative, rule-centered, functionally specific terms analogous to those of European-American law.

As long ago as 1957, Bohannan argued that it is inappropriate to transfer in this manner conceptual and institutional categories of Western law to non-Western societies (he was speaking specifically of West African agricultural societies; see also Bohannan 1965). In that same year, V. Turner (1957), following on Colson's (1953) earlier study, demonstrated that in at least some African societies cooperation in and competition for such assets as land are constrained by a prevailing structure of relations that can be understood only in the context of extended social processes. Gluckman, beginning in 1955, elaborated these insights.

Moreover, in former colonies, like Botswana, that are populated and governed by predominantly indigenous peoples, native institutions continue to provide—as they did in the colonial and precolonial past—the first avenue of redress, as well as the lower levels of appeal, for all common law, most civil law, and some criminal law cases. Traditional Tswana courts (*dikgotla*), presided over by a hierarchy of chiefs, local chiefs, and headmen (*dikgosi*, *dikgosana*, and *basimane*), hear disputes not only of Tswana litigants but also those of all subordinate groups within the country, including aboriginal San-speaking peoples who are belatedly gaining access to them. Only at the higher levels of state jurisdiction does introduced European law come into prominence. Land, and rights to its use, is allocated at one of these higher levels—through land boards operating under the aegis of the Ministry of Local Government and Lands. Again, only very recently have aboriginal institutions of tenure begun to be accepted as legitimate elements in the allocation process.

It thus becomes crucial to understand aboriginal relations to land, not only as coherent systems in themselves but also as legitimate vehicles for assertions by aboriginal peoples that they retain—or, as in most cases, ought to regain—undiminished rights in their native lands. The forms these assertions take and the legal processes by which they may be realized as actualities in the face of counterclaims are determined by the specific nature of each aboriginal and national system, by the history of their intersection, and by the current state of public opinion in the nation-state in which the aboriginal society is now situated.

With increasing frequency, anthropologists have played active roles in each of these facets of aboriginal land adjudications. The contributors to this volume address these roles critically, with an awareness of the uncertainties inherent in each. Running through the chapters— each with its separate focus—is a common theme, the commensurability of tenurality (as distinct from specific tenure systems) in what have heretofore been seen as separated stages of social development and complexity. The importance of this understanding to current and future negotiations of aboriginal land claims can hardly be exaggerated. Those peoples who have been classified as aboriginal, as foragers, face an obstacle uniquely applied to that classificatory status— the claim that they, alone among the peoples of the earth, have no institutions of tenure in land.

Other peoples, those who practice some form of domestic husbandry, even if they are still sometimes referred to as "primitive," are at least recognized as having some inherent form of land tenure that must be reckoned with in some fashion, both in academic and administrative arenas. There is a substantial literature on the tenure systems of these peoples and the rights to claims adhering in those systems. True enough, that literature contains innumerable instances of the dispossession of colonized agricultural peoples (pastoral peoples are often lumped with foragers in this regard), even from kingdoms and empires; one need not search far to find arguments by Europeans to the effect that some flaw rendered invalid and void the native tenure institutions of those who have been dispossessed. But these arguments centered on the *validity* of institutions, not on their existence, and in postcolonial times, agricultural peoples have generally had to argue for redress not in terms of law (i.e., whether they have legitimate tenurial relations) but in terms of fact (i.e., the force of their claim to a particular tract of land).

Aboriginal peoples, those who were formerly foragers, before they could proceed to terms of fact, have had to establish that their institutions of tenure were, in law, commensurate with other systems. The essays presented here illuminate that commensurability. Myers (chap. 2) unfolds the internal logic of Pintupi relations to property and land and describes how individuals assert and realize claims on each other. Similarly, Wilmsen (chap. 3) presents the internal logic of Zhu relations to land and shows how it is extended to encompass recognition of and by other systems indigenous to southern Africa. Feit and Hiatt (chaps. 4 and 5) document processes by which such recognition has been projected by Cree and Aboriginal peoples into the compass of English Common Law as interpreted in Canada and Australia. Asch (chap. 6) discusses proposals by the Dene to expand the scope of this projection to embrace a notion of local sovereignty within the Canadian state, a process requiring modifications in both systems while retaining crucial elements of each. Gordon (chap. 7) traces the sources in international law that are still called on in Namibia to withhold any recognition of rights in tenure from San-speaking peoples and demonstrates that this is a regression from earlier German recognition of San sovereignty over their land. Maddock (chap. 8) assesses the roles assumed by Australian anthropologists in helping to establish commensurability of Aboriginal tenure systems and finds them to be generally laudable at the same time that individual involvement in particular interpretations is often problematic; his conclusions can be extended to all similar situations in which anthropologists may find themselves and, in a sense, may be seen as a reflection on the offerings in this book.

A subsidiary theme runs through these essays. This theme posits that the operational dichotomy perceived to exist between forager and husbandman relations to land lies in European intellectual history in conjunction with the colonial experience as interpreted through that intellectual lens. That is, the dichotomy was constructed in European minds to serve European needs. To the extent that professional and public, anthropological and administrative, perception has been al-

tered—perhaps enlightened—by the activities and actions of anthropologists as recorded here, to that extent we have all gained in our
ability to recognize inherent integrity in diverse attempts to come to
terms with the conditions of social life.

This is not to claim that all such attempts are viable under continually transformed or radically altered political circumstances. Clearly,
aboriginal forms of tenure cannot, and do not, function in modern
nation-states as they did in the precolonial past. And national-state
forms have had to bend to accommodate awakened aboriginal demands. This raises the final theme addressed here: questioning of the
ultimate ability of current institutions in liberal-democratic states to
address adequately issues of equitable rights to land. Read in this
way, these essays as a unit constitute a critique of the idea of "rights
to land" as interpreted in capitalist terms.

The genesis of this volume was a symposium I organized for the
Third International Conference on Hunting-Gathering Societies held
at Bad Holmburg, Federal Republic of Germany, in 1983. The theme
of the conference was the sociology of land use among hunter-gatherers. Papers bearing family resemblances to, but of different content
from, those included here were presented by Asch, Hiatt, and Wilmsen. The three of us wish to express our appreciation to the Werner
Reimers Stiftung for their gracious, salubrious, and most attentive
hospitality during the conference. I wish to extend my grateful thanks
to Prof. Dr. Irenäus Eibl-Eibesfeldt for his organization of the conference and his untiring efforts to ensure its success, for his encouragement to pursue its results despite doubts about some of the directions
in which I have taken the issues, and for his continued friendship.
Polly Wiessner and Carmel Schrire assisted in organizing the conference and the symposia held in conjunction with it; without their skill
and spirit neither the sessions nor this book would have materialized.
Support for the conference was also provided by the Fritz Thyssen
Stiftung, the Max-Planck-Institut für Verhaltensphysiologie, and the
Maison de l'Homme.

My editorial task was lightened immeasurably by staff members of
the African Studies Center at Boston University who transformed the
contributions, most of which were submitted as typescripts in various
idiosyncratic styles, into word-processed documents of uniform for-
mat. All of the authors, accordingly, owe a debt to Joanne Hart, Jenny
Hochstadt, and Sonia Watterson as well as to the Center, which assumed the costs of this endeavor. Finally, I wish to express my thanks
to Sara Berry, John Comaroff, Karen Harbeck, Allen Hoben, Paul
Mattick, Jr., Pnina Motzafi-Haller, Johanna Schoss, and Eric Wolf, who

read different parts of the manuscript and offered critical advice on its construction, and to two anonymous readers, whose comments pointed me toward improving its presentation.

1
Introduction

Edwin N. Wilmsen

The notion of legitimate tenure rights in land for peoples once classified as hunter-gatherers or foragers has only recently gained legal
status, with severe restrictions and in a few countries only. In 1977,
the Aboriginal Land Rights (Northern Territory) Act, the first of its
kind anywhere, became law in Australia. In Canada, the Constitution
Act of 1982 for the first time "recognized and affirmed" the rights of
aboriginal peoples, thereby opening the possibility of significant land
adjudication in that country.

Hiatt reminds us, however, that just six years before the signing of
the Northern Territory Act, a group of native Australians in that very
same administrative district lost a challenge to the government's right
to dispose of their land at will. The court's ruling that "Aborigines
have no legal tenure of tribal lands" merely reiterated a view that had
prevailed since the settling of the continent by Europeans some 200
years earlier. Asch cites legal opinion as late as 1971 that Canadian
"aboriginal peoples had no aboriginal rights in law." And Feit emphasizes that although three years later the Cree gained extensive
usufruct and bargaining rights over a significant part of northern
Quebec, the provincial and federal governments retained ultimate
rights of disposition to all but a small reserved fraction of that land.
In Botswana, in that same decade, San-speaking peoples were found
by government council to have no rights in land other than to hunt
on certain portions of it.

The doctrine on which those earlier opinions were based is identified by Gordon and Hiatt as that of *territorium nullius*, empty land, which asserts that lands occupied by foraging peoples at the time of settlement by Europeans became the sole property of the "original [European] discoverers" because such native peoples were deemed to be even more primitive than others encountered in European expansion. Those foraging peoples were perceived to have had few institutions of civilized society. Furthermore, they were considered to be rootless wanderers without any ideas of ownership of fixed property. This doctrine is, of course, a subspecies of ideologies of racial differentiation. Without putting too fine a point to the question of whether such a doctrine is *necessarily* "racist," it is explicitly so in Namibia, as Gordon documents, where it continues to shape official attitudes toward San peoples and is applied in tandem with the overarching policy of apartheid to effect a sham recognition of land rights (in the form of a putative "homeland") for them.

Echoes of this doctrine are also still heard in Botswana despite constitutional guarantees of social justice for all citizens, regardless of ethnic background. In a government-commissioned evaluation of programs directed toward its peoples saddled with the label "forager" (and enshrined in the literature as San), Egner (1981:1) observed that

policy [of government toward "backward elements of the population"] has remained unchanged for almost a century. . . . The main similarity is that the independent government has since 1966 been as cautious as its colonial predecessor about the need to confront certain widespread customary attitudes which tend to perpetuate the impoverishment and dependence of the "backward elements," now known as remote area dwellers or RADs.

These "backward elements" are San-speaking peoples (the "Bushmen" of earlier literature, now called Basarwa in Botswana). They are said to be backward principally because it is claimed that they, too, have no fixed relationship to land. It should not be overlooked that this stance is taken here by an African ruling group, one that entered what is now Botswana only two and one-half centuries ago; Europeans have no monopoly on dispossessing aboriginal peoples. As Hitchcock (1982) makes clear, this is a convenient ideological stance in Botswana at this time when substantial portions of tribal communal land are being converted to de facto private commercial ranches, and there is no need to compensate for their removal from the land people who have no inherent rights in it. There is, in fact, no need to consult them about their removal.

On every continent where Europeans encountered peoples whose economies were perceived to be exclusively—or even substantially—

based on foraging, the same rationale was invoked to disenfranchise their land. Overlooked was the fact that all such peoples were actively engaged politically with a host of others through complex social and material exchange networks. It is at least arguable that this alienating doctrine has been nurtured in this century by an unwitting anthropological naïveté. For ethnographies, as traditionally written, construct alien cultures; they do not merely report on them. They cannot help but do so. It is the role assigned to them by a Western world that not too long ago, after discovering the far corners of the earth, set out to explore "the varieties of human experience." Many jewels have been unearthed in the search and displayed, often in settings of fine reporting. We are incomparably richer for this. The genuine advances Euroamerica has made in its evaluation of other peoples—however these advances may be debased, or even apparently lost, at times—have been fused by painstaking anthropological documentation of intrinsic value, inherent integrity, in other cultures. To exhibit the full scope of this integrity, anthropologists have polished the more esoteric facets of their finds. In reading ethnographies, varieties become exotics in the mind. As Gordon points out, citing the unprecedented worldwide box office appeal of the film *The Gods Must Be Crazy*, there are few more exotic peoples in this literature, and in the popular imagination, than those called foragers.

I (1983, n.d.) have argued that a long-standing overemphasis on ecological considerations coupled with a revived concern to clarify understanding of human evolution has had the effect of projecting a form of prehistoric primitiveness onto present peoples who were classified as foragers. As Hiatt (1984:22) has remarked, this approach undoubtedly has some value, but to realize that value, it is essential to address adequately the social dimensions of relations among the peoples it so classifies. Without these dimensions, the appropriation of current states of anthropological knowledge by those empowered to legislate and administer the disposition of a state's limited resources, such as land, requires no imagination on their part.

Let me emphasize that this is not a problem of the study of evolution or ecology but of the anthropological appropriation of these fundamental processes of life to one's own use. Ecological and evolutionary studies of social formations are valuable in themselves, but their integrity is subverted when they are extrapolated uncritically onto some projected past made present. Ecological studies are essential for specifying the nature and limits of natural forces of production with which members of social formations must contend. But neither an applied science nor even an advanced theory of ecology—in itself—can provide the theoretical framework needed to analyze the articulation and transformation of social systems. Godelier (1977:124) states the matter succinctly when he says that Marx was right "to declare that man's problem was not in his original unity with his conditions of production, but [in] his separation from them." In contrast to those applied to food-producing societies (a distinction that, itself, needs to be more carefully examined), anthropological models of "foragers" derived from ecological—and structural-functional—precepts alone are united in equating economic constraints on foraging production with the purely technical constraints of resource exploitation (see Asad 1978:58). The resultant simplification of production relations has nurtured a parallel simplification of social relations. Feit's contribution to this volume is a powerful illustration of this point.

Evidence that anthropological formulations are both sought and used in legislative and juridical processes is not hard to find; all the authors here mention such involvement or its prospects. Hiatt (1984:2) notes that the definition of "Aboriginal owner of land" in the Northern Territory Act was drafted after consultation of anthropological writings and advice; the definition adopted was strongly shaped by Radcliffe-Brown's structural-functional model. In fact, Maddock reveals the opinion of some observers that anthropological input into the Act far outweighs that of Aborigines. Elsewhere, Myers (1986*a*) underscores the reciprocal dialectic that has ensued. He notes that that input has itself been drawn into the inherently political process of traditional landownership: "What we as anthropologists write on paper, for example, becomes itself a ground for people's claims [on] each other." These anthropological interventions were what we would call benign; they were intended to further the cause of the peoples on whose behalf they were made.

In the course of events, clarification of the anthropological model, and legal process based on it, became necessary. Hiatt (1984:2) has noted that questions about the model's adequacy and its interpretation have engendered the liveliest debates among Australian academics. This debate has engaged popular attention on an unusually sophisticated level, as Peter Wier's critically acclaimed film *The Last Wave* attests; this is not unimportant, for public support is central to the fact that the debate took place at all.

We are at a time of reassessment. It is essential now to establish both that institutions of tenure exist among peoples called foragers as among any other kind of society and that these institutions have historic continuity and stability. On this basis, indigenous legal precedent for land rights claims by these peoples can be, and has been, offered. Paradoxically, efforts, developed largely in land claims cases, to articulate surviving forager societies equitably within modern states have pointed to the most rewarding direction in which to pursue analyses of these peoples' tenure systems. The roles of anthropologists in this process of correction—in both academic and constitutional contexts—have often been problematic and must, themselves, be examined not only on theoretic grounds but also in terms of practical applications. Fears over the loss of academic neutrality are misplaced; anthropological orthodoxy has in the past had its own, often hidden, share of ideological and pragmatic agendas. It is not value-free neutrality that we should seek but critical clarity in ascertaining where our values lie. The chapters in this book, separately and as a unit, explore some of the avenues leading to these ends.

In his contribution, Hiatt relates how he lost confidence in the structural-functional model because it distracted attention from regional variations and obscured the central role of social context in Aboriginal formulations of human relationships to land. His has been a leading voice in stressing the dialectic character of these relationships over the static idealizations of the orthodox model. At the same time, the Aboriginal Land Commissioner began to distance himself from the anthropological orthodoxy enshrined in the Act. He did so under the pressure of ironic decisions this orthodoxy forced on him in which claimants were denied rights in certain litigations, not because they failed to demonstrate a proper relationship to a particular portion of land but because their claim did not conform to the anthropological model. The course of this debate illustrates once more Friedman's (1977) thesis that the relationship between law and society is a dynamic dialectic; society itself is the prime mover of legal change, and law, in turn, continuously modifies social behavior. As Howard (1982:8) has remarked, there was a certain naïveté about the assumption that Aborigines needed to be integrated into Australian society, for it presupposed that they were not already part of it. Maddock evaluates the substantial role played by a large number of anthropologists in the achievement of this realization.

The use of anthropological work by lawmakers is neither always so amiable nor made with the participation of its authors. Hitchcock (1982:24) reports that, in Botswana, many government officials use their well-grounded knowledge of assertions by anthropologists that San-speaking peoples have no territorial affiliations to further their own interests in legislation. He records that he was challenged in a ministerial meeting by the then Commissioner of Lands, who cited anthropological opinion that "Bushmen have no territories" and demanded, "Why, then, are you trying to tell me that they do?" Hitchcock, himself, after a yearlong survey of a large area slated for commercialization of land, recommended the creation of "service centers" for San peoples amidst the privatized ranches—in essence, mini-reserves. This, despite his finding that the overwhelming majority of San people he interviewed opposed such a development and wanted instead a fair share in the development process (Hitchcock 1978). He did so in the knowledge that any more equitable proposal would receive no hearing. Parson (1981:252), in a sympathetic analysis of the situation makes this assessment: "It is a comment on the strength of the movement toward dispossession that this solution had the effect of an assisted proletarianization [of San] rather than an argument for the retention of the means of production already held [by these people]."

Because of these, and numerous similar experiences, it has become increasingly apparent that the study of foragers is a political matter. Indeed, it is inescapably clear that it always has been. There are two equally important ways in which this is so. From an external perspective, Western anthropology has created those societies labeled forager as scientifically sanctioned survivors of an evolutionary past, that is, *our* European past, or, as Asch alludes, at least a past rooted in Euroamerican conceptions about the passage of events. Anthropology has thereby aided the overarching colonial process in appropriating these societies to our own histories and our own intellectual and mythological use. In Wolf's (1982:3) apt phrase, these peoples have been left without history; the world of humankind has been disassembled and not put back together, falsifying reality. A corollary, putatively native view of the process has also been constructed, again drawn from a Euroamerican image. This view posits the supposed survival from a prior past as being the result of forager choice to remain detached from a larger, more complex world, protected behind their uncomplicated conceptions of natural, apolitical human relations. Left out is what foragers themselves think of the matter and what history tells of it.

This political grounding of forager studies has been successively— and successfully—disguised in a number of abstract models: evolutionary, ecological, and structural. All of these models assume a European understanding of group membership and claims to such things as land and the rights to its use. The merits of this perspective in the comparative study of adjudication systems is examined by several authors in this volume who find that the degree of required conceptual rigor has seldom been achieved (see also MacCormack [1983] for a discussion of this point). More fundamentally, these models are simply distractions when, as too often happens, they are encased as metaphors rather than elements in a comprehensive program for investigating social relations of production and the reproduction of social forms. What is essential is just this: the contemporary existence of foragers is due to the playing out of historical processes that has assigned dominance to some groups and subordination to others.

But foragers continue to be set in a world apart in our ideology, shielded from such processes as if time and our world had passed them by. A distortion has entered into our thinking—anthropological, administrative, and popular—about foragers, who are conceived as living closer to nature than do other societies; a corollary notion is that in keeping with their supposed simple form of social relations, they have only rudimentary forms of politics and rules of possession. Such thinking is as characteristic of those who purport to work with a forager mode of production in the Marxian sense as it is of those who espouse strictly structural-functional frameworks.

It is no distortion to claim that in all of these studies, phenomena such as kinship, land tenure, rules of possession, and so on, are analyzed as functional necessities in relation to the level of productive forces. Foragers are assigned the lowest level of development of these forces; as a consequence, they are conceived to have limited concepts of corporate tenure and political action. On these grounds, they have been denied a voice in contemporary jural proceedings to reallocate land rights in modern nation-states.

Historical reality is, however, radically different. Foragers were absorbed as outcasts in colonial social formations and cast aside as unneeded when the means to produce European bourgeois demands from their lands was appropriated by Europeans themselves. A process was set in motion which compressed native peoples into ever-smaller parcels of space, a process that made foragers marginal, not aboriginal. Their aboriginality stems from their prior existence and rights of possession in lands from which they were alienated, not from their modes of subsistence. A sharp change of focus is essential. We need to examine the relations of community within these subordinated groups and their relations to the larger civic arena in which they interact with dominant powers to establish the configuration of political functions within these groups and their cultural expressions. We must reincorporate political and social history into our narratives of these peoples if anthropology is to contribute to a better understanding of the nature of social divisions. Asch, Feit, Maddock, and I introduce a corrective balance into the discussion by emphasizing that forager systems of land tenure are not entirely distinctive but have substantial areas of congruence with other systems. As Asch remarks, "Aboriginal peoples see themselves as part of the same world as others . . . a viewpoint that does not receive enough comment in our discipline or currency in our ethics."

That there is an ethical as well as a theoretical imperative to this investigation can no longer be doubted. Anthropological studies that have given undue emphasis to supposedly isolated, nomadic, impermanent relations of persons to land among foragers have too often been used out of context by governments and business agents as legal buttresses for disenfranchising foragers further, both from their lands and from a share of the profits from capital development of those lands. Speaking in the Botswana context, Egner (1981:12) observes:

It becomes easy in the absence of detailed research findings or the mediating influence of [outside advocates] for politicians, planners, and implementors of projects to rig the agenda and exclude the real needs of the Basarwa [San-speaking peoples] from the planning process. The exclusion takes place because of the nature of the lifestyle *which has been imposed* upon the Basarwa by other ethnic groups. [emphasis added]

All authors in this volume address these issues. Their contributions fall naturally into four interrelated sets. Myers and I concentrate on indigenous, contextual modes of possession. Both, but Myers especially, stress individual autonomy in orchestrating personal interests in the formation of local group tenures. I emphasize historically mediated continuities and congruences among several southern African systems. Feit and Hiatt dissect the problems of translation and praxis in the interface between indigenous practice and English case law. Gordon and Asch address the increasingly discussed issue of an integration of native and national systems; Gordon in the context of Namibia struggling to attain national identity, Asch within the framework of Canadian liberal-democratic values. Maddock, though evaluating the course of a particular set of events, articulates the questions of professional and personal ethics surrounding an awareness of the ideological grounding of all anthropological engagement. As a whole, this volume presents a powerful illumination of the fact that false disarticulations of ethnographic endeavor lead to false disassembly of the human world.

A recurrent theme here is the question of translatability. Myers raises the issue immediately by expressing his "discomfort with the notion of property as being too concrete and specific" to encompass Aboriginal meanings. This is a long-standing concern; Bohannan,

Turner, and Gluckman voiced it for anthropology more than a quarter-century ago. But Gordon documents a far longer legacy in juridical law by tracing it to the American Supreme Court justice, John Marshall, who noted in 1832 that Euroamericans applied their own terminology, not only to Indians but "to all others," to subvert native sovereignty to themselves.

The problem has not yet been satisfactorily resolved. MacCormack (1983), a jurist, stresses that it is necessary particularly to investigate the native conditions of use of terms, for example, whether some are confined in application to land or have a wider domain. Roberts (1979), another jurist with considerable anthropological experience, cautions that the presentation of indigenous concepts in the form of legal rules organized in Western categories encourages the use of such distorted rules in artificial ways that will damage native intents and interests. These cautions are among the basic assumptions of this collection, which points to avenues of advancement in our ability to deal with them.

Asch and Maddock make convincing cases for the proposition that although specific native *terms* may "encapsulate a bundle of notions that are not readily transferable from a native language," nonetheless, native *"ideas* relate to the underlying concept of political polity" in democratic states, and their *relations to land* have "significant features in common with property rights as known in English and other major legal systems." They, along with Feit and Hiatt, specifically, and the other authors generally, argue that the talents and techniques of anthropology are essential to bring these areas of congruence successfully to the surface.

In my contribution, I insist that one necessary step in this direction is to remove our study of land distribution from "the arena of means to overcome necessity" (where it is located by both structural-functionalism and evolutionary ecology) and to situate it "in the cultural definition of how these means are to be pursued." It is here that criteria for admitting persons into production relations and for identifying those persons are specified. Similarly, Myers stresses that landownership is "not a special set of rights defining relationships to ecologically necessary 'living space' " but is "one more form of objectifying social relationships of shared identity." Tenure, therefore, should be seen as a complex of interacting concepts about land, property, resources, rights of access, and inheritance; it includes the processes by which individuals and groups obtain and defend their interests in these, as Hoben (1986) reminds us.

It is apparent, then, that land tenure relations for aboriginal peoples were neither merely "superstructure" nor "base" but entered directly into and structured relations of production. Asch quotes Dene and Metis leaders who enumerate collective ownership of land, language, customs, and resource management as essential elements, but "certainly not all," that is entailed in their conception of aboriginal title. That is, that which is most central in their minds pertains to political jurisdiction that includes a land base.

What is at issue here is a social geography relating persons to place. The ways in which membership in such political jurisdictions is acquired by individuals has become clearer during the last decade. Both Hiatt and I conclude that the mechanisms of inheritance and exercise of tenure result in ambilineal, rather than patrilineal, descent that provides a structure within which individuals create and manage their own effective social networks. It is this dialectic of structure and practice that regulates ownership. Myers illustrates in compelling fashion that Pintupi landownership is best understood as the negotiated outcome of individual claims and assertions. Common to all the systems examined in this collection is the theme that land and places are inalienable—in Aboriginal terms, these can be "given away" without being lost; among San-speakers, they can be shared without being relinquished. Individual responsibility to the group, however, is secured by the requirement that tenure rights must be exercised to be retained. Hiatt underscores the critical importance of these rights by emphasizing that "they constitute a set of credentials probably of the same order of usefulness to the individual as his tool kit."

At this point, another central question intrudes: of what use are such credentials in contemporary national states? There are those who argue that "traditional" social relations and cultural conventions, no matter how distorted in the colonial era and its aftermath, provide a sort of sleeping bag to insulate the continually dispossessed from their predicament. This is a passive stance that tacitly accepts both the structure of the status quo *and* its structural inevitability.

Clearly, neither the authors of this volume nor the native peoples whose aspirations they document find that to be a desirable or adequate assessment of possibilities. The position advocated here is that tradition forms only a part, albeit an essential part, of the basis for negotiation. This is an activist position and is buttressed by experience in the fifteen Australian cases reviewed by Hiatt and Maddock, who document that not only were social credentials the strongest—indeed, often the only—grounds for pressing an individual's claim but it was also repeated conflict between legitimate concrete credentials and their abstract embodiments in the Act that led to changes in interpretations of the Act. Equally demonstrable, there remain severe limitations imposed on the range of applicability of native credentials, for as Maddock (1982) details, as a result of colonially inspired dislocations, a substantial number of Aborigines find themselves without claim to the land on which they were forced to live against their will. In fact, D. Smith (1984) suggests that registration under the Act has set in train a process of creating an Aborigine elite class, a main concern of which will be to reproduce itself by controlling the Register, and thus land, in the Northern Territory. Myers provides an example, noting that in this case all claimants had long been dislocated from the land to which they attempted to gain precedence of claim.

Feit, after noting appreciatively the fact that the James Bay and Northern Quebec Agreement was the first comprehensive aboriginal rights agreement negotiated within a modern nation-state, discusses its liabilities. These are not insubstantial, resting, in the last analysis, in government's reservation to itself of final authority over land. Then, too, the native peoples of northern Quebec "have also come to depend on complex, extensive, and direct interactions with the Canadian market economy," to which, in fact, they have now become more closely tied. This has exacerbated strains in the internal native economy, and Feit notes that the outcome is far from predictable.

Analogous predicaments are detailed for Aborigines. The authors here are not alone in recognizing the potentially insecure status of the gains that have been made. Egner (1981:5, 15), in his consultancy report, notes this potential in Botswana and points to its political foundation:

Such rights to land, water, and wages as RADs [San in this context] have gained since 1974 are by no means entrenched and could well prove to be ephemeral in the absence of the firm political support which will be needed in the next decade. . . . [On the other hand] any attempt to upset carefully established priorities in order to cater for newly identified RAD projects would obviously be contrary to sound planning practice and would draw down the wrath of councillors.

In keeping with this observation, Egner recommended that central government support for such projects, which was never strong, be further reduced and responsibility assigned to districts, where, he notes, they are converted to the benefit of more powerful constituencies; that recommendation was the prefigured, but unstated, purpose of the consultancy under which he wrote. Maddock (1983b:177) observes in his major work on the matter that "a theory of native land rights is the obverse of a theory of settler rights." Piecemeal claims by particular groups to particular parcels of land obscure this larger issue (Beckett 1985:19). Although significant advances have been made, in the final analysis, these "hang on a moral premise, a shaky support in a world of realpolitik and the cold logic of capitalism" (Gartrell 1983, quoted in Beckett 1985:8). These circumstances simply confirm that the history of aboriginal gains in the past decade has been a manifestation of the "slack" in state legal systems which allows some change to occur as long as there is no radical impact on the status quo (Friedman 1977). Tyack et al. (1987:4–5) argue that "the ability to define an issue as a legal question is an index of the relative power of groups"; at the same time, they stress the significance of legal/ideological conflict that emerges when a minority group increases its power beyond the point of tolerance of ruling elites. Attempts by aboriginal peoples to gain juridical recognition and a measure of self-determination within guaranteed tenures have been mounted in just this arena of political struggle. It seems doubtful that their gains, limited as they are, could have reached the proportions they have without the active support of anthropologists.

On a different, but also cogent plane, what, if anything, has anthropology gained in this endeavor? As Maddock is quick to point out, echoing the points just made, anthropological involvement in aboriginal rights cases is "largely a consequence of policy and organization in the wider society." In other words, although anthropologists may work as agents for aborigines, they do so within the agency of nonaborigines. In such an environment, can anthropologists be in anything other than a double bind? Again, Maddock urges the view that they can. The forensic process can be, indeed has been, salutary. Hiatt (1984:6) noted earlier that anthropologists have been free to alter their descriptions and generalizations at will, while jurists have to wrestle with what is meant by anthropological words enshrined in law. Maddock does not equivocate on the matter: intellectual discipline has been absent from anthropological accounts of local organization and land tenure. Ownership (and all sorts of other social attributes, with almost no examination of what is meant by these terms) was assigned to abstract model idealizations, not to social persons: "One can hope that those days are gone, never to return." If they are gone forever, anthropology has been set on the road to conceptual clarity and has gained a recognition of the importance of rights. In the policy arena, anthropologists are confronted for the first time in the history of their profession with an unmitigating test of what they mean when they define the lives of others; in the scientific and humanistic domains of this discipline, nothing could be more salutary.

There are severe ethical dilemmas concerning personal and professional involvement in corrective efforts on behalf of the people we study, and doubts abound about the ultimate success of such efforts. None of the authors gloss these with pretty talk. Although it may be uncomfortable at this time, as Myers notes, anthropologists must come to terms with the fact that they are directly a part of the political scene in which they work, a scene that most emphatically includes the people we study. The pragmatic nature of our knowledge, the questions and answers we frame, are situated in these circumstances.

This can lead to difficulties. In Australia, some anthropologists have found themselves ambiguously placed, doing both lawyer's work in preparing a claim and appearing as expert witness in the hearing of that claim. In Botswana, those of us who have worked in ministerial consultancies have sometimes been placed in analogous, but not yet identical, positions. As Maddock asks, "How could it be disputed that such a dual role endangers intellectual integrity?" But Myers's question is inextricably bound to this: do we then "remain strictly accountable only to the canons and concepts of scientific reporting"? The ethical answer must be no; we can no longer maintain the fiction that arbitrary divisions of society dictate our responsibility. In pragmatic addition, everyone has too much to gain, for in the process of securing the rights of one segment of society the inclusive body politic redefines its own internal relations to itself.

There is precedent for such a stance in the struggles of our own minorities, of homosexuals, and of women where similar ethical conflicts have been noted. We enter into thorny ground here, some of the ramifications of which are raised by the authors of this book. The one certainty is that the disquieting question of accountability, and its more troublesome corollary, foreseeability, will not remain silent now. Ethical standards for constraining conflicts of interest have been built into the working charters of other professions; it would be sad to think that we could not do the same in anthropology.

A final crucial point that forms the rationale of the work presented here—and its consequences—is stressed by Asch in his contribution to this volume and more fully in his book, *Home and Native Land* (1984). Answering claims that aborigine awareness of basic rights is a product of assimilation, a claim that belittles that awareness, Asch argues eloquently that "aboriginal nations have always had the conceptual material available to create systems of alliance among member groups." Myers gives an illuminating illustration of Pintupi native negotiating strategies employed to "embody their contemporary shared identity" as a projection of their past associations. I show how the foundations for such negotiating strategies have been historically constructed to accommodate "ethnically" plural aboriginal groups. These are direct challenges to theoretical orthodoxy. Furthermore, "backward elements" and "crazy god characters" are but popular translations of ethnographic labels. All serve the conceptual and political segregation of peoples still called "foragers" that is sanctioned, if not condoned, by the crude evolutionary orthodoxy that has hampered anthropological thought for too long. This theoretical realization has its extension in praxis where it lends fundamental support to aboriginal claims to equality both in consciousness and in law.

This discussion has brought us full circle. Thus far, in considering social relations to land of peoples who once were foragers and have been conceived to exist in an uncomplicated past made present, we have been led by our own concepts of natural order and by our own ideological investment of the nature of relations; these are the products of our own creative reasoning. We must now turn to the creative reasoning of those we presume to study, whose concepts of natural order and whose ideological investment are of a different nature of relations. If we succeed in this intellectual effort, we may better find our way through practical negotiations of contemporary tenurial relations and in doing so enhance the reputation of our own discipline's ability to address some problems of this world.

2

Burning the Truck and Holding the Country: Pintupi Forms of Property and Identity[1]

Fred Myers

> If they are not given their shares, this denies their kin-
> ship. . . . A man's variegated relationships with others run
> through his chattels as well as his land; and the measure
> of how far he feels the correct sentiments in those relation-
> ships is the way he deals with his property and his produce.
> —[Gluckman 1965:45]

THE SOCIAL LIFE OF OBJECTS

I am concerned here with the indigenous meanings attributed to a variety of "objects" among Pintupi-speaking Aborigines of the Australian Western Desert. My argument is that "things" (objects, ritual, land, prerogatives, duties) have meaning—that is, significance or social value—for the Pintupi largely as an expression of autonomy and what I have elsewhere defined as "relatedness" or shared identity (Myers 1986b). In this regard, landownership is not a special kind of property, not a special set of rights defining relationships to an eco- logically necessary "living space."[2] Instead, it is one more form of objectifying social relationship of shared identity.

Among the Pintupi, as among many hunter-gatherers, the use- value of rights to things is not at all obvious. Rather than, as Radcliffe- Brown (1930–31) once thought, corporate groups forming around some valued property or estate, Pintupi seem to constitute social aggregations (see also Sansom 1980) and give them identity through time by projecting them into shared relationships to objects.

My essay begins, then, not so much in disagreement with Gluckman's views on property but in my discomfort with the notion of property as being too concrete and specific for the meanings that Pintupi give to objects. Legal language may be useful for characterizing certain similarities in the relationship between persons and things, but it does not make for entirely adequate translation. In exploration of this theoretical problem, and in search of deeper understanding of the social significance of things among hunter-gatherers, therefore, I want to focus on similarities and differences between land and other forms of property. The distinction on which I draw is not unlike the French contrast between *propriété* (personal property) and *immeubles* (real property), a contrast enshrined in Mauss's (1954) *The Gift* and recently resurrected in Weiner's (1985) article, "Inalienable Wealth."

Two basic issues arise. First, is land tenure different from relationships between (and among) people and other objects? Second, the question of concerns over temporal continuity is, according to Woodburn (1980) and Meillassoux (1973), central to understanding hunter-gatherers. Whereas Woodburn attempted to locate the source of Aboriginal concerns over enduring relationships in the "farming" of women (in bestowal), I see the basis of temporal continuity in the process of objectification. In articulating this process, some sorts of objects have different capacities than others. It is of critical importance, as I shall show, that a Pintupi can "give away" (or share) some rights to named places without losing his or her own intrinsic identity with the place. This inalienability of land, that it cannot really be lost, differs from the way most other objects enter into processes of exchange.

While these issues cannot be fully resolved here, I would like to begin by exploring the different ways personal identification with objects occurs in Pintupi social life. How is identity extended in the negotiation of shared rights to objects and processes of exchange? And why, for example, are "personal effects"—but not country—destroyed, effaced, and given away at death? What, if anything, is inherited, or what does inheritance accomplish?

OWNERSHIP AND IDENTIFICATION

A basic issue at all levels of Pintupi social organization is transaction in shared identity. What is most impressive to me about the Pintupi conception of objects is the continual negotiation about relationships to them and a willingness to include others as what, for the want of a better heuristic term, I will call "co-owners." Such ambiguity is deeply seated in the negotiated quality of much of Pintupi social life. Relationships among people are not totally given in the rules of a defining structure, not in landownership, kinship, or residence (Myers 1986b). Instead, the relationships must be worked out in a variety of social processes. The politics of Pintupi life, however, should not be confused with an aim for domination over others. Its roots lie in the emphasis placed on shared identity with others as a basis for social interaction.

This framework suggests a simple and obvious conclusion, namely, that "property" be viewed as a sign. The immediate material use-value of most forms of propertied objects among the Pintupi (tools, clothing, food, etc.) is not great. While such objects are clearly useful, that which is necessary for simple production is rather easily obtained, constructed, or replaced. The rapidity and ease with which things move through a network of relatives and friends show that objects are important as opportunities to say something about oneself, to give to others, or to share. Like any signs, however obviously "useful" they might be, objects are tokens that represent an opportunity not so much to sustain exclusive use but to constitute other sorts of values defined by a larger system of exchange. That these values are ultimately convertible to labor or political support, far from subtracting from the significance of a semiotic analysis, suggests that such analysis should be based on a temporal perspective that focuses on value as being constituted in the process of *reproducing* social life.

Analysis of the cultural relationships between persons and objects should begin appropriately with Pintupi ideas of "ownership"—a conception better translated as one of "identification." The Pintupi words most closely approximating "property" in English are *walytja* or *yulytja*. While the former may be translated as "relative(s)" or as "one's own personal effects" (see Hansen and Hansen 1977:152) and the latter as "baggage and personal effects" (ibid., 190), the significance of identification is clearer when one understands the entire semantic range of walytja. In addition to objects associated with a person, it can refer to "a relative," to the possessive notion of "one's own" (such as "my own camp" [ngayuku ngurra walytja] or "my own father" [ngayuku mama walytja]), or to reflexive conceptions like "oneself" (such as "I saw it myself" [ngayulu nyanju walytjalu] or "He sat there by himself" [nyinama walytja]).

Examining this range of meanings offers some perspective on the almost natural reifying of legal conceptions of rights and duties in our common usage of "property." Indeed, a similar foundation of property in rights deriving from some concept of personal identification is suggested by the shared root of "proper" (my proper father) and "property" in the Latin term *proprius*, "private or peculiar to oneself" (Partridge 1983:529).

There is a certain ambivalence or ambiguity about Pintupi relationships to objects. There is clearly a sense that objects might "belong to" someone—the idea that X is the walytja of a person contrasts directly with the idea that an object X is *yapunta*, a word whose literal meaning is "orphan," without parents. To follow the linguistic usage further, one's parents are said to *kanyininpa* one, meaning "to have," "to hold," or, more loosely, "to look after one." Thus, an object that is yapunta does not belong to anyone, but it appears that this might mean also that it has no one who is holding or looking after it. The question remains of what it means for something to belong to—to be walytja of—someone. An object becomes yapunta when it is no longer "held" but has instead been *wantingu*, "lost" or "relinquished," released from an active association with a subject. For objects to belong to someone means as much that they are expressive of that person's identity as it does that they are simply identified with or related to that person. To say that something is "one's own" implies, for the Pintupi, that one does not have to ask (or defer to) anyone about its use.

Leaving aside for a moment the issue of co-owners, the right to use an object without asking—even the claim that it is "my own"—expresses one's autonomy. By "autonomy," I mean self-direction, although we will have occasion to see that this is not necessarily self-created. In contrast, rights to objects that might be regarded as personal effects still seem less exclusive among the Pintupi than Americans, for example, would tolerate. The very notion of ownership as identification provides also a sense that rights to objects can, and should, be more widely distributed, a willingness (not always ungrudging, of course) to include others with oneself as co-owners.

Rights to objects enter into a system of exchange that constantly negotiates the relationships of shared identity. In the examples that follow, I want to show how negotiation of the meaning of ownership rights moves within a dialectic of autonomy (as in the right to be asked) and relatedness (exemplified in the tendency to include others and to share rights with others who one recognizes as identified). This sense of property as potentially providing a temporally extended objectification of shared identity has much in common with Sansom's (1980) treatment of fringe-dwelling Aborigines in Darwin as "people without property."

To Share, Perchance to Give

Let me begin with a simple and striking example of how Pintupi regard personal possessions. Cigarettes, purchased through the cash economy, are a popular item among Western Desert Aboriginal men. Men cadge each other's tobacco and cigarettes almost without thought. Although my Pintupi comrades were generous with me in sharing their cigarettes, I often found my supply depleted all too quickly. On just such an occasion, a young man named Jimmy came to my camp and asked if I had any cigarettes. Aggrieved, I replied with some anger that people had taken all of mine, more or less including him in the group of those who had taken advantage of me. Rather than taking offense, he was sympathetic and offered me some of his cigarettes. Further, he took it upon himself to explain how I should not give my things away so easily. Instead, he suggested that I should hide what I had. He showed me how he had hidden a packet of cigarettes in his socks under his trousers and suggested that if I did the same, I could simply tell people that, unfortunately, I had no cigarettes—although I would surely give them if I had. Giving me a whole packet, Jimmy told me he had several buried near his camp.

This example illustrates some common themes in Pintupi action about sharing, owning, and asking. I interpreted Jimmy to mean I did not have to refuse anyone overtly. It is clear that it is very difficult for Pintupi to simply refuse or to accept from others. Sympathy and compassion are the appropriate and moral responses to co-residents or relatives. Outright refusal, conversely, constitutes an open rejection of the other's claim to having a relationship with one (see Myers 1979). To "say no to someone's face" is something very unusual and dangerous in Pintupi social life. Those so denied may respond with anger and violence.

Were Jimmy's buried cigarettes to be taken by others, he would certainly be angry. In similar cases, people talk of "theft." That is, Jimmy might say, "Someone has taken my cigarettes, *mulyartalu* ("thieving"; ergative case)." Even though he might have been obligated on the basis of his relationship to a thief to give some cigarettes, to take "without asking" (*tjapintja wiya*) would be regarded as a violation of his personal rights to them. In other cases like this, people often argued that the owner got them with his own money. This is to say that the cigarettes were not a product of cooperative or joint activity through which others could claim identification with the product.

No one else would be very concerned about such an event, as long as their ox was not gored. Indeed, it might be claimed, in counter, that Jimmy should not have hidden (*yarkatjunu*) his cigarettes, or, as I have heard in "thefts" of radios and cassette players, that he should have hidden them better (so the thief would not be tempted). Jimmy's claim would be that he should have been asked. Under such circumstances, in which refusal is impossible, the only way to maintain one's possessions is to place them out of immediate reach. To give one's cigarettes in response to a request, however, is to build a right to ask others because reciprocity in these matters is expected. By not asking, it would appear, one is doing more than simply taking an object; one is denying to the "proprietor" the opportunity to give it, that is, to be generous and to thereby build a debt. "Theft," defined as taking without asking, is a serious interruption to one's ability to express the self, albeit through a gift, and to build through exchange an expanded shared identity with the other.

It is illuminating, finally, to reverse the conception offered here. Consider that one might claim a right to be given some object, claiming co-ownership or a relationship with the proprietor that obligated him or her to give. While the proprietor might choose to give, for propriety's sake, or to be diplomatic, he or she might still claim that the other was really "nothing to do" (*mungutja*)—having no basis for shared identity either with the object or with the proprietor.

The Exchange of Food

It is obviously not possible here to circumscribe the entirety of Pintupi relationships to things. Nonetheless, consideration of rights in food that is gathered or hunted can inform us more deeply about what is at issue in establishing one's primary identity with things.

While women frequently forage for vegetable foods and small animals in a group, each woman has exclusive rights to what she produces—when the actual productive activity is not cooperative. Much of her production is brought back to the residential camp for final preparation and consumption. Characteristically, women prepare what they collect themselves. In camp, the product is (1) shared with the immediate family, (2) given in exchange for child care services rendered, for example, while a mother was foraging (B. Clark, personal communication), and/or (3) distributed to co-residents who had not fared well. While such people may have claims on the producer's services, they have no special claim to the product itself. What she gives is conceptualized, therefore, as exchange. Although co-residents in this situation are expected to share with each other, the sharing often takes place only on request, giving to the distribution of production a character of "mutual taking." Based on their technology and resources, cooperation in production among Pintupi men is unnecessary, though beneficial, in certain circumstances. When men engage in cooperative drives, the kill is distributed among all who participate. Most hunting, however, takes place alone or in small groups, and when a man is successful in hunting large game, it is distributed interdomestically, to those others in the residential group who have shared their production with the hunter. Gifts of meat could satisfy other exchange obligations as well, namely, to one's in-laws or parents.

Anthropologists have frequently pointed out the practical economic benefits of such interdomestic distribution, so I need not emphasize that point here. In any case, the preparation of large game treats it as a social product. A hunter is supposed to give the kangaroo he kills to others for preparation, although his activity in the hunt provides for him the right and responsibility to direct disposition of the cooked animal in exchange (if he uses another's spear or rifle, the owner of the hunting implement has this privilege). Success in the hunt provides food for the hunter, of course, but this does not exhaust its significance. His success also secures a particular set of rights to the animal, providing him with an opportunity to give—to engage in interdomestic exchange that establishes or promotes a kind of moral identity with recipients.

The social value of this exchange of meat is not simply that of caloric satisfaction. Rather, these exchanges among individuals provide a moral basis for continued and ongoing co-residence and cooperation among members of a group. They constitute, that is, a moment in the reproduction of shared identity (people who "help each other") that is the foundation of band organization. Failure to share or, as I would prefer to describe the activity, to exchange within such groups, has predictable consequences. The idiom of shared identity sustained through exchange provides the very basis of possible criticism: conflict ensues as those neglected make accusations of being rejected or neglected as "relatives" (*walytja*). Such neglect is understood as "not loving," not regarding people as related.

Distribution of foraging production in a large group does present a problem. Frequently, the conflicts that develop in such aggregations concern sharing and are brought on by the difficulty of allocating products and services among a large group of co-resident "kin." Since all such co-residents have claims on each other, at least to some extent, large groups place a considerable strain on individuals, producing conflicts of loyalty as well as continuous imposition on one's generosity (not to say diminishing people's incentive to overproduction). Thus, the rights to the kangaroo as property are involved immediately with an exchange used to maintain one's relatedness to others. It is possible, of course, for a person to assert his (or her) autonomy, the right to decide who gets a kangaroo. Rights exist, but what do they mean? Insofar as exercise of choice may defy other people's claims about their relationship or obligations, these choices are likely to create a threat. Herein lies the tension between a valued autonomy and the claims and necessity of shared identity.

How Pintupi manage this tension is clear in a case of "hidden meat." In 1979, I lived at the small outstation community of Yayayi, then, population 15. Having been successful the previous day in hunting kangaroos and bush bustards, we were enjoying the cooked fruits of our labor on one cold midmorning when we heard the approaching sounds of the tractor from the nearby community of Yinyilingki. Long-time and frequent co-residents with the Yayayi mob, the Yinyilingki people were close and often generous relatives only temporarily separated. To my surprise, the male leader of Yayayi decided we should hide our cooked meat, which we did, inside the many flour drums around the camp. When the Yinyilingki people arrived, they asked, of course, whether we had any meat. One of the Yayayi, Ronnie, sitting on top of some drums, replied that we were, unfortunately, empty-handed. His good friend from Yinyilingki, Ginger, was not fooled, since he could plainly see the evidence of recent cooking as well as the feathers we had plucked from the birds. Laughing and without any rancor, he opened a few flour drums until he found what he was looking for. Inescapably, for better or worse in his case, Ronnie's identification with the cooked meat truly spoke to the world about him—communicated, that is, about his identity. Nonetheless, the case is instructive about the cultural meaning of "property" as an expression of identity, a node of personal identity caught at once in webs of shared identity.

Materially, Ronnie's strategy of the polite rejection through hiding was a failure, although it did not lead to the conflict or antagonism that shatters the sense of shared identity. I believe this is so because often enough he was generous. Indeed, the strategy of hiding one's property to avoid either having to give it away or having to overtly deny the other is a common enough practice. Ginger recognized Ronnie's rights to the meat, but these rights did not really sustain exclusive use. What Ronnie did with the meat was necessarily and unavoidably meaningful, a sign of their relationship, just as Ginger's jocular but insistent demand highlighted his sense of a closeness that allowed him to intrude. The potential dangers of such selfishness, however, are clearly outlined in Pintupi myths, where long cycles of vengeance follow on a constant failure to share. And conflict over food has altered the relationships in many Pintupi camps, so that the continued identity of a community, what the Pintupi call "the people with one camp" (*ngurra Kutjungurrara*), is essentially a temporary objectification of these relationships of exchange.

MOTOR VEHICLES AS MEDIA OF IDENTIFICATION

Among the most valuable objects in contemporary Pintupi life are motor vehicles, especially the trucks and four-wheel drive Toyotas that are able to carry large loads (and people) in difficult terrain. Vehicles are necessary and valuable for getting supplies from the store, for hunting expeditions, and for visits near and far. The problem of ownership is compounded in the case of such objects, of which there are few, in that Pintupi recognize two categories of "property"— what they call (in English) "private" as opposed to "community" or "company."

Vehicles that are private are those purchased with money that belongs to an individual or, occasionally, to some individuals who jointly buy a car. The purchaser is understood to be the proprietor of the vehicle, that is, to have the right to decide on its use and nonuse. It is unlikely that the proprietor will be the sole user of a vehicle, but as in the case of other personal effects, relatives and friends must ask permission to gain its use. The very autonomy of ownership (the possibility of giving) is the basis for the establishment of extending shared identity with others. To have a car, one might say, is to find out how many relatives one has.

Those without their own vehicles draw especially on their kin relations for help, placing those in possession of a car under almost constant pressure of such demands. Where the moral rubric of shared identity guides the relationships of those who live in the same camp, such requests are difficult to refuse, and open rejection is impossible. Those who refuse are said to be "hard" or "jealous" for the motorcar. Anyone who has lived in a Pintupi community will recognize just how much conflict, how many fights, are occasioned by relationships to motor vehicles because of misuse and requests for and refusals of use. Indeed, sometimes owners are relieved when their cars break down, only then seeming to be free of demands. Disputes among kin about the use of a vehicle have, I understand, led proprietors to set fire to and destroy their own cars as a desperate and angry resolution.

In contrast, "ownership" provides an opportunity for a person to "give," and one who helps his relatives is not only understood to be generous but also gains a degree of respect and authority for having "looked after" them. The demands on a proprietor are not entirely a bad thing, then, insofar as they provide one with an opportunity to "be someone." Proprietorship can make a person central to the planning of activities that require transportation. More important, however, is the general attitude toward personal possessions. No matter what they cost, it would appear, Pintupi regard vehicles as replaceable, like spears or digging sticks. Thus, even when a $4,000 car is destroyed after only a few weeks of use, they say, "There are plenty more motorcars; no worries." To be sure, this reflects an expectation that someone else will have a car, that another relative will help one to obtain the bare necessities—that is, an expectation of long-term reciprocity prevails.

I believe this attitude to property underlies much of Pintupi social life. Put in familiar terms, if faced with a choice between caring for their property or for their relatives, they prefer to invest in people rather than things. Without granting this any special moral status, let me say that under the conditions of settlement in the traditional life of hunter-gatherers, such "investment priorities" may be a realistic appraisal of resources. Nonetheless, the conception of property as replaceable guides our attention to a conception of things as relatively transparent signs of social relationships, vehicles for another sort of value. Many Pintupi recognize a difference between their conception of the relationship between persons and things and that of whites. A long discussion I had with a middle-aged man resulted in his contemplating the difference thus: "You white people are always worrying for money. You don't think about who will cry for you when you die." This is a salutary comment on commodity fetishism as Marx comprehended it. The accumulation of private objects, while not entirely ignored (Pintupi do work and save to get cars), is not the means through which one's identity is transmitted through time. That is secured in part through giving such things away.

If it is difficult to refuse help, private cars are the basis on which a sort of shared identity is constructed, those with whom one shares the use reflecting an ongoing exchange. Pintupi themselves regard particular vehicles as representing a cluster of associates who, often for the life of the car, travel together: a certain blue Holden is "that Yinyilingki motorcar," identified with a group of young men. The car is the occasion for the temporary realization of their relationship and obligations to each other. When driving past old wrecks on the road,

Pintupi habitually identify them with the persons, communities, and events they were involved with. Cars become, in other words, objectifications of a set of social relationships.

The other category of motor vehicle, the "community" one, has been the occasion for conflict and confusion in many settlements. Such objects are usually the product of government or foundation grants, not the result of a community's joint, voluntary contribution to a collective enterprise. The problem with community vehicles is, who actually can be said to own something that belongs to a community?

Ordinarily, Pintupi have assimilated this problem of property to their ambiguous notion of kanyininpa ("to have, to hold, to look after"), and they recognize that Pintupi Village Councillors "look after" such vehicles. Indeed, in all the cases I have seen, a particular councillor assumes responsibility for a vehicle. "Shorty," they might say, "is looking after that Bedford truck." They do not mean, of course, that he is its "owner." Their conception, as I understand it, is that Shorty must be asked, but conversely, as a Village Councillor he *must* help them. Although he might try to explain that there are other uses for the truck and try to relate these to everyone's benefit, he cannot really refuse.

These community vehicles are interesting from another point of view. To the Pintupi who are granted them, such vehicles seem to embody a recognized "community" identity. When Pintupi refer to the Yayayi Toyota or the New Bore Toyota, they are saying more than that the vehicle belongs to that place. In a particular Pintupi sense, such objects represent the community's collective identity as an autonomous social entity. They do not do so, however, legally; if it crashes, the community is not held liable collectively, and individual members would undoubtedly claim that they were "nothing to do" (*mungutja*) with the action.

For historical reasons, Pintupi associate the founding of past outstation communities with the granting of four-wheel drive Toyotas by the Department of Aboriginal Affairs or the Aboriginal Benefits Trust Fund. As a result of this association, it appears, they believe that a community's autonomy will be recognized in the granting of such a vehicle. Men often say that they are the "boss" of an outstation at such and such a place, but they are waiting to go there because the government has not yet given them their Toyota. Possibly, the attraction of gaining control over such a vehicle is the very reason that people have been eager to establish outstations. Much of the politics of autonomy that matter so much to men gets worked out around control of the motor vehicles of the community. At the first Yayayi community where I worked in 1973, there were two community vehicles, each associated with historically and geographically distinctive segments of the camp, one for the people "from the east" and the other controlled by those whose traditional country had been farther "from the west." The controllers of these resources became the nodes of community organization.

The ambivalence about proprietorship of community vehicles is made clear in the case of the death of a person who controlled a vehicle. When the "boss" at Alumbra Bore died in 1981, the community was faced with the problem of what to do with the orange Toyota that was theirs from a community grant. Personal property of a deceased is always destroyed or given away to that person's "mother's brothers" from far away, because a person's effects are identified with him or her and make close relatives sad. The Alumbra community planned initially to swap vehicles with another community in order to remove their truck from sight because it reminded them of the dead man. They eventually thought better of this, realizing they would still have to see this truck often since it would be in the area. They decided to burn it and thus efface its association with sad memories.

OWNING THE COUNTRY

If the objects considered so far are recognizable as personal effects in their extendibility to others, landownership is not a special kind of property. Among Pintupi, shared identity is readily extended to others in the form of recognizing their identity with named places, an identification formulated through a particular cultural logic.

In contrast to traditional views of Aboriginal landowning groups as patrilineal, Pintupi landownership is better understood as the negotiated outcome of individual claims and assertions. Maintaining relatedness with others is a striking feature of this organization. The emphasis on sociability underlies the variety of claims that individuals make to multiple affiliations to landowning groups and gives an omnipresent quality of negotiation to the processes of local organization. Through allowing others to become joint custodians of one's own estate, people maintain important ties with each other throughout the region. Landownership, then, is not first an ecological institution but rather an arena in which Pintupi organize relations of autonomy and shared identity with others.

Ownership as the Pintupi understand it—that is, "holding a country" (*kanyininpa ngurra*)—provides opportunities for a person to be the organizer of a significant event and the focus of attention, albeit in limited contexts. Owners are in a position to exercise equality with other fully adult persons, to offer ceremonial roles to others (as part of an exchange), and to share rights in ritual paraphernalia. At the same time, people view "country" as the embodiment of kin networks and as a record of social ties that can be carried forward in time.

Various means exist by which individuals may make claims of identification with the "country" (*ngurra*) as their "own." But the fundamental notion of "identification with country," rooted in the fact that places always bear the imprint of persons and their activities, refers to the whole range of relationships a person can claim or assert between himself or herself and place. These provide the cultural basis for its ownership. Thus, if the place is called A, the following constitute bases for such a claim:

1. conception at the place A;
2. conception at a place B made by and/or identified with the same Dreaming ancestors as A;
3. conception at a place B whose Dreaming is associated mythologically with The Dreaming at A (the story lines cross);
4. initiation at A (for a male);
5. birth at A;
6. father conceived at A or conditions 2-5 true for father;
7. mother conceived at A or conditions 2, 3, and 5 true for her;
8. grandparents conceived at A or conditions 2-5 true;
9. residence around A;
10. death of close relative at or near A.

Through this logic, individuals can have claims to more than one country, but it is through political process that claims of identification are converted into rights over aspects of a country and knowledge of its esoteric qualities. Identification is an ongoing process, subject to claim and counterclaim, dependent on validation and acceptance or invalidation and nonacceptance. It is by such political processes that claims of identification are transformed into rights over related aspects of a country. Such rights exist only where they are accepted by others. The movement of the political process is along a graduated range of links or claims of increasing substantiality, from mere identification and residual interest in a place to actual control of its sacred associations. The possession of such rights as recognized by others, called holding a country, is the product of negotiation. Ultimately, owner-

ship is not a given here but an accomplishment, although this his-
toricity is disguised by the fact that the cultural basis of claims is the
ontological priority of the Dreaming (*tjukurrpa*; see Myers 1986*b*, chap.
2). In the end, ownership of country, denoting close association
among a set of individuals, is a projection into transhistorical time of
the valued social relations of the present. This is accomplished, however, without calling attention to the boundaries it draws.

In substance, ownership consists primarily in control over the stories, objects, and rituals associated with the mythological ancestors
of the Dreaming at a particular place. Access to knowledge of these
esoterica is requisite, and the creative essence they contain is restricted; one can acquire it only through instruction by those who
have previously acquired it. Important ceremonies are conducted at
some sacred sites, and other sites have ceremonies associated with
them which adult men (particularly) may perform to instruct others
in what happened in that important period (the Dreaming) in which
all things took on their form. Because such knowledge is highly valued
and vital to social reproduction, men seek to gain it and to be associated with its display and transmission. Their major responsibility,
in fact, is to "follow up The Dreaming" (Stanner 1979), to look after
these sacred estates by ensuring that proper rituals are conducted.

From the Pintupi point of view, the emphasis is just as much on
the social production of persons who can hold the country, that is,
on initiating young men and teaching them the ritual knowledge
necessary to look after the country, as it is on getting the country.
The Pintupi image of social continuity is effectively one in which
"country," as an object, is passed down, is "given" as a contribution
to the substance and identity of the recipient. This is a kind of transmission of one generation's (or person's) identity to the next. By
learning about the Dreaming and seeing the rituals, one's very being
is altered. People become, Pintupi say, "different" and stronger. One
cannot become adult without the help of others; to be sure, no one
can become a man by himself. Certainly, while younger recipients
are supposed to reciprocate for the gift of knowledge—in hunting
meat for the givers and in deference—they cannot really repay what
they have been given. They have, as it were, acquired an obligation,
a responsibility that they can repay only by teaching the next generation. Pintupi stress that men must hold the Law and pass it on.
Men are enormously concerned to pass on their knowledge and identification with places to their "sons" and "sister's sons."

This was evident on a trip to the Gibson Desert that I made with
an older man, Wuta Wuta tjangala, and several others. On our return,

Wuta Wuta decided he wanted to take us all to see an important place
to the north where his father had died in order to *nintintjaku* ("show"
or "teach") his *katja* ("son" or "sister's son"), Ronnie (his brother's
son), Morris (his own son), and Hillary (his sister's son). Two other
older men opposed this, saying they were afraid the young men would
use the sorcery spells from this place when they were drunk. Keen
for knowledge of his country, Ronnie objected in a noteworthy fashion. "All right," he said, "then nobody will ever know about that
place when you all die. If people travel around out here, they'll just
go up and down this road only." In other words, this place would be
lost. Wuta Wuta hoped to establish an outstation near the place where
his father had died. His brothers, he told me, were nearly dead; only
he was still strong enough, and he was concerned to "give the
country" (*katjapirtilu witintjaku*) for these descendants to hold.

Ownership derives from such processes as well as those by which
in-laws and other distant relatives come to be attached through exchange of obligations. Since knowledge and control of country are
already in the hands of "owners" (my gloss for the Pintupi term
ngurrakartu, referring particularly to custodians of named place), converting claims to an interest in a named place requires convincing the
owners to include one in knowledge and activity. Identification with
a country must be actualized and accepted by others through a process
of negotiation.

A group of individuals, then, can affiliate with each significant
place. The groups may differ for each place considered; the corporations forming around these sacred sites are not "closed." Instead,
there are descending kindreds of persons who have or had primary
claims to sites. Of all those "identified," only a portion are said to
hold (*kanyininpa*) a country and to control its related rituals. These
primary custodians are the ones who must decide whether to teach
an individual about it; it is they who decide on the status of claims.
Men are quite willing to teach close kin about their country and to
grant them thereby an interest in the place.

For claimants who are remote genealogically, or are not co-residents, there is less persuasiveness to claims. These processes make
it likely that claims of a patrifilial core will be acceptable. It is men
who control these rights, and because at the height of his influence
a man is likely to live in his own country, it is predictable that he will
pass it on to his sons. Rights are also passed on to sister's sons, who
are also frequent co-residents. If such persons or those with other
sorts of claims (conception from the Dreaming, a more distant relative
from it, etc.) take up residence in an area and convince the custodians

of their sincerity, they can become important custodians too. Conversely, failure to maintain some degree of regular association with a place seems to diminish one's claims. As I have written elsewhere (1982), this is a process, then, by which cooperative ties among frequent co-residents ("those from one camp") may be transformed into a more enduring one.

The fact that men do seek rights for many "countries" leads to extended associations of individuals with places, surrounding a core of those with primary claims. The Pintupi data show not only numerous individuals with extensive estate rights but also individuals having very different personal constellations of such rights. One's identification with a named place is, in this sense, at once a definition of who one is and a statement of shared identity with others. In most cases of conflict, the agreement and disagreement about who should be accepted follows closely current ties of cooperation among people, attempting to project their associations into the past and to embody their contemporary shared identity in the same objective form.

Thus, it is often difficult to determine exactly who is and who is not a member of a Pintupi "landowning group." Rather than being given, membership is usually negotiated, often extended to include those present with one who is already an owner. If others show an interest and a willingness either to participate with owners in activities or to exchange with them, Pintupi seem inclined to include them rather than to negate the proffered shared identity.

I have written at length elsewhere about the processes and politics of landownership (Myers 1982, 1986b). Here, I would like to offer an example to show how Pintupi reasoned about landownership as a form of identification, as they began to consider moving west to establish a new community in the Kintore Range. For most of the Pintupi, the possibility of a settlement in that area raised the question of who could live there and who would be the "boss" (*mayutju*) of the place. No one had lived out west in their country for twenty years, and no one had lived at Kintore for at least thirty. Its traditional custodians probably deserted the area in the 1930s, moving east to the missions. Warna Tjukurrpa tjungurrayi, a man in his sixties who was anxious to move out of the Papunya area, had written to the government for help in setting up a community out west, and the grant of a truck had been promised. While he assumed that this would be under his control, the question of rightful ownership of Kintore brewed. (Two named places in the Kintore Range are central, Warlungurru and Yunytjunya.)

Warna explained to me that Wiri tjungurrayi and his brother Willy

Nyakamparla tjungurrayi were important owners. Their father, Murruntu tjapaltjarri, who died at the settlement of Haasts Bluff, was associated with Kintore, and his brothers Ngapa Tjukurrpa tjapaltjarri (Warna's own father), Naapi tjapaltjarri, and Kurupilyaru tjapaltjarri were all from Kalipinnga (a place distantly to the north of Kintore) and Warlungurru. It is noteworthy that most people identify Warna closely with Kalipinnga; he has named an "ownership" base for Kintore that includes people associated with his own country *and* with Warlungurru, implicitly linking them to him. These places, he insisted, were not far apart; they were "one country." This was in reference to the fact that people traveled frequently and easily between these places, residing, as it were, in a single range. Furthermore, Warna's grandmother, Marrawilya nangala, was the mother of Murruntu and Naapi. Also, Charley Tarawa's father, Nuunnga tjapaltjarri, was identified with Kintore. The "older brother" of all these tjapaltjarri men, Tjangaratjanunya, according to Warna, died at Ngutjulnga, which is only a few miles from Kintore. Warna described the place as "part of Kintore." The father of all these men, he said, was Kunkunnga tjungurrayi, an owner of Kintore. Other genealogical information makes it clear that all these tjapaltjarri men, while they consider themselves to be brothers, are not in fact biologically related. The "descent" imputed by Warna is culturally constructed in the sense that Kunkunnga looked after these men, either when their fathers, his "brothers," died or as part of a group of "brothers" who considered their sons to be sons collectively.

The ultimate basis of the claim is not really explained in Warna's account. From another man I found out that Murruntu tjungurrayi, the very man with whom Warna began, was really "from Kintore" in the sense that it was his own conception Dreaming place. His Dreaming was the monitor lizard (*Ngintaka*), the mythological ancestor who created the hill known as Yunytjunya. This would, in the cultural logic of claims, make sense as a powerful starting point for ownership rights for his descendants. It is a measure of the multiplicity of means through which people establish and argue claims of identification that Warna did not even mention this.

Other people were also related to Kintore, according to Warna's reckoning: Marlkamarlka tjupurrula, the grandfather of Pantjiya nungurrayi and of Charley Tarawa (their "mother's" father; Pantjiya's mother was Charley's father's second wife), and Wartaru tjupurrula were from Kintore—providing another link. Charley himself subsequently described Wartaru as being conceived at Putjanya, midway on the Dreaming track the *Tingarri* ancestors took from a place called

Mitukatjirri to Warlungurru, and from these relatives he says he "grabbed," or took on responsibility for, the place. This Dreamtime line I take to have provided a basis on which his descendants, who are deeply identified with Mitukatjirri, can argue their claim to Warlungurru and the Kintore Range as well. Thus, through Marlkamarlka and Wartaru, for example, based on genealogical connections, I could predict that Billy Baku tjupurrula and his children, his sister Tartuli and her children, Mikini tjupurrula and his children, and many others could lay claim to Kintore, all as grandchildren of the brothers Marlkamarlka and Wartaru. Indeed, this large related group continues to act together in visiting, residence, and marriage arrangements. Even in this incompleted reckoning, it is possible to see how a country owning-group objectifies past and present shared identity. The country stands for the relationship among those who are related through an earlier marital exchange and who continue to cooperate, based on that tie, as relatives.

As Warna was giving me this account, Willy Nyakamparla, a classificatory brother whom he had imputed to be a co-owner with him, approached us. Whether he perceived what we had been talking about I do not know, but he immediately began to tell Warna that "some people are jealous for Kintore," such as Nolan tyapangarrti. "He is nothing to do," Warna replied; "his father is buried at Turkurrnga [another place]"—implying that Nolan belongs elsewhere. Willy tells me, then, that Kintore is the place of *his* mother and mother's brother (Warna adds, in explanation, that it belonged to Willy's grandfather), who were from Mitukatjirri and Nyurnmanu, two relatively nearby places. Papulu and Mikini tjupurrula (descendants of Wartaru) might go too, he thinks, because they are owners of the country. The men tell me Papulu's father was from Nyurnmanu and Mitukatjirri, a brother-in-law of the tjapaltjarri people Warna had described. Warna regards Papulu's father, Ngungkuyurriyurri tjakamarra, as the brother of his own mother's brother, Wintarru tjakamarra (Mikini's father). Finally, Willy explains to me that his father's country was Nyirpi and Kunatjarrayi, places ordinarily considered to be Warlpiri, north of Kintore and actually near Kalipinnga (as Warna had said). People of their country traveled regularly to the north and south to Kintore, meeting each other.

From their accounting as a whole, it becomes clearer that Kintore was a central place to which northerners came to visit and from which southerners traveled north. While Warna emphasized Kintore was their country through the father's tie, Willy emphasized connection through his mother, talking about how his father came south to visit with in-laws. The basis of their claim, then, is that their fathers married women who had close association with Kintore and as a result spent a lot of time in the area, coming to take on ceremonial responsibilities for the country of their wives and brothers'-in-law. More important, however the claim is ultimately decided, the conceptualization of country represents it as an objectification through time of a complex set of past activities. Kintore represents a node of shared identity for all of these people, the descendants of these marriages of several generations ago. Obviously, Warna and Willy have claims in other areas that represent their identity with other persons as well.

According to Willy and Warna, Nolan was not an owner of Kintore, but Nolan firmly believed himself entitled to claim identification with the place. He had several reasons for this. First, he derived a claim from Long Jack tjakamarra, his cross-cousin (his father's sister's son). "In the bush" (i.e., before white contact), Long Jack was the custodian (*ngurrakartu*), presumably somehow through his father. Second, Nolan maintained, his "father" Tatjiti tjapanangka died at Tjukanyinanya (i.e., Sandy Blight Junction), very close to Kintore. This man was Nolan's actual father's younger brother, and his death and burial in the area is a source of identification. Nolan's own mother was from the south, so he has important ties to that area as well, but Long Jack's father, he argued, belonged to Kintore, and Nolan was related to him through his father's sister's marriage. Long Jack and Nolan should cooperate in ritual. This is not to say that Nolan rejected other people's claims. Turkey Tolson tjupurrula (a descendant of Marlka-marlka and Wartaru tjupurrula, like Mikini), he suggested, had rights in Kintore and in Mitukatjirri. Nolan said that Long Jack was the proper custodian but that he had already "gotten" (*mantjinu*, obtained) a place in Pitjanytjatjarra country, so he was not concerned about taking control of Kintore as a community. Part of what was at issue for Nolan and what may have been inspiring conflicting claims was the question of who, rightly, should be given the Kintore truck.

Even before this, however, a variety of claims of identification for Kintore had been bruited about. Shorty Lungkarta always claimed it as "his country" (but not exclusively) because his mother and her sisters (nakamarra, women) were from there and because he had lived around here as part of his range. According to Shorty, Likili tjapaltjarri was a "holder" of Kintore—*mamangkatja kanyinin*, holds through the father. Likili's "father," Kamutu tjungurrayi, one of the earliest Pintupi migrants to Hermannsburg (see Lohe et al. 1977:49, 53), is generally considered to have been a primary owner, although he was conceived further north at Tjunginnga. Likili's own Dreaming-place (conception) was Nyurnmanu, to the east of Kintore. Likili died, however, before anything was settled in the control of Kintore, and his own children seem not to have been interested in pursuing their claim. Long Jack himself, when the question of moving to Kintore arose in a meeting, insisted that the people who were really from Kintore were dead. The people who were talking, he said, were all "from outside." His own country was not far either, but he was not worrying about that country; then again, Long Jack did not think people should move.

What is important to recognize in the Kintore case is that claims to ownership are fairly widespread. Almost none of the claims are really those of direct genealogical descent, not only because members of the original landowning group have died out or disappeared. Instead, most of the claims to identification are traced through extensions in the past, established through affinal exchange and prolonged residence. Furthermore, the agreement and disagreement about who should, and should not, be accepted follow fairly closely current ties of cooperation among people, attempting to project their associations into the past, to embody their contemporary shared identity in some objective form. Conflicts emerged but were never vocalized overtly in a challenge that would have definitively excluded the "opposing" claimants from having a relationship. In subtle ways, despite their opposition, the two major protagonists in the conflict, Nolan tjapangarrti and Warna tjukurrpa, came to support each other as both having an influential relationship to Kintore. At last report, however, neither was actually in a position of control over the community.

The significance of country (ngurra) as a cultural entity is twofold, both given form in processes of exchange. With its origin in the Dreaming, it is defined as a form of valued knowledge that is esoteric, transmitted—or, as the Pintupi say, "given" (uyungu) to younger men, but restricted in access. At the same time, country constitutes an object of exchange between equal men. Moreover, in this light, for Pintupi, country provides an (perhaps *the*) embodiment of identity that allows for the performance of autonomy in exchange.[3]

If we consider how people become "members" of landowning groups through politics of persuasion and exchange, it is clear that these groups represent an objectification of shared identity. That is, people's joint relationship through time to a named place represents an aspect of an identity they share, however limited. The process through which membership is established is precisely one in which people attempt to convince others that they are already related, that they care. Each named place, then, commemorates, records, or objectifies past and present achieved relations of shared identity among participants. Each place, however, represents a different node of re-lations.

The ultimate expression of this principle whereby shared identity among participants is projected out into the object world (and seen as deriving from it) is the way Pintupi verbally extend identification with a place, describing some important site as "belonging to every-body, whole family" or, as they say alternatively, "one country." In reverse, one may and should read this as representing their sense of the Pintupi as a unity; that is to say, of themselves—people with no distinctive organization as a political entity—as "all related" (*walytja tjurta*), as one group, albeit this context-dependent claim is not to imply an identity for all time. Land is, for them, a sign that can carry expressions of identity. What Pintupi refer to in this fashion, it is critical to add, is not a "community" in the sociological sense of people who physically live together; rather, each place represents an aggre-gation of individuals from a wide area of the region in which they live, a form of regional integration through individual ties.

SHARING THE BOARDS

A powerful example of the tendency to inclusion and proferring of shared identity is presented in rights to "sacred boards" (*turlku*), the sort of object referred to by Strehlow (1947) for the Aranda as *churinga*. As Lévi-Strauss (1966), among others, has noted, these objects may constitute title deeds for rights in land, although they are not reducible to this. Throughout Central Australia, sacred boards represent, for men at least, the epitome of value, objects said to be "left by The Dreaming" (although fashioned by men) and which men are permit-ted to know about and view only after initiation. Individual boards are always associated with particular Dreaming stories and usually with one or more named places created by that Dreaming. Rights to such objects, as to songs and stories, are part of the "estate" associated with mythologically constituted places. Presumably, a man has rights to manufacture and/or possess boards related to his own conception place.

A number of men have described to me their conception, for in-stance, in the following terms: such and such a Dreaming was trav-eling at a place, performing ceremonies, and they forgot or left behind one of their sacred objects, which (eventually) became the person.

The value of such sacred objects is constituted by their imputed indexical relationship to the Dreaming, by the restrictions on knowl-edge about them, by the difficulty of acquiring them, and by their historical associations with the subjectivity of people who once held them and have since died. Pintupi men often emphasize how such objects were "held" by people who are now dead ("ancestors") and how seeing the objects makes men "sorrowful" and the objects "dear." In some sense, a sacred object is a powerful representation of one's identity, hidden from the sight of women and children and shown only to initiated men of one's choosing. A man keeps his sacred objects in several places, many of them being held jointly with other men in one place or another. Only authorized men can manufacture a sacred object, that is, only a person who has passed through all the stages of initiation and has been granted ("has been given" [*yungu*]) the right to make a board for a particular site by being taught the design by a legitimate custodian. This is a province of Aboriginal life about which our understanding is unsatisfactory.

Knowledge of such matters, as with much of religious life, is restricted in access, not only difficult to learn about but also problematic for publication because of the desire for secrecy. Nonetheless, it is clear that the exchange and circulation of these objects is a matter of intense interest and concern among men. Indeed, while such boards come "from the country," more or less representing the country, as it were, they are detached from it and movable. In this lies part of their power. Their exchange among men who may live far apart may constitute a distinctive level of organization, a transformation of marriage exchange, ritual exchange, and the like, through another medium that has the capacity to constitute a common identity among those not in daily contact. While it is much like these other "levels" of exchange, the negotiation of identity through sacred objects has its own properties.

Among the Pintupi, boards are frequently exchanged as a result of bestowals between a man and his male in-laws, sometimes as a result of initiation, sometimes to settle long-standing disputes (such as murders). Obviously, access to sacred boards is an important condition of autonomy and equality with other men. A young man must, consequently, rely on elder male relatives to supply him with sacred objects for marriage and for fulfilling his social obligations. What is involved in such transactions, however, is not completely revealed by this. Basing his analysis on Strehlow's (1947) ethnography, Lévi-Strauss (1966) likened the exchange of such objects to the loaning out of one's basic identity to the care of another group, the ultimate sign of trust.

The first point I should like to make is that a Pintupi man has rights to more than one sacred board; his total identity is not wrapped up in one. Second, it was enormously difficult to find out who were the "owners" of the sacred boards that I was shown. While this derived partly, no doubt, from the secrecy surrounding boards, it is also the case that boards are rarely owned by a single person. When I was shown and told about boards, I noticed that a man would tell me this one belonged to him and also to such-and-such other men, that another one belonged to him and X, and so on. Frequently, a group of "brothers" (rarely genealogical, however) "held" boards in common. The way in which I was told made me feel that, as in landownership, there is a tendency for individuals to extend ownership of sacred objects to men with whom one identified. This is consistent with Pintupi stress on the enormous dangers involved if one should try to make a sacred object by oneself. To do so, I was told, would inevitably arouse the jealousy of other men who would kill him. Making a sacred object oneself, it would appear, is to assert one's total autonomy, to deny other people's relationship to oneself and to the object. One should have *kunta*, that is, "shame" or "respect" for others.

Thus, I believe, Pintupi are inclined to share out ownership of, and responsibility for, sacred objects with men they regard as close. Conversely, their planning of, and participation in, cycles of exchange with other men always involves a set of men who cooperate as brothers as a node in the exchange, just as a group of brothers will stand as a party in arranging marriage bestowals. Joint participation in exchange, then, constitutes an identity among the men who jointly accept a responsibility: the boards they possess in common are an objectification of their shared activity, their joint responsibility, of who they are. Failure to fulfill one's obligations in a board exchange is described as "having trouble" (*kuunkarrinpa*, i.e., being under threat of revenge and retaliation); fulfilling one's obligations is described as "clearing oneself" (*kilinipa*) or being free. Joint participation may reduce the danger of failure.

What happens in the exchange itself is equally illuminating. Men often described to me, for instance, how they had lived in other people's country for some time (as young novices or in bride service), and when they made ready to return to their own country, "owners" of the host country "gave" them sacred boards. What they meant by this, they explained, was that the owners drew designs on a fashioned board that a young man then carved; he then took this finished object back with him to his own country. Effectively, he had been taught the design and given the right to reproduce it, although it appears, not the right to teach other people. His possession of the board from the host country recognizes his prolonged residence and shared identity with other owners of that country, converting residence and cooperation through time into an identity projected into landownership. It is important to recognize also that in "giving" the board, the original owner had not actually lost it, indeed, had not lost anything. While he recognized or granted to another rights in the country and shared identity as embodied in that object, he still retained his own identification with the place.

DEATH, MEMORY, AND THE SOCIAL TRANSMISSION OF IDENTITY

My argument has been that the tendency to extend rights to property through exchange and the extension of rights in land bear much similarity. As objects, land and other forms of property have the capacity to embody the relationships among people in outward form. Proprietorship, then, provides a basis on which identity can be built through exchange, both establishing one's autonomy through the possibility of taking part in an exchange and creating the possibility of expanding that identity to include others. Both possibilities are encoded in the meaning of walytja as "relative," "oneself," and "something owned." Nonetheless, these objects have very different potentials as constituting identity through time. I believe this becomes clear when we consider how the Pintupi deploy them in the case of a proprietor's death.

In death, accumulation of personal effects throughout a lifetime is denied, not transmitted as an estate or as personal mementos, to those heirs most closely identified with the deceased. Because, in the Pintupi view, things associated with the identity of a dead person make the relatives of the deceased sad, such things are effaced. All of a person's yulytja and walytja are given away to distant relatives, preferably of the mother's brother kin category. Typically, these effects include a person's blankets and swag (the bedroll in which the living person camped), his or her hair (which is cropped close at death), and his or her tools and personal items—even including an automobile if one had been owned. Objects are given away or destroyed. In the "finishing up" ceremonies, as Pintupi have called the distribution at death, the carefully rolled up swag of the dead person seems to stand for the body and is placed in front of the mourners as the silent and untouched focus of attention. For one such ceremony at least, it was the dead man's wife who oversaw his swag, while it was the group of women mourners who carried it about preparatory to each performance of finishing up (i.e., for each arrival of groups of kin from other places whose willingness to take part shows they are not guilty of ill will). Invoking the identity of the dead, the swag occasions elaborate expressions of grief and anger at loss. The camp or house they inhabited is abandoned; relatives in other communities may move their own camps as well if they remind them of the dead person.

In the seminomadic life of traditional times, the place of death and burial would be avoided for years until all traces of the dead were gone. For similar reason, the personal name(s) of the dead person, and anything sounding like it, is avoided, substituted for in everyday speech by synonyms or the avoidance phrase *kunmarnu*. The deceased is subsequently referred to by the name of the place where he or she died. As an example of the degree to which such effacement may be extended, when Likili died, his relatives proposed burning the nearly new truck that had been granted to the outstation community he led. Sight of the truck, even if they gave it away to distant relatives, would cause them grief.

Despite the dramatically enacted grief at the loss of a relative, the symbolic effect of these practices is quite the opposite of commemorating the dead through inheritance. Relatives of the deceased's own generation, rather than parents or children (in the case I was best acquainted with the deceased's own close younger brothers), are responsible to collect his or her goods and to see to their dispersion among other distant relatives. As far as I could tell from the activity after Likili's death, the sending off of the yulytja is the primary responsibility and activity for close relatives; the funeral, albeit a Christian one now, could not take place until this had been completed. Likili's brothers collected his bag (which, I presume, contained some of his personal ritual paraphernalia—hair string, arm bands, small sacred objects), and his close mother's brothers (who had actually been living with him) seem to have overseen the planning and organization of the sorry business of distribution of goods. The sense of obligation is pressing during such occasions. It was important, Likili's mother's brothers told me, to send this bag off to the mother's brothers in Yuendumu quickly, lest people begin to talk about them (*wangkakuturripayingka*, "to avoid moving toward talk").

In a sense, these goods are not allowed to carry the deceased's identity forward in time. This is accomplished in the grief and lives of those whom he or she "held" (or looked after), especially those he or she "grew up." The Pintupi man who criticized white concerns with money and accumulation by asking "Who will cry for you when you die?" was pointing to this alternative form of accumulation, of investing identity in and increasing the social value of people through caring for them as a relative. This is the focus of Pintupi social reproduction, which emphasizes so strongly the role of seniors as "nurturing" those who come after. Pintupi often explain their grief at loss by referring to the way the person held them. Further, the people who have been looked after by the same person seem to consider themselves related as if they share substance by that contribution. It is also through such links to some shared predecessor that groups of people formulate their shared identity, referring to themselves as "real siblings," for example, because they have "one father" or "one grandmother."

Unlike the personal effects (related to a transient historical identity) that are dispersed at death, men particularly strive to pass on to their successors an identity formulated through ties to named places. Shorty Lungkarta, as a case in point, placed constant pressure on his son Donald to attend his ceremonies and to learn so that he could pass on his country. As Shorty and a number of other Pintupi explained to me, the process they desire is one in which *"Mamalu wantintja, katjapirtilulpi witininga,"* that is, "The fathers having lost (relinquish) it, the group of sons grab it." What they pass on, or transmit, in this way is not a personal property that they have created or accumulated themselves but an identity that is already objectified in the land. Recipients acquire rights to a named place that has preexisting relationships with other named places on its Dreaming track, and through rightful possession of this knowledge, inheritors gain the possibility of taking part in equal exchange with other men and the capacity to nurture the coming generation of men with the gift of their knowledge.

This knowledge of country and the rights to place represented in knowledge is a form of inalienable wealth, as Weiner (1985) describes it. Unlike the spear one has made or the kangaroo one has hunted and cooked, one can "give" one's country to others, take part in exchanges, without really losing it. One has accepted others as sharing identity, represented in the shared relationship to an object that stands for one, but one has not lost the ability to give it away again. Indeed, by including more people as "co-owners," one has to some extent increased the value and importance of a place, as long as one is recognized as the principal custodian. As Munn (1970) clearly realized, the country is perceived by Western Desert Aborigines as symbolically bearing an identity that when taken on (or "held"), comes to be possessed as one's own identity. On death, these special "objects" with which a person came to be associated in life remain in the landscape, and those to whom that person contributed, by growing them up and teaching them, are precisely the people able—even obligated—to carry on responsibility for this country. This is the identity that endures and is reproduced through time in the social production of persons, an identity that each generation takes on from its forebears mediated through the "inheritance" of place.

The freedom with which Pintupi are willing to part with their personal possessions owes something, I believe, to this enduring dimension of identity. Spears, rifles, clothing, food, even the costly automobile—these are all, in the Pintupi view, replaceable. There are always "plenty more motorcars." While such objects provide a basis through which identity can be created and extended, the Pintupi take part in such exchanges with an assured foundation. Everyone, according to their conception beliefs, comes into the world with an association with the Dreaming at a place. In some critical way, Pintupi regard themselves as having an assured identity no matter what happens to personal possessions. This is very different from a world in which accumulated personal property constitutes the only medium in which identity can be realized. Several years ago, when the Native American activist Vine DeLoria spoke to a class I was teaching, a student with a beginner's ethnocentric background in psychology tried to question him about the way in which some Indian religious concepts provided for them a sense of self. "The Self," DeLoria snorted, "is not an Indian problem. That's something white people worry about."

A recognition of hierarchy in Pintupi organization of relationships to objects takes away from "property rights" the simple notion of legal problems and suggests that objects, as property or not, have meanings for these people which cannot be limited to the analytic domains too often prescribed by our own Euroamerican cultures. For Pintupi, I would maintain, identification with place as an object assures an identity in the world whereby the more transient exchanges of daily life can take place without threatening to reduce participants to the emptiness of pure despair that economic failure too often brings to us.

NOTES

1. Fieldwork with the Pintupi has been funded by the National Science Foundation, the National Institute for Mental Health, and the Australian Institute of Aboriginal Studies at Yayayi, N.T. (1973-1975), Yayayi and Yin-

yilingki (1979), New Bore (1980-81), and the Central Land Council at Kintore and Kiwirrkura (1984). This chapter is an expanded version of a paper that was first presented at the Fourth International Hunting and Gathering Societies Conference (London) in September 1985; that version appears in the volume originating from that conference, *Property, Power, and Ideology in Hunting-Gathering Societies*, edited by T. Ingold, D. Riches, and J. Woodburn and published by Berg Publishing Company, London. The present version is dedicated in "whitefellow way," to my close friend Shorty Lungkarta, who died after it was written.

2. The focus here is on the logic of relatedness. This is not to deny entirely the ecological significance of landownership but rather to point out that the uses to which land is put for the Pintupi are equally cultural. For more detailed discussion of the relationship to foraging uses, see Myers (1982, 1986a, 1986b).

3. The possibility of handling "country" in this way arrives for men through initiation and the very possibility of two other basic forms of autonomy through exchange, marriage, and fighting.

3
Those Who Have Each Other: San Relations to Land[1]

Edwin N. Wilmsen

It should raise no controversy to state that anthropological approaches to social mechanisms of San[2] land distribution have tended to treat San groups as sociocultural isolates that have been insulated until comparatively recent decades from contacts with other peoples, whether African or European. Accordingly, the relations of San-speaking peoples to land have been seen as entirely autochthonous in origin and development. The underlying motive forces forming these relations have been attributed principally to ecological imperatives centered on resource procurement necessities (Meillassoux 1967, 1972; Lee 1979; Silberbauer 1981; Tanaka 1980; Cashdan 1982).

San land tenure, however, far from being an ecological given, is part of that social universe negotiated by San persons in their day-to-day interrelations with each other. Furthermore, these people are not "free from fundamental conflicts of interest," as Leacock and Lee (1982:10) contend. Lee's own descriptions, as well as those of other authors whose work will be cited later, forcefully show that negotiations to resolve interpersonal and intergroup conflicts are a constant aspect of San life. Land, and rights to its access and use, is a continually recurring factor in these negotiations. Of course, San-speakers have developed inherent political structures for organizing these negotiations both in their internal dimensions and in relation to other peoples whose distribution overlaps or interlayers with their geographic space.

In Botswana, San-speakers (who constitute approximately 3 percent of that country's population) are particularly disadvantaged with respect to recognized rights in land as compared with other groups in the country. The grounds on which that disadvantage is rationalized was that they did not in the past, and do not now, have inherent land tenure and political structures that would admit them to equality in claims to land. To correct this imbalance, and to bring San-speaking peoples into active participation in Botswana's political economy, it is necessary to examine, first, the native legal frameworks of all peoples concerned, not only those of San-speakers; second, the history of association of these peoples; third, the colonial system superimposed on these frameworks; and fourth, the anthropological interpretations that have been offered concerning these frameworks and this history. These considerations have both theoretical and practical entailments. Theoretically, they add a social-political dimension that has been subordinated in the evolutionary-ecological models uniformly employed in recent forager studies. Practically, they contribute to current debates over the status of San-speaking peoples in the modern national state of Botswana, to further extension of that debate in an eventually independent Namibia, and, by association, to similar debates elsewhere.

To begin with, it is necessary to examine the systematic similarities of San social relations to land to those of other southern African groups. In stressing these similarities, I am aware of the danger of imposing structural uniformity where none exists and have tried to avoid tendencies in that direction. I do not envision anything like a unitary San system of land tenure much less that it might be simply a subspecies of southern Bantu—or specifically Tswana or Herero or whatever—systems. Nor by drawing on some principles adduced for other societies do I intend to suggest that the structure of San land tenure can be comprehended entirely in models derived for those societies. Indeed, I specifically reject the applicability to San systems of significant parts of those models. I wish only to demonstrate that these systems, although exhibiting important distinctive features, share with other systems a number of equally important common principles for relating persons to place. These common elements have their ontogeny in a long history of association among these groups, a history that has been distorted by colonial interventions that have obscured long-term regularities. This has been a result both of the administration of policies intended to foster political differentiation and of a corollary consequence of competitive capitalism.

Also obscured is the fact that San social relations to land and the structures for confirming these relations are as fully developed as those of their neighbors with which there is significant congruence. The establishment of this point undermines arguments of San inequality in this regard. It is to this rather than to a postulated unproblematic relationship or a shared corpus juris among the examined systems that this discussion is addressed.[3]

ECOLOGICAL AND MARXIAN MODELS

Current approaches to San relations to land claim to draw inspiration from some combination of ecological and Marxian models. Not accidentally, there is virtually nothing to distinguish these models as they have been applied to San-speaking peoples. Both are founded on the premise that for foragers, "reproduction of the means of subsistence is left to nature" (Lee 1979:117). On this base rises a superstructure of sociality and ideology: "foragers must fit their organization into the niches afforded by nature" (ibid.). I have criticized the ecological components of these models elsewhere (Wilmsen 1983); it is enough to observe here that San-speakers have been particularly tyrannized by attempts to find in contemporary foragers insights into cultural evolution (Lee 1965:1–3), the original configuration of human society (Tanaka 1980:xi), and the technological cum environmental drive that L. White (1943) and Steward (1955) saw to be primary in shaping human social life (Silberbauer 1981:30–31). Lee (1979) makes a serious effort to wed these ecological components to their Marxian analogues. We may turn directly to the Marxian models. Meillassoux (1967, 1972, 1973) anticipated Lee; his construction is based on a literal reading of Marx's ([1867] 1967) distinction between land as a subject of labor and land as an instrument of labor (Meillassoux 1980:194). He says, "The use of land as *subject of labor* amounts solely to the extraction of the necessities of life from it, as it is the case with hunting or collecting (ibid.; original italics). Such use fosters "instantaneous" production, which, once shared, frees the hunters from "any further reciprocal obligation or allegiance" (ibid.). There is no ground for the emergence even of extended family organization at this forager level: "The basic social unit is an egalitarian but unstable band with little concern for biological or social reproduction" (ibid., 1972:99). Only with the emergence of agriculture is the material base available for "the emergence of the '*family*' as a productive and cohesive unit and of '*kinship*' as an ideology" (ibid., original italics). Obviously, there can be no basis for land tenure among foragers so conceived. This conception was in error when it was born, as even a superficial examination of the results of decades of research condensed in *Man the Hunter* (Lee and DeVore 1968) reveals. Earlier, Sahlins (1965), dismissed by Meillassoux as a "liberal economist," had offered a theoretical formulation of the role of kinship reciprocity in forager society. Prior to that, Marshall (1957, 1961) had presented an empirical description of such reciprocity for Zhu, whom she called !Kung San. Both absolutely contradict Meillassoux's formulation.

Lee does not fall victim to this error when he appropriates key elements of Meillassoux's construction. He recognizes forager social integrity (Lee 1979:117ff.), but he subordinates it by offering a forager mode of production, the five components of which are a hierarchical construct based on environmental constants. In this, he follows quite faithfully the lead offered a decade earlier by Meillassoux as well as by Terray (1972). Taylor (1979:150–163) carefully dissects this approach and finds it to be reducible to the identification of elements and their combination in a process of production, in simpler terms, a typology. As with all typologies, this one obscures the basis for analyzing social relations, which is presumably its intended purpose. Similarly, Godelier (1973, 1975) reduces human social relations to the product of the evolution of chronologically antecedent forms that develop in response to functional constraints imposed by a combination of environmental and technological forces (cf. Taylor 1979:157–163); foragers are way down on the scale (cf. Kahn and Llobera 1981:298). Clearly, these constructions are all legacies of Morgan ([1877] 1963) descended through Engels ([1891] 1972) in the Marxian genealogy and through Steward (1955) in ecology to their multilineal standpoints of today (Wilmsen 1983; Schrire 1980; Perper and Schrire 1977). Attempts to insert social dimensions more firmly into these Marxian-evolutionary schemes (cf. Keenan 1981) have been hampered by both inadequate ethnography and underdeveloped theory.

This is not to assert that social dimensions are categorically excluded by students of San-speaking peoples. Silberbauer (1982:28, 33–34) speaks of factions, cliques, the exercise of political power, and strategies for decision making among the Gcwi (G/wi in his orthography). Lee (1982:52–53) mentions multiple options exercised by Zhu individuals in a number of social situations and—in apparent contradiction to the denial, mentioned above, that foragers may have fundamental conflicts of interest—strategies of competition among Zhu groups for recruitment of members. Silberbauer (1982:24) sees this as Gcwi manipulating their society to fit their environmental requirements, while Lee (1982:53) finds that the characteristics of foraging life lead to shallow spans of social continuity (1979:60–61) and to political egalitarianism (1982:53–55). This brings him back suspiciously close to Meillassoux's position. Similar views are expressed by Yellen (1976) and Tanaka (1980). Barnard (1979:131) correctly identifies the environmental determinism of these authors (cf. Wilmsen 1983).

It is thus no distortion to claim along with Taylor (1979:162; original emphasis) that in all these studies "phenomena such as kinship, religion, etc., are analyzed as *'functional necessities' in relation to the level of productive forces."* Or, in R. Williams's (1977:75–82) terms, an economic/ecological productive "base" is objectified with the result that all variations in social relations are reduced to secondary consequences. From this perspective, it is easy to view continuity in social relations as reflecting stability in ecological conditions with perturbations tending to oscillate around some equilibrium state and for change to be seen as adjustments to external impositions—either drastic alterations in the productive base or injection of disruptive forms. There can be no doubt that conditions of both continuity and crisis have characterized the past and continue to characterize the present for forager societies. These societies have consequently developed a repertoire for anticipating and managing a wide range of contingencies. What has been missing in studies of these repertoires is close attention to the constraints that social relations themselves impose on the forces of production, or, more cogently, the dynamic connection—the dialectic—between social relations of production and the productive environment. Attention to these connections opens the way to analyzing their integral coordination in specific societies.

THEORETICAL CONSIDERATIONS

The constitution of land tenure in San societies is the logical locus for this investigation because, in contrast to the ecological concept of territory, which focuses on productivity and the means of production, it locates people in the social matrix of relations to land within which productive activity must take place. Hitchcock (1982:23) notes that virtually every anthropologist who has worked in the Kalahari has mentioned the existence of San territories; however, the distinction between these applied model concepts of ecological territoriality and indigenous San conceptions of land tenure was posed first by me in a report to the government of Botswana (Wilmsen 1976) and later by Hitchcock, Vierich, and Wilmsen (1977) at the first Botswana National Migration Workshop. Theoretical arguments on which this distinction is based were developed further at the Botswana Society Symposium on Settlement (Wilmsen 1982*b*) and in the final compilation of the National Migration Study (Wilmsen 1982*a*).

It is not surprising that the structure of San land tenure has been overlooked. Marshall (1960, 1976), Lee (1965, 1979), Yellen (1976), and Yellen and Harpending (1972) include discussions on spatial distributions of Zhu (whom they call !kung), as do Silberbauer (1965, 1981) and Tanaka (1969, 1980) for the Gcwi, Heinz (1966, 1972, 1979) for the Kqo (!xō), and Cashdan (1977, 1983) for the Gxanna (g//anna). All these authors view their subject group in isolation and offer no more than generalizations drawn from limited descriptions of a few particular cases. Barnard (1979) makes a similar point. Moreover, Marshall and Lee—whose publications on this topic are the most extensive to date—limit their understanding of underlying San conceptions of ownership because they consider the peoples they studied to be members of separate enclaves, dissociated from their neighbors until very recently. They have not noticed, therefore, that these peoples share structural elements of ownership and tenure common to a number of societies in southern Africa; accordingly, they misconstrue San land tenure practice as well as its interdigitation with other systems. However, Wiessner (1977, 1982) successfully places some aspects of Zhu settlement dynamics in a broader social context, and Hitchcock (1978, 1982) firmly anchors contemporary Kwa relations to land in eastern Botswana in the context of dominant Tswana systems. Hitchcock gives excellent descriptions of interlocking Kwa and Tswana customary claims to land ownership at the local level and shows how this differs from higher-level administrative views on the matter. He does not, however, attempt to develop a basis for San customary claims (other than presence on a specific parcel of land, an argument that can be, and is, negated by assertions that this presence is the result of squatting, not tenure).

We must search elsewhere. By definition, nonliterate societies do not keep written codifications of their constitutive principles of ownership. The only avenue for comprehending these principles in such societies is to examine the logic of social relations that governs their ownership and its extensions without forcing it entirely into a Western model.

The argument may be distilled as follows:

Property law in tribal societies defines not so much rights of persons over things, as obligations owed between persons with respect of things. . . . The crucial rights of such persons are demands on other persons in virtue of

control over land and chattels, not . . . any set of persons, but persons related
in specific, long-standing ways. . . . To understand the holding of property,
we must investigate the system of status relationships; we must deal constantly with relations to property. (Gluckman 1971:45–46)

Ownership in such societies cannot be absolute because property
acquires its critical role in a specific nexus of relationships. Under
these circumstances, there can be no definition of ownership in a
sense of incontestable control over property. Rather, ownership involves being bound within a set of reciprocal obligations among persons and things; everything, especially land and the right to its use,
must be subject to a complex of claims arising from the social matrix.
In essence, ownership is a flexibly defined right over someone or
something in terms of social status: "rights to property . . . are attributes of social position" (Gluckman 1975:163).

Gluckman did not employ a dialectic vocabulary, yet the essential
dialectic dynamic of property is apparent in his formulation—the
reciprocal discourse among members of a social universe conducted
in historical, not mechanical, nature. It is this dialectic element that
I take from Gluckman. For foragers, as for anybody else, persons
create property. They create it in reference to each other, not in reference to space or the use of objects in space. Production takes place
within a conception of property—within a conception of persons in
relation to each other with respect to place. Within that conception,
the social rules and processes of the relation of production are as fully
articulated for foragers as for anybody else. This crucial and self-
evident point is subverted in ecological-Marxian models of forager
cultural order. Harris and Young (1981:117–128) relate Gluckman's
analysis of links between kinship and ownership to labor processes
and thus carry it a step further into the realm of social production. I
shall return to this extension as it applies to San peoples.

I should make it clear, however, that I depart from Gluckman's
construction in two important ways. First, no codified *corpus juris*,
such as he seems to have found among the Barotse, can be attributed
to any San group or, for that matter, to Ovaherero or Botswana (Comaroff and Roberts 1981) who will also be considered here; I neither
make that attribution nor follow an analytical procedure that requires
it. Second, Gluckman assigned major importance for property relations to the status hierarchy inherent in Barotse social organization
and considered rights to land to be held in a graded arrangement of
administrative estates. Aside from the fact that this assessment has
been criticized (C. White 1963; Biebuyck 1963; see Comaroff and Rob-

erts 1981:5–11 for an extensive evaluation of the controversy), the status distinctions that can be discerned in San and Herero social relations are not characterized by the graded administrative estates that Gluckman attributed to the Barotse. I do not adopt that aspect of Gluckman's model.

I take the "attributes of social position" by which rights to property are obtained to be entailed simply by virtue of native membership in a group, that is, by ascription at birth or adoptive incorporation into a specific set of related persons. Acquisition of new status by a person is constrained in scope and direction by that person's initial membership in such a group and hence is an extension of ascription (cf. Comaroff 1978). Abandonment of hierarchical ladders does not impair the theoretical foundation for the argument to follow. On the contrary, it opens the possibility of a more fundamental analysis of the way in which property is woven into the social fabric of forager society. As will become clear, flexibility of spatial organization for San-speakers— and for Ovaherero and Batswana—rests on a fluid and negotiable social field in which a repertoire of rules is constantly activated and continually reassessed by individuals in the course of everyday interactions. In this social field, "norm and reality exist in a *necessary* dialectical relationship" (Comaroff and Roberts 1981:247; original emphasis) that gives form to the San universe. That social field must be brought into prominence to set equally variable functions of production in their proper context. For San-speaking peoples, it must also be made comprehensible within the broader social sphere of southern Africa in which it has always existed. This is especially urgent today when a centuries-old legacy of precapitalist and capitalist disenfranchisement is being legitimated in legislation for lack of well-grounded and persuasive arguments that this dispossession should be corrected rather than concretized (cf. Hitchcock 1982). Gluckman's insight, modified as mentioned, provides an indispensible first guide to this endeavor.

As I see it, the principle heuristic value of Gluckman's effort is that it stresses the flexible quality of property rules and the leeway allowed in their application during negotiation of individual cases. Theoretically, by identifying the dialectic between person and property mediated in a social field, it restores kinship to that central logic of cultural relations from which it has been analytically divorced by ecological-Marxian models of "foragers."

Beyond that, and more important in the overall scheme of things, interpreted in this way, property is removed from the arena of pursuit of means to overcome necessity and is situated where it is, in fact, created: in the cultural definition of how these means are to be pursued. Forager relations to property (land, chattels, etc.) can then be seen as inhering not in a different natural order but in a cultural order that organizes persons and relations of production differently. To at once rescue San-speakers from Western legal institutions and to dig them out of the teleological grave in which they have been buried before they are dead is to open the way to their culture in terms of its own structure set in the concrete locus of its African history. The initial discussion will center on Zhu relations to land as perceived by people at CaeCae (/ai /ai or NxaiNxai); subsequently, the systems of other San groups and of Herero will be summarized and their congruence with that of Zhu will be made clear. Finally, the underlying principles of kinship and membership in a group as the basis for tenure rights in these systems will be shown to be compatible in essentials with those of Tswana land tenure.

ZHU SPATIAL ORGANIZATION

There is agreement among researchers on the ecological-geographic correlates of Zhu land division: space is partitioned such that each demarcated section of land contains enough food and water resources to sustain the user group in all but the most unproductive years. The basic unit is called *n!óré* (pl. *n!órési*).

To move more deeply into the meaning of this term, it is necessary to recognize that the word *n!óré* (hereafter, *nqore*) is associated with a group of etymologically allied words carrying the primary sense, "belonging to place." Snyman (1975) formulates a standardized orthography in which to couch the discussion; he also provides independent confirmation of my glosses of the lexical items to be considered. Placing the word nqore within its etymological group will help clarify the conceptual connotation it has for Zhu. The noun, *n!am*, is translated into Afrikaans as "plek" by Snyman (ibid., 57); plek, in turn, is rendered "place/position" in English by Bosman et al. (1982:592), who associate it with the sense of location (plaas). The verb, *n!ang*, is glossed "vasmaak" (Snyman 1975:57); Bosman et al. (1982:817) translate this as "attach/secure." As an adjective or preposition, n!ang is given as "binnekant" (Snyman 1975:57), "inside" (Bosman et al. 1982:91); for example, *g!un!ang* combines *g!u* (water) plus n!ang, literally, "waterinside" = pan/well. All these words have the connotation of attaching or securing something to its place. In contrast, the verb, */'u*, is used more casually "to put" (insit) or "to stick" (insteek) (Afrikaans from Snyman 1975:98) something somewhere. A Zhu person distinguishes between the use of n!ang (to place) and /'u (to put) in a way analogous to the distinction in English between "place it properly" and "put it there." Thus, nqore may be glossed "place in land" and has the primary connotation of attaching persons properly inside locations of land. Snyman (ibid., 62) captures this sense in *n!óré!xáiyàsì*, "landgrens" = land frontier/border [of a country] (Bosman et al. 1982:407). A Zhu person refers to some locality—some demarcated land—as nqore mima (nqore plus mi = self plus ma = possessive: my place), meaning "the place where I belong/ was born."

There is, however, disagreement among anthropologists about the mechanisms of place affiliation. Marshall (1976:184) notes that a person, no matter where he or she resides, identifies primarily with nqore of origin (birthplace); Lee (1979:338) agrees. While this is true, it must not be construed to imply denial of rights in subsequently acquired nqoresi, as we shall see. Such identification is made to locate a person in an appropriate social geography; anyone familiar with that person's network will automatically fill in many kinship details without further prompting. Nqore affiliation is said by Marshall (1976:184) to be inherited unilaterally through either parent. Lee (1979:338) says that inheritance may be unilateral, bilateral, or neither with a strong unilateral bias. Wiessner (1977:50–51) says inheritance is strictly bilateral but that additional affiliations are acquired through marriage. This lack of agreement arises because nqore inheritance is considered by these authors to be primarily a means for associating individuals with geographic territory.

Marshall (1960:344–345) brings a thoroughly commodity view to her depiction of Zhu relations to land. Although she does recognize that kinship plays a role in forming these relations, she holds that relative adequacy of resources causes people to flock around an "owner" of productive land. She has altered her view to the extent that she no longer thinks of an owner as a headman (1976:191–195; see, however, Wilmsen, n.d.), but the resource function of Zhu spatial organization has been retained in her most recent presentation. Lee (1979:58; 334) also defines nqore in resource terms; he again uses "territory" here as he did in his original discussion (Lee 1965:137–148) of what he then called Zhu territories. He has now reversed his interim view that Zhu have no concept of land ownership (Lee 1972) by asserting that "the !Kung do own the land they occupy" (Lee 1979:337) but does so in an anecdotal manner that puts him in a position indistinguishable from Marshall's. Lee (ibid., 58–63) envisions a core group of owners who compete to recruit members in order to increase productive output (ibid., 457; 1982:53) and thus create a radiating chain of affines who may stay together for two generations or so (Lee 1979:60–61). The main adhesive holding some people together, while keeping them well spaced from others, is personality (1982:52) and observance of rules of conduct (1979:338). But the adhesive dissolves in the unpredictability of rainfall with its consequent variable resource production. This becomes a "powerful argument against territoriality" (ibid., 352), which induces "!Kung [to] *consciously* strive to maintain a boundaryless universe" (ibid., 335; original emphasis). In this contradictory ecology, Lee says "ownership of *land* passes from parent to child" (ibid., 339; emphasis added). Even so, since he investigates only one generation of such passages, he finds shallow and diffuse inheritance and guesses that a significant rate of moving about in the nqoresi occurred in precontact as well as in contact time (ibid., 333–339). It is true that Lee's respondents, all male, were of different ages and generations, but he reports inheritance from their immediate parents only, not for earlier or subsequent generations.

But it is not land itself that is inherited. What actually is inherited is a set of status positions binding an individual to a network of obligations owed between persons with respect to land. It is through this network of associations that persons become associated with geographic space. Among Zhu, a person's primary (in the sense of identification, not necessarily of foremost acquired rights) nqore is always birthplace. As I shall demonstrate, there is a very high probability that this birthplace will be in at least one parent's nqore. Thus, an individual Zhu's tenure rights in land are a dynamic function of a regional kinship net defined initially by ascription through birth into a social unit and later expanded through acquisition of membership in other units either by marriage or adoption. Ascription is bilateral, with rights at birth vested equally in the nqoresi of both parents.

Hitchcock (1982:24) documents the fact that in Botswana, government officials invoke published works of anthropologists in support of their particular positions during debates over land reallocation. He cites a case in which anthropological conclusions that San peoples do not have territories in the classic ecological sense were used by the then Commissioner of Land to argue that these peoples have no vested tenure rights in land and therefore have no basis for claims to land other than as a subject of resource exploitation. Simple resource exploitation is, of course, completely compatible with a squatter existence: use of land is appropriated by the currently present group, but tenure does not accrue. Lee (1979:337), by recognizing that Zhu land ownership is collective rather than individual, had the right answer for an African context. His discussion, however, obscures this collective ownership: "land . . . because it is owned by no one exclusively, is available to everyone who can use it" (ibid., 445). Lee clearly does not mean just everyone; he, of course, is thinking of foragers in a world of foragers—of Zhu in a land of Zhu—despite his approving citation (ibid., 16) of Sahlins's remark (Lee and DeVore 1968:4) that such people could no longer be found.

Policymakers, however, do not think in terms of such isolated worlds; they think in terms of competing interest groups. In this context, customary tenure systems of all Botswana's people have subsequently been expressly recognized in their constitution as a basis for adjudicating rights in land within the country (Hitchcock 1982:24). But, as we have seen, customary tenure systems of San-speaking peoples are not recognized within the country; consequently, they cannot be brought forward as a basis for claims to land. We must establish that basis for San-speaking peoples. To do so, it is essential to elucidate the kinship matrix in which their land tenure is set. I shall begin with the Zhu case.

ZHU KINSHIP

Since Marshall (1957), no one has reported fundamental work on Zhu kinship and marriage. Fabian (1965) and Barnard (1978) identify contradictions in her work, and Marshall (1957:14) herself noted that some critical points remained to be clarified. The contradictions, however, do not lie in Zhu kinship relations as has been supposed.[4] Marshall (1957) gives male-centered consanguineal terms correctly. It was her decision to exclude kin-term suffixes, which she considered to be strictly diminutives (despite the fact that she retains the suffix *n!ā'à* [n!a in her spelling] meaning big), that led her astray, especially in association with her second decision to adopt an exclusively male egocentric paradigm. She was consequently unable to discern the systematic relation between terms, especially those applied to affines, nor did she recognize the reciprocity in male- and female-centered terms that lie at the terminological heart of transformation from kin to affine.

Marshall's Diagram 1 (1957:6) gives these male-centered terms, which I employ in the following discussion. To facilitate comparison with Marshall's work, I will enter Zhu terminology through male-centered terms for consanguines and then move on to the female-centered paradigm. Terms in ego's adjacent generations are the same for both sexes, and there are only two: *g//a* (*gxa*, adjacent generation female colateral), parent's female sibling and generational equivalent plus sibling's and cousin's female child and equivalent, and *tsu* (adjacent generation male colateral), parent's male sibling and generational equivalent plus sibling's and cousin's male child and equivalent. In ego's and alternating generations, however, there is a fundamental difference; terms here are linked to gender of ego. For males, male offspring of tsusi-gxasi are in the *!u* (qu, name) relationship as are female offspring of these parents for female ego. In her Diagram 1, Marshall makes female ego's parent's fathers as well as all male cousins *!un!a'a* (qunqa, name-giver) to her; as Zhu names are gender linked, this cannot be true in the consanguineal terminology, although, as we shall see, it is true in the affinal terminology.

Complementary to this qu relationship is a *tru* relationship that is also gender linked: opposite sex persons in ego's and alternating generations are *trug!a* (trugqa) to female ego and *truma* to male ego. Again, Marshall assigns affinal terms in the female consanguineal paradigm, as she must, having placed male cousins in the qu category.

At this point, it is important to summarize. In ego's first ascending generation, father's brothers (FB) and mother's brothers (MB) are termed tsu by both male and female ego; in this generation, father's sisters (FZ) and mother's sisters (MZ) are termed gxa by both sexes. These terms are also applied to male and female kin, respectively, in generations alternate to this one. In ego's generation, however, male ego applies the term qu with appropriate suffix to male offspring of both parents' siblings (FBS, FZS, MBS, MZS) as well as to male relatives in parents' parents' (FF, MF, etc.) and childrens' childrens' (SS, DS, etc.) generations. In these generations, female ego applies the same term to the female counterparts of these persons (MZD, MBD, FZD, MM, FM, etc.). Male ego applies truma to female offspring of parents' siblings (FBD, FZD, MBD, MZD) as well as to female relatives in parents' parents' (FM, MM) and childrens' childrens' (SD, DD) generations; female ego applies trugqa to their male counterparts (MZS, MBS, FZS, MF, FF, etc.). These terms are indefinitely extendable, paradigmatically, both laterally and vertically.

It is also important to note that trugqa and truma are not primitive terms but are compounds of a stem, tru, and a suffix, *g!a* (gqa) or *ma*. The stem component will be considered when affinal terms are introduced. The suffixes are possessive particles; ma, as in *dshau mima* = my wife (cf. Snyman 1975:42) and gqa associated with *ga*, as in *zhu a ga* = your/his/her relative (ibid., 10).

Support for the possessive character of these suffixes is found in the term *mámà*, which Marshall (1957:15) notes is used as a term of affection, as is qunqa. It is also, however, a kin term denoting parents' mother (Snyman 1975:43 gives "ouma," grandmother). The stem, ma, is associated with a whole set of lexical items (ibid., 42–44) expressing incorporation in a group: *m̀* = us, *mà* = own child, *mà'á* = to give birth or to carry a child, *mhīsī* = own children, *mi* = self, and the possessives *mà* and *m* as in *mba* = my father; mama, thus, is a reflexive possessive that may be glossed "she who bore us," or "she who carries us."

For purposes of understanding Zhu marriage and inheritance, these are the only consanguineal terms that need be considered and we may move on to affinal terms. The trugqa—truma reciprocal pair has affinal, as well as consanguineal, denotations: on marriage into a group, a man's consanguineal trumasi in that group remain his affinal trumasi, but his consanguineal qunquasi/qumasi become affinal trugqasi. In like manner, a woman's trugqasi remain as such, while her qu relations become trumasi. For both sexes, consanguineal tsu becomes father of spouse and is termed ≠*xum* (tcum), as are all other affinalized tsu. It has already been noted that trugqa and truma are compounds; their stem along with tcum may be glossed "in-law." Thus, trugqa and truma denote "belonging to in-laws."

There are only three other affinal terms, and these are also compounds. The consanguineal gxa (when married to tsu) becomes /'*utsu* (tcutsu, from *gu* = take, marry + tsu, hence wife of tsu). Parents of child's spouse are !*untae* (quntae, name + *tae* = mother, hence name-mother) and !*unba* (qunba, name + father, hence name-father). Notice that these two affines were respectively already in the consanguineal qu name relation with the same-sex parent of child's spouse: quntae was qunqa to child's spouse's mother, and qunba was in the same relationship to the father. And, of course, opposite sex parents of this offspring pair had been in the tru relation. This set of co-parents-in-law contains the four persons for whom their childrens' children will usually be named, hence the terms name-mother and name-father. These co-parents-in-law apply the term !*uma* (quma, name-receiver) to all their mutual grandchildren, regardless of sex (Wilmsen, n.d., gives the reason), by whom they are reciprocally called qunqa. Thus, the puzzling aspects of the name relation (Marshall 1957:7–14) becomes clearer; this system operates in a straightforward way, not only to override consanguineal relations but to recognize terminologically a bilateral local descent group that functions as a kindred for individuals. The tendency of descent groups to exclude is balanced by individual interests to expand networks.

We may now consider Zhu marriage. Any opposite sex, same generation descendant of a person's parent's parent's sibling (PPsCC) or parent's parent's parent's sibling (PPPsCCC) is called by a term (trugqa—truma) that connotes persons "belonging to in-laws," and such persons—and only such persons plus their terminological equivalents in alternate generations—are permissible marriage partners and sexual mates. Appropriately, Marshall (1957:21) notes that a joking relationship exists between these persons. She also records that persons in a joking relation, and who apply the reciprocal tru terms to each other, are permissible marriage partners (ibid., 19). The name relation, as illustrated above, serves to reduce the probability of first cousin (PsC) marriages because both partners will have a primary name-relative pair (grandparents) in common. It does not eliminate such marriages, however. The lines of reckoned descent will be orchestrated by the principals to the marriage according to their perceived interests. Adjacent generation primary kin of trumasi—trugqasi are never eligible mates for them, but are accorded respect and, after being linked through a marriage, are addressed by an in-law possessive term (tcum or tcutsu according to gender) by affinal ego.

Marshall (1960:332–333) provides some evidence that this is indeed the system operating among the people she studied. Her Figure 3 is a chart of partial relationships among 108 persons in what she calls 8 band segments. Among these persons, there are 58 spouses of whom 19 are without information regarding their kin; of the remaining 39, 37 have at least one primary kin link (parent or sibling) in the group. As this information is confined largely to a single generation (there are only 8 living persons in the eldest of 3 generations shown, and only 5 marriages in the youngest) and is, no doubt, also incomplete (an unknown number of persons is said to have been omitted), this number of links is even higher than may have been expected. Furthermore, Marshall (ibid., 344) confesses that she has no data on second and third cousin relationships and therefore can say nothing about marriages among persons related in this manner. In the single case she gives that can be worked out, 25-tsamgao is engaged to marry 54-kushay, his MFBSD, as he should.

This discussion has been sharply abbreviated; however, it is fully apparent that Zhu marriage takes place within a clearly defined bilateral descent group in which affines are simply recategorized kin. This overlapping of consanguinity and affinity distorts any assumption of a dichotomy between these categories. There are different lines of reckoning kin, and a person falls into one or the other category according to contingencies of the moment. Kinship in Zhu society, rather than being a static straitjacket, is a dynamic keyboard on which individuals play variations on a theme of options. It is, as Comaroff (1982:164) notes, up to the individual to "create and manage an effective social network."

ZHU LANDOWNERSHIP

Within this incorporative structure of kinship, the corporate unity of Zhu landholding devolves from one generation to the next. Property right transfers consequent on marriage are, accordingly, largely matters of reshuffling priorities among latent claims by members of a kin consort. Negotiations for, and legitimation of, marriage ties are important moments in this creative process. To condense Bourdieu (1977:34–36; original emphasis): "to treat kin relationships as something people *make*, and with which they *do* something, is not merely to substitute a 'functionalist' for a 'structuralist' interpretation . . . it is radically to question the implicit theory of [kin relationships] 'in the form of an object or an intuition' as Marx puts it.

In this perspective, Zhu bride service can be seen not in the decontextualized structural-functionalist terms usually offered (Lee 1979:240–242, 1982:42–43) but as a form of devolutionary marriage payment that mediates the conflicts over land that inevitably must occur among mutually interdependent groups. San bride service has long been recognized as marriage payment in traditional Tswana law and is specifically related to *bogadi*, the Tswana form of marriage payment. In 1930, Tshekedi Khama, then regent of the Bangwato, testified before the British Resident Commissioner that "Bogadi [marriage payment] is a tradition and a right of Masarwa [San]: bride service of one or two years or, if a man owns a cattle, he can pay in stock" (see Wilmsen, n.d.). Schapera (1970:138) notes that when, in 1875, under missionary influence, Khama III abolished bogadi among the Bangwato, he specifically did not ban the practice among his other subjects including San-speakers, who continued to practice their traditional forms of marriage payment.

For Zhu, bride service resolves the question of personal status and locates a marriage union with its offspring within the structure of relations between persons and places. The devolution of property begins with negotiations and prestations between principals to a future marriage, primarily future co-parents-in-law. Wiessner shows this process in action through hxaro (haro) prestations, primarily of beadwork and other symbolically valued materials. This process may extend over a period of many years, as Marshall (1960:351–352) and Lee (1979:240–242) confirm. Devolution begins to take more concrete form with the establishment of a new household located in association with the woman's parents. The period of bride service is measured in terms of offspring, its conditions having been satisfied when two or more children have been born to the union.

Children born during this period in the woman's nqore will have that locality as their primary nqore. This confers lifelong mutual obligations between the woman's natal group and those children and, indeed, on their descendants. It is the inheritance of land that is at issue in bride service and initial residence with wife's parents, not some few pieces of meat that a newly recruited hunter may provide. Lee (ibid., 240) stresses the surface function of hunting prowess. He refers to bride service as a period of probation for the man and fails, thereby, to comprehend its deeper significance. Economics and nutrition are, of course, unassailable necessities in corporal and social life, but the large animal that the young husband is expected to kill and present to his parents-in-law provides not only protein and calories but, more important, symbolically mediates the new relational status of families.

That it is not hunting ability per se that is specifically at stake is confirmed by the fact that domestic animals (either owned or obtained from employers or even purchased with mine labor wages [Lee 1979:241]) are readily substituted for hunted animals. Such substitution does not, however, free the husband from uxorilocal residence obligations. This transferred animal, hunted or herded, should be seen as signifier of commitment by the parties concerned (acceptance is as much an active act as is giving) and has its analogue in the transferred *mokwele* (betrothal) animal among Batswana (Comaroff and Comaroff 1981:34) and *onjova* (wedding) sheep among Ovaherero (Gibson 1959:7). An employed man may more easily evade his commitment than his hunting brother, but he knows this commitment is reciprocal. Half the social and material support for his household resides in his wife's social matrix, for he not only shares with them, they share with him. He may manage his end of the commitment differently, but ultimately his status devolves in the kinship defined network of nqore relations. Without that base, he has no status.

During the period of bride service, devolutionary rights in husband's nqore are kept open by visiting his primary kin who reside there; after that period, if household residence changes to husband's nqore, rights in wife's nqore are kept open by visiting her kin who remain there. Such visiting is undertaken not only to enjoy each other's company. Lee (1979:377, 389–391) documents that nearly 70 percent of all homicides occur when groups are visiting each other and that a high proportion of fights and killings occur between affines. These risks are counterbalanced by the need to keep options open through active participation in social relations to land; expectably, many conflicts arise over the exercise of those options, although they may be masked as simple marital disputes.

It is probable that the frequency and, perhaps, the violence of such Zhu disputes has increased under colonially induced disruptions of relations to land. The source of these disputes in the interpretation of rights and obligations must always have been present, however. For foragers, as for anyone else, these relations, if they are to persist, must be unambiguously expressed even if they are ambiguously practiced. "Because the status of property holdings and exchanges conveys a range of messages concerning social linkages and individual rights, their definition and designation are always critical to the parties involved" (Comaroff and Roberts 1981:175). It is in this dialectic of structure and practice that Zhu regulation of ownership lies.

It is now possible to demonstrate that Zhu kinship and land tenure are stable in space. To begin with, the majority of Zhu marriages take place between people who live in closely contiguous nqoresi. Harpending (1976:161) plots marital distances for a large number of marital pairs who are parents, that is, whose marriages have been stable. Harpending stresses the large distances over which marriages may be contracted. Equally striking, however, is the fact that 53 percent of all partners were married within 30 kilometers of their birthplaces and 78 percent within 60 kilometers; in other words, more than half of all marriage partners were born within the same nqore space and more than three-quarters within the same or adjacent nqoresi as were their spouses. In addition, Harpending (1976:161) states that parent-offspring birthplace distances (distance between birthplace of respondent and that of respondent's parents or children) are even less dispersed. Supporting evidence is provided by Lee (1979:338) who found that 77 percent of his respondents inherited their nqoresi from one or both parents. To this may be added that I (1976:4–7, n.d.) document five-generation continuity of kin-based owner groups at CaeCae.

Thus, the probability of a Zhu person being born in a parent's ancestral land is at least 0.8. This is precisely the result one would expect under a structural system that incorporates primary relatives into spatial entities and puts colaterals into contiguous units linked through reciprocal, bilateral marriage. A high degree of generational continuity of tenured family groups is evident from these data. If anything, events of recent history, which have introduced pressures from European and *difaqane*[5] induced movements, have reduced these probabilities. For example, these pressures are responsible, in conjunction with ecological changes that may be linked to more intensive pastoralist land use keyed to market production, for bringing half of the current rural inhabitants of western Ngamiland to their current places of residence.

Exchange networks play important integrative roles in this social-spatial structure. Wiessner (1977:119, 178; 1982) found that 62 percent of haro partners (persons who engage in reciprocal exchange) are traceable to same grandparents and 82 percent to same great-grandparents. Given the marriage preference and spatial distribution noted, these people will be contiguous, consanguineal relatives among whom are potential as well as actual affines. Wiessner (ibid., 246) gives the spatial distribution of partners by area and distance for a sample of people residing at CaeCae and at Tchumqwe in Namibia. She found that 48 percent and 55 percent, respectively, of haro in these two places is transacted within the home location and 70 percent and 67 percent within 60 kilometers of that location, that is, within same or adjacent nqore. Wiessner also found that a high proportion of this exchange is associated with marriage negotiations.

Thus, kinship, space, and exchange describe an interlocking system of status relationships in which individuals are bound within a set of reciprocal obligations among persons and things. The internal boundaries within this system are zonal rather than incisional but are well known and are open to those with appropriate social ties. Ownership, in the sense in which I have been speaking, is vested in all members of a group who apply a reflexive set of reciprocal terms to each other and refer to themselves as "people who own [have] each other" (Marshall 1976:214). It is this group of people who form the stable set of descendant owners of a place. They are the *n!óré k'àosi* (possessors of place); that is, they are those who have generationally continuous, inherent rights of tenure in their ancestral land.

OTHER SAN SYSTEMS

Schapera (1943:5–7) speaks of "this system of land tenure characteristic of Bushmen" in exactly this way, and the compatibility of other San tenure systems may be indicated quickly. Cognate terms for locational place are: in Nama, *n!u:s*; in Gcwi, *n!ūsà*; in Nharo, *n!û:bà*; in Kqo, *n!óle*; in Kwa, *ņ'ū:*; in Gxanna, *ngo*. All of these terms are clearly derived from a common root. Traill (personal communication) has confirmed the essential meaning to be locative, referring to a person's or group's possessed placed. Common origin and common meaning do not, however, guarantee that terms are parts of otherwise identical systems; other evidence must be called in support.

Silberbauer (1981:99) records that Gcwi attitudes to land are centered on "the fact that the primary bond is between the individual and his band, whereas the link between the individual and territory is derived from the bond between community and land . . . rights . . . flow from band membership." Landownership is vested in band members for whom elders act as intermediaries when nonmembers enter and ask to use the land, "a formality that clearly indicates that the use of territorial resources and residence have to be granted before they are gained" (ibid., 141). Silberbauer is not so clear, however, on the question of the social determinates of membership. He applies a normative, rule-centered approach to his strictly ecological frame of reference, looks for lineal descent groups with nameable ancestors, and finds only shallow lineages in this sense. Nevertheless, he recognizes that, inevitably, real and classificatory kinship links are established, and a high probability of a kinship bond among members exists (ibid., 142). It is apparent that this high probability is the product of Gcwi marriage arrangements in which bilateral cross-cousins are preferred mates. Silberbauer (ibid., 183) lists thirty-four relationship positions, in addition to MBD and FZD, covered by the term glossed "cross-cousin" including, among others, MMBSD, FFZDD, MMMBSSD, and FFFZDDD. He confines his analysis, however, to first cousin marriages despite the fact that all first marriages are between terminological cross-cousins (ibid., 149–150); he of course finds relatively few current first cousin unions among adult males but tells us nothing about the status of other-cousin unions.

Without going into further detail, it is apparent that this cannot be a shallow or divisive system. For any person to know that a descendant of someone probably long dead and never met (perhaps never having been specifically mentioned)—along with terminological equivalents of that descendant—is a potential mate that person must comprehend the system in considerable depth. This requires membership in a group that is stable, although not necessarily static, in person and place. Fragments of texts from the girl's menarcheal ceremony (Silberbauer 1981:151–152) make it clear that such stability is, in fact, conceptually inherent and actually realized in the Gcwi point of view. At menarche, a Gcwi girl's mother introduces her to the group's land: "This is the country of all of us and of you: you will always find food here." And her father introduces her to the group: "See your people . . . see [them] where you go." Tanaka (1980:127–134) presents data that conform to this analysis. He demonstrates that residence groups are tied in a regular manner to kinship: of his residential groups (N = 18), 11 contain 20 parent-child links, 9 have 14 sibling links, and only 3 have no kin ties to the rest of the total group (2 of these are composed of a single married pair each). Tanaka shows further that primary kin ties link adjacent groups and that the relationship among residence units is structured in space as a direct function of kinship distance.

Cashdan (1977:22–24) states that "among the Bag//anakwe, a person has an automatic right of access to an area that is part of his 'lefatshe' (ngo) meaning 'place' or 'territory'" [lefatshe is Setswana]. She discusses the process of the inheritance of land based on "birth and/or residence and/or parentage" and makes clear the kinship matrix that controls access to land, whether for resource exploitation or residence, noting that "the absence of [a claim to kinship] may prevent a person from choosing to use an area even if it is geographically convenient."

Heinz (1972, 1979) documents an equivalent system for the Kqo, as does Barnard (1976, 1979) for the Nharo. Barnard (1979:72–75) details the devolutionary nature of transferral of rights among Nharo: "Kamane, or marriage and childbirth prestations, mark the change in the disposition of rights over individuals." Gifts are exchanged during negotiations for marriage, at marriage, and at the birth of the first child. People are said to be "owned" by their grandparents, ownership being inherited bilaterally. Kamane symbolically mediates transfer of sexual and residence rights at marriage and establishment of primary rights at birth. As among Zhu, Nharo marriage prestations enter the larger gift-giving cycle where they serve to reinforce the continuous association of persons and place. The case for the Ghanzi area of these people has historical documentation. Hahn (1895) concludes the report of his investigation for the Imperial Secretary of Cape Town as follows: "Ghanse can only be claimed by the Bushmen, who admittedly and indisputably from time immemorial, lived on it and never left it." Heinz (1972:412) records the fact that even today Ghanzi ranchers recognize San land divisions that intersect their own holdings and employ San persons in relation to those land divisions. Identical systems for San-speaking Kwa (Hitchcock 1978, 1982) and Tsaase (Vierich-Esch 1982; Hitchcock 1978) in eastern Botswana are recorded. Hitchcock (1982:25–26) emphasizes that even today local

Ngwato wardheads and cattle owners respect Kwa land ownership, if only to the extent of consulting Kwa owners before using the land for their own purposes.

HERERO LAND TENURE

The relevant features of Herero land tenure will be summarized briefly. The principal unit is the *onganda*, a settlement unit constituted by a set of patrilineal affiliates with their wives and children; matrilineal kinsmen and affines may be included, and may even be more numerous, but never organizationally dominant (Gibson 1959). Ozonganda have associated sections of land for grazing in which are located *ozohambo* (sing., ohambo), cattle posts conjoined to water sources of varying permanence.

Almagor (1980:50) vividly documents that a Herero's rights in land are traced exclusively through kin networks. Rights to pasture derive from the concept of locality; a person attached to a specific locality cannot utilize another except by activating his structural links to individuals in the other locality (Almagor 1978; Luttig 1933:96–97). A person's identification with natal household and locality is lifelong, but links to kindred households and localities may be invoked to change residence. Ownership—again, in the sense used here—of land and chattels is vested in the kindred group (Vedder 1938; Luttig 1933:96–97). Marriage is preferred between bilateral cross-cousins, and children are born preferentially in the mother's natal onganda to affirm the spatial-social solidarity among generations of the group (Luttig 1933:69). Possessive particles are applied to persons and things, and, once established, rights to land, water sources, and chattels remain in the group. The wells at CaeCae, for example, are the contemporary states of natural springs that have been progressively deepened by Ovaherero since the mid-1930s; each well has passed in ownership among a set of patrilineally related men. Furthermore, the division of grazing land among CaeCae cattle owners—Herero, Zhu, and Tswana—is such that each set of households has its own section. Similar settlement-tenure rules have been described for the Bakgalagadi (Campbell and Child 1971; Hitchcock and Campbell 1980).

INSTITUTIONAL EQUITY OF TENURE SYSTEMS

Despite significant differences in details, the underlying principles of affiliation and legitimization are compatible among these systems with Tswana institutions of land tenure. Schapera (1943:46–59) encapsulates the essential determinates of place in Tswana law: the location of a Motswana's home is determined primarily by group affiliation, not by income, occupation, or social ambition. Tribal land is apportioned among social units constituted as wards under the administration of headmen. The basis for establishing a ward was initially kinship or ethnic identity, although this is no longer invariably the case. Areas *mofatshe* (rights to use specific sections of land) are allocated to members of a ward and may be passed to descendants, but the land remains the property of the tribe under the administration of the chief and his headmen. Rights are acquired by membership in the tribe and are activated by application to the headman of the ward to which one belongs (Schapera 1938:195–213). Schapera (1963:164–169) further notes that in precolonial times, fission, as a result of tenure disputes, was common among Tswana, for whom in such cases assassination or secession was the principal recourse. As a Motswana recently put it, "It's just that we moved around a lot looking for good land" (Kiyaga-Mulindwa 1980:85). Thus, it would appear that before direct colonial intervention, San and Tswana tenurial systems had as much in common as they now superficially appear to lack.

The important thing to note is the structural commonality of land tenure among San, Ovaherero, and Batswana. The only conclusion that can be reached is that San tenure has been, and continues to attempt to be, generationally stable and sanctioned by traditional native rules that are congruent with other southern African systems. The basis of rights to land is membership in a kinship group whose history is associated with a specific parcel of geographic space. That related persons are admitted to an owner group's land in order to share ecological resources reinforces, rather than weakens, the fact of tenure rights based in group sociality. For only certain persons who can claim participation in the social polity are admitted and then only after presenting their kinship credentials for examination.

Multitiered ownership of places and things have characterized the remembered and recorded past. Space associated with one particular group was layered on that of other groups. This was possible not because of some altruistic urge for accommodation but because the tenure systems of the different competing peoples were intelligible to each other, and their ecological requirements were to some extent complementary rather than conflicting. Displacement and display were the usual modes of defense of these tenures, with considerable negotiation based on detailed examination of genealogies given an important part in the process (see Comaroff 1973). Fights over land did, and do, occur, of course; all the Zhu cases given by Lee (1979:336–

338) illustrate this, although he chooses to interpret them as revealing paucity of structure rather than structural articulations of persons in place. The literature of conflict for Ovaherero is vast (Vedder 1938; Tlou 1972, 1976; Estermann 1976) as is that for Batswana (Parsons 1982 gives an extensive summary). And the history of subjugation of San-speaking peoples by Batswana is well documented (Tagart 1933; Joyce 1938; Silberbauer and Kuper 1966; Tlou 1977; Hitchcock 1978; Wilmsen, n.d.). Nevertheless, a striking feature of current settlement in the Kalahari is its continuity—a continuity that transcends time and space and ethnicity despite some major displacements of peoples. The current distribution of groups in the region is clearly the product of a very long process of interaction involving congruent social concepts and complementary economic systems. If this were not the case, current debates within Botswana over the reallocation of tenure rights (Hitchcock 1982; Wilmsen 1982*a*, n.d.; and Kerven 1982 give extensive overviews) would not be necessary. These systems were able to maintain their integrity until disrupted by the penetration of commodity capitalism in this century. It appears that even during the initial colonial period of mercantile capitalism in the nineteenth century, they were able to retain significant parts of their former structures that—though continually modified in relation to each other—continue to be realized today.

NOTES

1. A short, preliminary version of this chapter was presented to the Third International Conference on Hunting-Gathering Societies held at Bad Holmburg, Federal Republic of Germany, in May 1983. The research on which it is based was supported by the National Science Foundation, the National Endowment for the Humanities, the Social Science Research Council, the Wenner-Gren Foundation for Anthropological Research, the Max-Planck-Institut für Verhaltensphysiologie, the Rackham Graduate School of the University of Michigan, and the government of Botswana.

2. I use "San" instead of the discredited "Bushmen" as a general categorial term to encompass those southern African peoples who speak Khoisan languages and are known in the anthropological literature as hunter-gatherers or foragers. This term, if unqualified, is also increasingly difficult to defend because it lumps together peoples with different social and economic histories. To avoid unnecessary terminological confusion, I retain San but solely as an adjective to designate those peoples who speak Khoisan languages other than Nama; for my present purpose, I take these to be those called foragers. When referring to speakers of a specific San language, I use their self-referent name for themselves. Those with whom I am most familiar call

themselves žu/'hōasi; they are better known in anthropological literature as !Kung. They now live in Botswana and Namibia between roughly 19°S–22°S and 19°E–22°E. This area has been labeled variously the NyaeNyae (Marshall 1976) or the Dobe (Lee 1979) region. The word !kung is an anglicized rendition of !xū, which means 'person' in a regional variant, spoken mainly in Angola, of the language group known as !Kung. This word (!kung) is used by linguists to designate the group of northern Bush languages (Vedder 1910; Bleek 1929; Westphal 1963) spoken in Botswana, Namibia, and Angola, of which žu!'hōasi is a dialectical variant. Snyman (1970) originally used !xū to designate žu!'hōasi in his grammar of this language but has since changed to the latter term (Snyman 1975). The San people within the coordinates indicated invariably use žu!'hōasi as the designation for themselves and their language (žu = person, people; !'hōa = real, true, complete; si = plural suffix: hence, completed or true people). For this reason, I use žu!'hōasi as the name of these people and for simplicity in presentation abbreviate it to Zhu, a convention that is in keeping with their own usage. For proper names of peoples and places, I use Setswana spelling as found in the *Third Report of the Place-Names Commission* (1984), which establishes standard usage for Botswana. Setswana uses 'c' for the dental (/) and alveolar (≠), 'x' for the lateral (//), and 'q' for the palatal (!) clicks.

3. The encompassing background for this examination, the histories of the peoples considered and the colonial system as it impinged on them, is presented in my forthcoming book, *Land Filled with Files: A Political Economy of the Kalahari* (Wilmsen, n.d.).

4. Thorough reconsideration of Zhu kinship and marriage may be found in *Land Filled with Flies*; only the outlines necessary to comprehend the active dialectic among Zhu kinship, marriage, and inheritance of land are presented here.

5. The "time of troubles," a series of wars that engulfed southern Africa during the 1820s and 1830s. *Difaqane* is Sotho-Tswana; *mfecane* is the Nguni form.

4

James Bay Cree Self-Governance and Land Management[1]

Harvey A. Feit

The recent trend toward anthropological perspectives that locate foraging peoples within history and within the context of relationships to wider economies and polities is the major development transforming recent scholarly literature on hunters and gatherers. It is a purpose of this discussion to document the diversity and complexity of those relationships, which have not been fully recognized in recent studies. A parallel goal is to document the fundamental conflicts that are inherent in foragers' relationships with developed liberal-democratic states. A third objective is to assess the extent to which it may be possible to resolve or moderate those conflicts in the context of efforts to restructure the relationships between the James Bay Cree and the political and economic systems with which they have extensive interactions.

Within the anthropological literature there are varying, often covert, assumptions about whether the developing linkages between foraging peoples and wider economies and nation-state institutions are desirable. Some liberals and some conservatives want to isolate foraging peoples in an effort to maintain their autonomy or their cultures. Some radicals and some Marxists want to isolate foraging peoples in an effort to maintain their egalitarian relations and/or their modes of production. Some liberals and some conservatives want to integrate foraging peoples into the wider systems so that they may better benefit from the national prosperity or future national development. Some radicals and some Marxists want to integrate foraging peoples into the wider systems so they can find needed allies with those who share their present or future class interests.

The list could go on, but the point is that none of these formulations tell us much about the range of views we might find expressed among foraging peoples themselves. In my experience, the views of foraging peoples include all the above but also many other perspectives as well. These peoples have a wide variety of goals and means to these goals, means with which they seek to make their history. Their choices among means and goals are often unexpected; at the same time, their responses to these choices are often insightful and farsighted in addition to being pragmatic. To participate more effectively in whatever roles they are invited to play and are capable of playing in these historical processes, anthropologists will have to examine more precisely what the experiences have been with various strategies of response to the linkages of foraging societies into wider systems. This is a modest contribution to the latter need.

I present a case study of one foraging people's efforts to restructure their linkages to wider systems of economy and nation-state polity within a developed liberal-democratic nation. I show that the linkages that already exist in such states are more complex than has generally been recognized in the existing prescriptive discussions on how foragers should respond. In doing so, I show that the James Bay Cree Indian people of northern Quebec had a distinctive set of aspirations for their linkages to the non-Cree world.

I also explore the limits for short-term restructuring within a liberal-democratic state. These limits are sufficiently narrow that fundamental conflicts between Cree aspirations and state aspirations and practice do exist which cannot be resolved in the short term. Nevertheless, within the limits of a liberal-democratic state, there are quite diverse and important short-term means by which a foraging people can enhance their opportunities to pursue their aspirations in the longer run. The future outcomes, however, remain decidedly uncertain.

The James Bay Cree have a long history of linkage. The mercantile fur trade reached them indirectly through Indian intermediaries, probably considerably before the Hudson's Bay Company set up its first trading post in North America on Cree lands, three-fourths of the way through the seventeenth century. And specific government Indian policies and programs also reached them indirectly through the Hudson's Bay Company and through Christian missionaries decades before a governmental administration was established in their region in the 1930s and 1940s. Their lands were opened to industrial exploitation of wildlife and mineral and forestry resources following the building of a railway one hundred miles south of their lands in 1914-15. But industrial resource exploitation was limited in scale by problems of accessibility until the transportation networks for large-scale activities were greatly expanded in the 1960s. From that point on, a growing number of mining and forestry operations and towns was established, along with development of the hydroelectric resources of the region (Feit 1982, 1986).

The commencement of the James Bay Hydroelectric Project in 1971-72 represented to the Cree a critical expansion of the rate of resource exploitation and of threat to their own society and economy. Responses to the project became a focus of concern and challenge to the external agencies initiating resource developments in the region. A group of young Cree mobilized the Cree population to support opposition to the hydroelectric project, while soliciting advice from Cree elders on goals to seek in opposition (Richardson 1975). The elders saw current development schemes as part of a long historical process going back to the arrival of Europeans. The problem they focused on was that throughout this history, resource development was solely in the hands of outsiders and the needs of Cree people had been given little or no consideration. In short, Cree had no voice in decisions about the development of the resources of their region (Feit 1985*a*).

In response, the elders saw the opposition to the hydroelectric project in the context of the need to restructure long-term relationships with nonnatives. The goal was not to completely stop the project but to have an effective voice in modifying it so it would be acceptable to the Cree and to have an effective voice in all nonnative development in the region. Opposition to the hydroelectric project in the courts or in negotiations was an essential immediate means toward the long-term goals. The tone was conciliatory, the desired means were negotiation, but the change being sought was fundamental.

In a Cree view, the goal was obvious and reasonable as it expressed the essence of a responsible reciprocity that Cree value in all relationships: reciprocity that permits others access to resources they need but within a mutual respect for the autonomy and needs of each, so that all can survive in security and well-being. In this view, mature and responsible relationships respect the needs of others and demand such respect in return. The Cree thus neither sought sole control of land and resources nor did they deny access to nonnatives. Neither did they seek to retreat into a self-imposed isolation. In a Cree view, it was possible to maintain autonomy within an ongoing relationship.

They therefore did not see as incompatible outcomes the possibility of maintaining an autonomous self-governing society while participating in wider linkages so as to permit, and to benefit from, developments by nonnatives. Elders sought the security and wealth that would prevent the starvation known in earlier decades and that would give them a share of the wealth accumulated by nonnatives during centuries of fur trading. Younger Cree sought productive work for those who could not hunt full-time and a share of the wealth they knew was a taken-for-granted feature of everyday life for the sections of Canadian society they could see around them. And Cree did not see these as contradictory goals that could not be achieved simultaneously.

Cree opposition to hydroelectric development in negotiations and in courts led over a four-year period to the James Bay and Northern Quebec Agreement (JBNQA, also referred to as the Agreement) (Anonymous 1976). Completed in 1975, it was the first modern comprehensive aboriginal rights agreement in Canada and the first such settlement to explicitly specify a set of aboriginal rights, including the means thought necessary to maintain the relative autonomy of a group of indigenous hunters within a modern nation-state (Hunt 1978; Feit 1980, 1985*b*; Asch 1984). The negotiation process was a difficult one because while the Cree and Inuit were determined to maintain and enhance their self-governance and their hunting cultures, societies, and economies, they had to accede to the asserted rights of provincial and federal governments to promote the general development of the natural resources of the region and to assure a clear national sovereignty over the land and all the peoples thereon. These conflicts structured the framework in which the negotiations with Quebec provincial and Canadian federal governments proceeded.

The conflict was defined by two issues: development, which hinged on control of economic resources, and sovereignty, which hinged on the distribution of political power. On the one hand, government insisted that it retain the final authority over all development in the region, except on lands reserved for Indians, to assure that aboriginal people could not block regional development; government also retained final jurisdiction over legal and administrative authority applying to lands and peoples, although this authority was divided between the two levels of government and could be delegated to other governmental institutions. On the other hand, Cree insisted that the maintenance of their hunting societies depended on continuing access to, and protection of, the wildlife resources of most of the lands of the region, not just to those of the reserves, which covered only a limited portion of their hunting lands. Further, they insisted on their need to continue, and indeed enhance, the areas over which they exercised self-governance, although this particular term was not used at the time (Feit 1980).

These positions had to be discussed through negotiation because neither side had the power to impose its views absolutely and without significant cost. From government's point of view, it was forced, by a partial Cree and Inuit victory in a court case against the James Bay Hydroelectric Project, to accept the fact that the aboriginal rights of Cree and Inuit had not been extinguished by any government action and therefore the aboriginal litigants were able to effectively ask the courts to intervene on their behalf against developers (Malouf 1973; Richardson 1975).

From the native standpoint, it was unclear whether the courts would maintain a strong definition of aboriginal rights and actually prevent development or merely recognize a usufructuary interest in the land, which would have a more limited impact on development activities. Given the parliamentary system, it was also clear that government legislation could extinguish, or more likely unilaterally define, what the aboriginal right was although not without a public outcry. These considerations made undefined aboriginal rights effective levers for court challenges to disrupt—if not permanently stop—development and for political protest. The same considerations made it unlikely, however, that a strict insistence on legal pursuit of aboriginal rights in the short or medium term would result in a fundamental redistribution of power within political structures or in adequate protection of the indigenous peoples from the immediate impacts of the ongoing development. In addition, the ongoing construction of the project put Cree and Inuit under significant pressure, because during the years a court case would take, they would suffer the impacts of the development, many of which would have long-term consequences.

The distribution of power and legal resources available to them, the ongoing construction of the James Bay Hydroelectric Project, and the overall package of benefits negotiated to support their hunting societies led the Cree and Inuit to seek a compromise within the framework of the negotiations when it became clear that they could not achieve a more comprehensive or just fulfillment of their goals. The main body of this chapter is a discussion of the short- and medium-term experience with the JBNQA and, more specifically, on the means it explores for reconciling conflicts over control and use of wildlife in the James Bay region of Quebec. This case material is used to examine the possible limits of aboriginal autonomy within a developed liberal-democratic state. Before proceeding to specific case materials, I provide below a brief, general outline of the Agreement provisions.

OUTLINE OF THE AGREEMENT

The main areas of Cree concern, and therefore the main areas addressed by the Agreement, were (1) modifications to the plans for the hydroelectric project; (2) native control of land; (3) protection of hunting rights and resources; (4) enhancement of Cree self-governance; (5) establishment of a balance of government powers between Cree and provincial and federal authorities; and (6) control of future developments. In each of these areas, Cree negotiators worked extensively to explore possibilities for achieving goals within the constraints of the negotiation context. And although several innovative and important measures were developed, in other areas no effective agreements were found.

The insistence of federal and provincial governments that the James Bay region be open for development significantly limited the land base the Cree could negotiate. The provincial government took the position that land under Cree control, effectively owned, be limited to areas immediately around the settlements and adjacent hunting locations. No satisfying arrangement was reached on this issue. The maximum land the province would transfer to Cree control was only 5,500 square kilometers, called Category I lands, of the approximately 375,000-square-kilometer region. This area was sufficient to provide an effective base for community sites, some buffer against adjacent development projects, and protection that mineral developments in the areas could only proceed with native consent. Cree local governments would generally control access and residence on these reserve lands as well as use of forestry resources. The land provided through the negotiations, however, gave only limited natural resources that could form a basis for economic development and only very limited protection for the hunting economy.

Cree negotiators sought to reduce their dependence on government authority and administration and to take more control of their own affairs through enhanced self-governing institutions. They thus negotiated with the governments for recognition of their rights to govern their own affairs in their communities and the need for new regional government structures but within the sovereignty of the existing Canadian state. Cree were a minority in their region, comprising approximately 7,000 people distributed in seven settlements in the James Bay territory, as opposed to 20,000 Euro-Canadians. They therefore sought regional autonomy and self-determination through the formation of distinctive, ethnically defined governments and boards with authority over Cree lands, which would assure native control and administration of their affairs under legal provisions established in the negotiations. This pattern was generally acceptable to government because it was compatible with their sovereignty; it transferred the Cree from federal to provincial jurisdictions, a goal being sought by both levels of government; and the province was prepared to accept the decentralization of provincial responsibility to regional boards and governments.

At the community level, the Cree got agreement that there would be special legislation for a Cree Act extending the powers of their band councils in new community governments and replacing the provisions of the existing national Indian Act. Among the provisions were (1) communal decision making, a reallocation of powers between the community as a whole, the band council, and the Minister of Indian Affairs to better conform with Cree values, and (2) additional powers over lands. In addition, a Cree Regional Authority would be established, controlled by representatives elected by the communities and mandated to manage compensation funds provided by governments. Several regional service administrations were also to be established, a Cree school board, a health and social services board, and police units within the provincial system; also, changes were to be made to the existing administration of justice. The education board would be established under provincial legislation but would be run by Cree members who would hire the school administration and teaching staff. In addition to the regular authority of provincial school boards, the elected Cree board would also have several special powers including discretion for hiring native teachers without completed teacher qualifications, instruction in their own language, development of a special curriculum, and alterations to the school year schedule. Similar special modifications were provided for other boards. The effect of these provisions was to give Cree substantially increased control of their own government and of the administration of basic services (for a different assessment of the effects, see LaRusic et al. 1979).

These complex and detailed negotiations also emphasized the diversity of the linkages that already existed between the Cree and the political and economic institutions of wider Canadian society. Key institutions of Cree self-governance, including existing band councils and new regional authorities, were already then established in Canadian law and required specific negotiations to modify or establish them. Basic education, health, social, and security services were already common in Cree communities, but their terms needed to be further negotiated to establish adaptations both to Cree needs and values and to Cree control. The extent of the shift, in the previous few decades, from relatively "traditional" foraging societies to societies with relative and changing forms of autonomy within a network of ties to wider systems was clear as Cree sought to systematically restructure those relationships.

The discussions also provided for monetary compensation and economic development for Cree. Their share of compensation funds was to total $137 million (Canadian, hereafter C$) over twenty years. This was over and above the several tens of millions of dollars spent each year by governments for education, medical care, social services, housing, community infrastructures, and other services provided to Indian peoples by the Canadian state. In addition, specific moneys were to be available for the promotion of economic enterprises, and special funds were to be used for remedial works. With respect to project modifications, the Agreement included several changes to project plans. But these changes were not numerous or of large scale, so it was essential to provide funds for remedial works to be undertaken as future impacts were experienced. Cree negotiators, however, agreed only to a detailed description of the hydroelectric project. Because the project was still being planned, this assured that any future changes would require the consent of Cree regional authorities; in fact, this has provided an opportunity for occasional Cree responses to ongoing project design. These project modifications reduced the direct consequences around villages and assured future participation for Cree; but they also meant that the project would go ahead, substantially as planned, and that substantial impacts on the land and wildlife of the region would result. Despite major efforts by Cree negotiators, no other major project modifications could be agreed on.

The main legal provisions of the Agreement provided for eventual Cree and Inuit withdrawal of legal opposition to the hydroelectric project and of claims to other undefined land rights; they also provided for recognition by both governments of the rights spelled out in the Agreement. The detailed legal structure of the Agreement, involving over 450 pages of text and eventually requiring dozens of new laws and modifications to existing legislation to give it force of law, is also a testimony to the complexity of linkages in which aspects of Cree society had become embedded.

The agreement reached after two years of negotiation and discussion in Cree villages was taken back to each Cree community for approval or rejection as a whole. People did not consider the Agreement to be fair or just but thought it would increase their chances of maintaining their culture, society, and economy—given the alternatives—and all Cree communities accepted it. The key parts of this acceptance were provisions for the hunting, fishing, and trapping rights of Cree.

PROVISIONS OF THE JBNQA FOR MANAGEMENT AND USE OF WILDLIFE

I will examine the provisions of the Agreement relating to hunting, fishing, and trapping in some detail to better identify the constraints on Cree self-governance within Canada and to assess the opportunities and effectiveness of negotiable measures designed to enhance long-term pursuit of self-governance within the existing constraints. Discussion of the provisions of the Agreement relating to self-governance and management of wildlife focuses on five areas of conflict: recognition and definition of basic rights of native hunters; management of wildlife resources; allocation of resources among conflicting users; provision of adequate cash incomes for indigenous hunters; and protection of renewable resources from the effects of nonrenewable resource development. Each problem area, with its practical responses, is set briefly into three contexts: (1) the relation of the problem to capitalist or nation-state formations is identified; (2) the possibilities for relative autonomy inherent in those formations that the responses try to exploit, as well as the constraints on those possibilities, are identified; (3) the extent to which these responses have mobilized and enhanced, or endangered, Cree autonomy is also indicated.

RECOGNITION OF RIGHTS OF NATIVE HUNTERS

Throughout much of Canada, no basic and inalienable native right to harvest and use wildlife resources is recognized. Native peoples are accorded various rights to use renewable resources by the Crown; the rights so accorded are, in the view of government, subject to change by the will of the Crown alone. In the past, the exercise of the Crown's authority has been constrained only partially, mainly by political considerations and by treaty obligations in certain areas. Indigenous peoples, however, have consistently asserted their aboriginal rights, including a right to harvest and use renewable resources, not subject to government authority (Usher 1984). The aboriginal peoples' rights and responsibilities arise through spiritually and socially sanctioned relationships to land, animals, and God (Feit 1986). In the view of Cree hunters, their rights are received from God and are grounded in the order of the world; to them, these rights and responsibilities extend to all humans. Reciprocity is the central idiom of resource use—reciprocity between men and animals, reciprocities within Cree communities, and reciprocity between Euro-Canadian and Cree users of the land (Scott 1983). Such reciprocity is manifest, in the Cree view, in the respect shown to God, in the respect with which animals and environments are treated, and in the respect with which each resource user should treat the needs of other resource users.

The standard Canadian formula of recognizing hunting rights on unoccupied Crown lands is clearly inconsistent with this view as well as inadequate for maintenance of renewable resource-based economies, as the history of nonnative occupation of southern Canada has indicated. It was therefore necessary to develop alternative legal formulations of indigenous harvesting rights during negotiation of the Agreement. The Agreement had also, in the Cree view, to recognize the Cree's own culturally distinctive system of rights and privileges. The negotiated agreement provides for a native right to hunt, fish, and trap—called a right to harvest—all species of fauna, at all times, over all categories of land in the entire territory used by Cree, wherever this activity is possible physically. The right to harvest includes the right to conduct all of the hunting, fishing, trapping, and related activities that the Cree people are now pursuing and have traditionally pursued. This was intended to codify, in modern terms, aboriginal hunting rights and to give them legal force binding on governments at all levels.

The one significant constraint on the right to harvest is that it is subject to the principle of conservation, which is specifically defined in the Agreement; "Conservation means the pursuit of the optimum natural productivity of all living resources and the protection of the ecological systems of the Territory so as to protect endangered species and to ensure primarily the continuance of the traditional pursuits of the native people, and secondarily the satisfaction of the needs of non-native people for sport hunting and fishing." In essence, the principle of conservation provides that the right to harvest may be limited only under specific conditions in order to protect endangered species and ecological systems. These limitations are essential to the reconciliation of the interests of the governments and those of the indigenous population. The principle signifies the acceptance by both indigenous peoples and governments of the priority interest in protecting wildlife and environments, and it binds all action by Cree and governments.

The rights and the principles were binding because they are stated both in the Agreement and the laws that give legislative force to the terms of the agreement. The legislation is subject to parliamentary politics and discretion; however, because this legislation does not replace the Agreement, because the Agreement states that the legislation must reflect the provisions of the JBNQA, and because the Agreement is a legally binding contract between the Cree and the governments of Quebec and Canada, any change in the provisions must involve changes in the Agreement. Changes can be made only with Cree consent. Recourse in the event of a breach of this contract would be to the courts. More recently, the JBNQA has been given standing under the Canadian constitution, placing it beyond the powers of parliament and effectively denying the possibility of unilateral changes by any one government.

The right to harvest, as set out in the JBNQA, was also intended to give legal recognition to the Cree system of hunting and to provide the basis for hunters to pursue their way of life according to their own culturally ordered knowledge, decisions, and activities. The agreement does not try to codify or define the Cree cultural system but recognizes its existence and its key structures: the system of hunting territories and of "owners" of territories, which are called, respectively, "traplines" and "tallymen" (Tanner 1979; Feit 1986). A trapline is defined as an area in which harvesting is conducted under the supervision of a Cree tallyman. A tallyman is defined as a person responsible for a trapline and recognized by a Cree community. These definitions incorporate the essential cultural concepts and practices of Cree use and management of wildlife without forcing the specific features of the system to be codified; these features are, therefore, left flexible for definition and adaptation by Cree. The complex system of socially distributed rights and privileges to land and resources, expressed as normative rules as well as in everyday processes of dispute and decision, is thus alluded to but not directly altered.

The agreement that was struck by the JBNQA definition of harvesting rights was accepted because it provided an acceptable series of compromises on several issues but especially those relating to sovereignty: (1) it recognized Cree rights but left open the question of the source of those rights, a form that did not make them dependent on a delegation of government authority but that also did not challenge government sovereignty by asserting an alternative source of legitimacy; (2) while not challenging sovereignty of government, the rights limited governments' claimed rights to unilaterally change Cree rights and thereby limited future exercise of government sovereignty; (3) both Cree and governments submitted themselves to a principle of protecting animals and wildlife; and (4) government recognized the indigenous Cree system of management of land and wildlife resources. These provisions have generally worked to date, although I will note below problems in the pursuit of conservation.

MANAGEMENT OF WILDLIFE RESOURCES

In northern Canada, values, goals, and methods of conservation and wildlife management differ among the culturally distinct populations of the area; in turn, these differ from goals of and methods used by government-mandated wildlife managers (Berkes 1977, 1981*a*, 1982). My own research among the Waswanipi Cree of Quebec emphasized the structure of one indigenous Cree hunting system. This system not only serves to constrain the use of wildlife resources but also, at least under certain conditions, serves to manage the resources (Feit 1986).

In general, the research on Cree hunting activities supports the conclusion that the Waswanipi seek to manage resources, and biological indicators support the conclusion that they usually achieve this objective. An important factor in this success is the extensive knowledge that senior hunters have of the land and wildlife they hunt. This knowledge comes from observing trends in game population indicators and harvests over many years. Harvests are adjusted in response to these trends. The observed indicators of moose and beaver populations include trends in numbers of animal signs and sightings, numbers of moose yards and beaver colonies, sizes of aggregations or colonies, age and sex structures of animals, frequency of births along with frequency of twinning in moose, the size of cohorts among beaver (judged in part from observations of placental scars during butchering), and the general health of animals. These are precisely the kinds of data that nonnative game managers try to get in order to manage moose and beaver populations. Senior Cree hunters who have returned frequently to the same hunting territories and who know in great detail these distinct tracts (which average about 1,200 square kilometers) have more detailed knowledge of the game populations they hunt and manage than nonnative game managers can usually have for the vast tracts under their management and intermittent observation (Feit 1986). Cree argued that their capabilities as managers should be acknowledged in the structure of the JBNQA.

Cree knew that their indigenous system of wildlife management was also highly resilient and adaptable but that this did not mean it was complete or sufficient in itself. Research has identified several conditions under which indigenous management systems require alteration: loss of control over resources, rapid technological change, commercialization of subsistence uses, and rapid population growth (Berkes 1981*b*). In northern Quebec, the indigenous management system, based on hunting territories or traplines, has existed at least since the beginning of this century, and there is good evidence of its existence at the beginning of the last century as well as plausible grounds for assuming it to have existed under certain conditions in the period before contact with Europeans. During this century, there have been successive intrusions by outsiders who have threatened conservation of the resources. There has also been extensive technological change, increased pressure for commercialization, and rapid population growth. Moreover, there has been the introduction of new consumer demands, nonnative-controlled education, more sedentary life-styles, extensive land-based development, and increased bureaucracy. The wildlife management system has, however, been maintained.

Cree have had to respond to these various changes. Although it has not always been possible to maintain the system with respect to all species, they have abandoned it only in those times, under those circumstances, and for those species for which it was temporarily not possible to continue management practices. For example, when there were competing fur trappers in the 1920s and 1930s, the Waswanipi Cree feared loss of control of the resource and appear to have trapped out beaver and marten. However, they did not overhunt moose or other furbearers. Simultaneously, they petitioned the government to restore their exclusive use and effective control over resources so that they could reestablish beaver populations and return to good management practices (Feit 1984, 1986). Various changes resulted from these events, some of which made it appear to outsiders, especially government wildlife managers, that fundamental control of wildlife had shifted to government. In practice, only the Cree had a sufficiently detailed knowledge of trends in local game populations to be able to manage them, and any local and detailed management by government agents was not enforceable if it was not supported by Cree tallymen.

In the widely decentralized system of hunting territories (there are about 300 in the James Bay region of Quebec), only the most general and ineffective regulations can be enforced by a centralized authority. This situation provides an incentive for reconciliation between competing interests in the management of wildlife; Cree cooperation is essential for effective management.

But if the fact that it can be regulated only by decentralized "owners" of hunting territory is a strength of the Cree system, this is not to say that it can be isolated from outside interventions. History shows that the actions of nonnatives can disrupt the system. The historical limitation of the system lies in its ability to regulate only the activities of members of the indigenous community, and this is why recognition of the system in the JBNQA was insufficient. Means were still needed to regulate non-Cree use and the effects of this use on wildlife. Governmental authority and cooperation were therefore also essential for effective management. This situation provided additional incentive for the expansion of efforts to achieve reconciliation. There was a need to articulate the indigenous systems with management systems designed to regulate nonnative activities; there is mutual benefit in recognizing both systems. Therefore, the JBNQA, besides protecting hunters' autonomy by recognizing Cree rights and their culturally defined system, also recognized that there would have to be new structures and principles for articulating that system with government powers. Most of the specific provisions of the JBNQA are designed around this latter need. The structures are needed to continually regulate nonnative hunting and resource use with respect to the numbers of hunters and to the times, places, and sizes of their catches. The establishment of such structures was acceptable to Cree because it recognized primarily the need to regulate nonnative wildlife resource use and only secondarily Cree uses.

Given the effectiveness of indigenous management, the Agreement recognizes that there should be as little interference with Cree use as possible. Because harvesting is limited by the principle of conservation, so long as Cree conservation is effective, Cree are considered to be complying with this condition. Interference with Cree practices can occur only if and when one party—native or government—claims (and can plausibly show) that a conservation problem exists, whether it is caused by native or nonnative peoples. Depending on the nature of the problem, its solution may or may not involve alterations in Cree practices for the short or long term. When it does involve alterations, conservation decisions affecting native peoples will be implemented first through guidelines or advisory programs or both, which amount to specific encouragements within native self-regulation. If these mechanisms are not effective or if they are inappropriate, government regulations may be used. However, regulations must be used in such a way as to create a minimum of interference with native peoples and harvesting activities. If regulations do not conform to this pattern, they are unlikely to be fully or even extensively enforceable. The underlying assumptions are that the new structures will come into play only when problems arise and that, when they are needed, the Cree people and the appropriate governments will wish to see the problem resolved to protect the resource.

The major area of conflict was the relative authority of native and nonnative institutions in these regulatory structures and processes. Cree wanted final decision-making authority or shared authority; federal and provincial governments claimed such authority as an aspect of sovereignty. The idea of coordinating management through a joint committee developed in response to this confrontation but failed to settle the issue of who would control the joint system and have the authority to take and implement decisions. With little common ground on this issue, the only proposal on which Cree negotiators could obtain agreement was that for the establishment of a coordinating committee with equal representation for the interested parties. This would be primarily a consultative body. The provincial and federal governments retained a final decision-making authority for most, but not all, issues; however, their authority would be constrained. The goals and principles for management decisions, such as conservation and minimal impact on Cree activities, are legally binding on government decision makers, and a complex procedural system of consultation must be followed before advice of the joint committees can be set aside. This system respects government sovereignty while significantly constraining any exercise of that sovereignty which might negate Cree rights or benefits.

Although key tests have not yet arisen, this system appears to be only partially workable in practice. The system is complex and bureaucratic; when it is not used in an atmosphere of goodwill, those using it can lose sight of issues in a plethora of procedures and rights. Futhermore, where there are significant conflicts between interests expressed by Cree and those expressed by governments, the system tends to inaction or slow action on the part of governments. Inaction has become a major tool of the governments for avoiding their legal obligations, thereby making it more difficult for Cree to bring court challenges based on contentions that government has acted in violation of the Agreement. Government does not, therefore, always respond effectively to Cree needs and sometimes undermines Cree rights (Feit, n.d.).

Beyond this, government has not always acted in the interests of conservation and has often responded primarily to political pressure from nonnatives rather than to conservation needs. To this extent, a fundamental assumption of JBNQA negotiations—that conservation was a shared priority goal—has not been systematically confirmed by experience with the implementation of the Agreement. Furthermore, the coordinating committee is still often treated as a body that is consulted only casually and after major policy decisions have been made rather than as an integrated system of advice with a role in all stages of government policy development and implementation. While some improvements have occurred as the process has been longer in place and as experience with it develops, it has, nevertheless, remained a largely paternalistic and only sometimes responsive process. The extent of governmental and bureaucratic backtracking and violation of specific provisions of the Agreement has raised questions about whether inherent trust in the responsibility of the governments to fulfill their commitments, essential to the effectiveness of even a detailed and legally forceful agreement, can be expected (Feit, n.d.). This finding has important implications for the use of legal structures to formalize and regulate relationships between indigenous peoples and nation-states, a point not lost on other indigenous groups seeking negotiations within Canada.

REGULATION OF CONFLICTS BETWEEN NATIVE AND NONNATIVE USERS

Conflicts between native and nonnative users of wildlife are common in many, but not all, areas of the North (Brelsford 1980, 1982, 1983*b*; Usher 1981, 1984). In the James Bay region of Quebec, where the conflicts have long standing and are already deeply entrenched, the basic question of how resources will be allocated is of central concern to the Cree. The first key to dealing with these conflicts is agreement on the relative merits and strengths of claims made by various user groups. This relative ranking is largely a political process, shaped at various times by legal and ideological features of both societies. In the last decade, the principle of priority for native use has gained ground. It is still clouded, however, by questions of whether it applies equally to all indigenous peoples or only those with treaties or specific legal statuses within Canadian law, whether there should be an economic means or subsistence test, whether the priority should include nonnative peoples with similar life-styles if not similar social communities, and whether the priority applies to only subsistence uses or includes various exchange, monetized, or commercialized uses.

Recognition of native priority was a key to agreements on each of these points, as indicated above and as codified in the definition of conservation previously cited. Various mechanisms were established to regulate conflicts and allocate resources according to these priorities. One provision was intended to limit the extent of potential conflict by reserving certain species and geographic areas for native peoples; the second was to establish a mechanism to put into operation the priority allocation of resources for native harvesting over sport hunting and fishing; and the third was to design an outfitting regime that would provide an important degree of practical native control over aspects of nonnative hunting and fishing activities.

The measures for priority of harvesting guaranteed the native peoples a minimum fixed level of harvest, if permitted by animal population levels. This provision would effectively cut off sport hunting or fishing when animal populations declined and would reserve the entire available catch for the native peoples, thereby protecting subsistence production during the period of greatest vulnerability. The fixed level of guaranteed allocation was acceptable to the native peoples, however, only when it was linked to additional provisions stipulating that larger kills were possible when warranted by game populations and that allocations to native and nonnative hunters above the guaranteed level would be based on need. Because it is impossible in practice to guarantee actual harvests over time, the mechanism finally adopted provides for governments and native peoples to establish fixed, guaranteed levels of permissible harvests to natives. These levels are to be based primarily on the results of a joint research project concerning native harvests of wildlife during a seven-year period (James Bay and Northern Quebec Native Harvesting Research Committee [JBNQNHRC], 1982). Once the guaranteed level is established, it will determine partly how the permissible kill in any one year may be allocated among native and nonnative users. When the estimated permissible kill from a wildlife population in a given year is equal to, or less than, the guaranteed level, the entire kill will be allocated to the native peoples. When the permissible kill of a wildlife population in a given year is higher than the guaranteed level, native peoples will be allocated at least the guaranteed level; the balance of the permissible kill will then be divided between the native peoples and nonnatives according to their needs, provided that some of the balance is allocated to nonnatives. This mechanism for giving priority to native harvesting should provide a major means of controlling the actual kill by sport hunters and fishermen and of limiting conflicts with native hunters. The mechanism will be used only when conflicting uses create a conservation problem. Furthermore, although quotas are given priority as the means of implementing allocations, other management techniques can be used in ways consistent with these principles.

The legal and technical complexity of these provisions indicates the difficulties of formally encoding in specific and potentially legally defensible procedures even a simple principle, such as the recognition of the priority of native rights and needs over those of other resource users. It was thought that this combination of measures could regulate and restrict conflicts between native and nonnative users and that if it did not, the provisions were such that they could be the basis for court challenges to government violations. In practice, the verdict is not yet in, but two items have become problematic—the lack of personnel and funds for policing nonnatives and the tardiness of governments in enforcing the provisions (Feit, n.d.).

The compromise provisions of the JBNQA are based, in part, on the assumption that governments and native peoples take the conservation of renewable resources as an important objective. The extent to which provisions of the Agreement have not been quickly or fully implemented by responsible governments, particularly provincial government, reflects the fact that government sometimes has ignored its responsibility for the conservation of renewable resources of the territory or has made it subsidiary to its political interests, as indicated above. Legal action has already been required to enforce certain of these provisions of the Agreement and more may be required in the future. Legal and political action will test the defensibility of these specific Agreement provisions.

PROVISION OF ADEQUATE CASH INCOMES

Native peoples in the Canadian North who continue to depend extensively on renewable resources have also come to depend on complex, extensive, and direct interactions with the Canadian market economy. They now depend on imports of some, although clearly not all, important and sometimes specialized components of their hunting technology and of materials to operate and maintain these components. They depend on the use of various commercial services, particularly in transportation and communications. They depend on use of imported foodstuffs to make up any difference between harvestable resources and the subsistence requirements of a growing population. All these imports require substantial annual cash incomes (Berger 1977; Asch 1982*a*, 1982*b*; Salisbury et al. 1972*a*, 1972*b*; Feit 1982).

Cash incomes have come from several sources. Income from the sale of harvested products—most important are furs—is highly unstable because prices respond to unpredictable variations in international economic cycles as well as shifts in fashion and, more recently, the market impacts of public movements protesting the killing of animals. Government transfer payments have, since the 1940s, cushioned the effect of the unregulated market cycle on incomes but have not always kept pace with rises in import outlays. In addition, governments have attempted repeatedly to use dependence on transfer payments as a lever to force northern native peoples to comply with government development policies. Because these policies have typically either sought or assumed the demise of the harvesting economy, the effects have, in most cases, been detrimental to the support and maintenance of harvesting and income from harvesting (Feit 1986). Some important counterexamples can be cited, but it was clear to Cree negotiators that some insulation from economic markets and from economic effects of changes in government administration and policy was required.

The economic problems of hunting were addressed in JBNQA sections dealing with the Income Security Program (ISP), the Cree Trappers' Association (CTA), and the provision for a corporation to undertake compensatory and remedial works, the La Grande Complex Remedial Works Corporation (SOTRAC). ISP is the key provision here, intended to provide sufficiently generous cash payments to Cree hunters to reduce their dependence on fur prices in the world economy and on government controlled transfer payment programs. JBNQA states that the objective of ISP is to "ensure that hunting, fishing and trapping constitute a viable way of life for the Cree people and that individual Cree who elect to pursue such a way of life shall be guaranteed a measure of economic security" (Anonymous 1976). ISP could only be used to accomplish this objective, however, because it was integrated into JBNQA, which contained the other provisions briefly mentioned above. The effectiveness of a cash payment to hunters depended on hunters having a right to hunt that could not be removed at the initiative of governments, on a continued priority access to wildlife resources, on continuing Cree wildlife management, and on regulation of the effects of future development (see below; Feit and Scott, n.d.; LaRusic 1979).

The general effectiveness of ISP payments depends also on the availability of the goods, services, and infrastructure necessary for hunters to make effective use of the funds available to them. This is the role of SOTRAC and CTA. These organizations, individually and jointly, can provide infrastructure, needed goods and services, and wildlife and harvest monitoring services. SOTRAC is funded by the James Bay Energy Corporation. CTA has been funded by joint contributions from the governments of Quebec and Canada and from the Cree themselves. Without these provisions of JBNQA, ISP could not contribute effectively to reducing the dependency of Cree hunters on world economic conditions and government welfare policies. Even with these provisions, it can only reduce, not eliminate, such dependencies (Feit 1983).

The actual amounts paid each year are indexed to the cost of living; in 1982–83, they amounted to C$23.64 per adult for every day spent in harvesting or related activities outside a settlement. The minimum number of days that can be paid to an individual is in effect 90, and the program establishes a limit of 240 paid days per annum per recipient. To the per diem amount, a second amount may be added, based on the difference between a basic guarantee, related to family size, and the total income of a family unit. The average ISP benefit paid during 1982–83 amounted to about C$8,500. And total benefits paid during the year amounted to about C$9.5 million.

The program is often justified in government literature as a means of reducing welfare payments and at the same time increasing productive employment. It should be noted, though, that the employment it creates is effectively outside the labor market (Scott 1979). Eligibility for the program is based on hunting activities of the previous year, and although the rules offer diverse criteria, most beneficiaries establish eligibility by spending at least 120 days in hunting or related activities, of which 90 are spent outside the settlements. The agreement established an overall limit to the total number of man-days payable annually under ISP so as to set an upper limit on costs to government. Since its initiation, this limit has been raised three times, and a procedure for future changes is now being discussed.

The incorporation of ISP into the framework of Cree claims settlement made it possible for the program to be structured in a way that would limit some of the dependencies inherent in other transfer payment programs. The costs of ISP, both program benefits costs and administrative costs, were to be paid by Quebec under the terms of the Agreement. In this sense, ISP is another transfer payment program and runs the risk of creating dependency of the kind experienced by Cree under previous welfare programs—dependency on funds controlled by changing government policies and politics. When the Cree negotiated ISP as part of JBNQA, they attempted to use the negotiations and the Agreement itself to limit this kind of dependency. As ISP is defined in the Agreement, it cannot be unilaterally changed by governments. In addition, ISP is not administered by the government that funds it but by a separate corporate entity, the Cree Income Security Board, made up equally of Quebec and Cree appointees, with a rotating chairmanship. The obligation of the Quebec government is to transfer the funds needed each year to the accounts of the ISP board. The board is also given considerable authority to implement and, where necessary, interpret and review ISP and its operations, in accordance with legislation and the Agreement (Feit 1983).

To summarize, the incorporation of negotiations over ISP within the framework of comprehensive aboriginal land claims negotiations permitted integration of ISP into the package of regimes, programs, organizational structures, and benefits thought to be necessary to assure the economic viability of hunting. It also made it possible to establish a program that, although funded by government, is significantly independent of government policy and politics, is jointly controlled and administered by the government and representatives of the beneficiary population, and legally encodes the specific rights of individual beneficiaries.

The actual impacts of ISP have been quite extensive. It has increased the number of Cree people who make hunting their main activity by about one-third. During the first year of ISP operation, people who had not hunted intensively during previous years could still register for ISP, if they declared an intention to hunt intensively. ISP initially, and almost immediately, increased the number of people hunting intensively from approximately 700 to 900 on average, or about 29 percent. The program therefore initially met the goal of enhancing participation in hunting activities by Cree (Scott 1977). To put the overall level of ISP participation in perspective, in 1982–83, when 1,122 beneficiary units were registered, they represented about 43 percent of the resident adult population of Cree villages. Variations between the eight Cree communities were considerable, however, ranging from approximately one-fourth to over one-half of community population of ISP. The amount of time hunters spent in the bush also increased significantly with the introduction of ISP and has risen slowly since that initial increase. In the first year of operation of the ISP program, the average amount of time beneficiaries spent in the bush increased about 25 percent over the time they had spent in immediately previous years. Since then, there has been a further 10 percent increase.

To give some idea of the extent of participation in bush life typical of ISP beneficiaries, the average number of days spent in the bush by hunters in 1978–79 (the last year for which there are full data) was over 235, or almost eight months. Over 50 percent of ISP hunters spend more than 7.5 months in the bush, and more than 75 percent spend more than half the year. The substantial increases in average time spent in the bush, therefore, came on top of an already time-intensive pattern of hunting that was common in Cree communities.

ISP has enhanced traditional social forms and practices. In particular, there has been a modest increase in the numbers of families going to the bush as groups, and the practice of women staying behind in the settlement, which had been growing, is now relatively infrequent, except when motivated by medical or employment concerns. There has also been a continuation of the practice of multifamily hunting groups as the main residential units in the bush. In some communities, there are clear indications that the numbers of women and children in the bush have increased and that the number of bush camps established has risen with the increased number of hunters and families. In this respect, the program has met another explicit Cree objective, the general maintenance of the traditional social organization of hunting (Scott 1977, 1979; Feit and Scott, n.d.). However, at the community level, there have also been several changes in social organization, most related to the emphasis the growth of hunting activity has put on coordinated decision making. As a result of the needs for greater coordination, community level decisions concerning hunting land and wildlife have become more formalized. Such decision making has developed because it meets a need that results from the increased intensity and use of land and resources.

Nevertheless, knowledge of the Agreement, and therefore of French and English, and knowledge of the administration structures set up after the Agreement, have become important resources in this decision-making process. As a result, middle-aged, and some younger, men probably have greater influence in the process than formerly. But it is also important that all of the active participants in decisions are intensively engaged in the hunting economy, so that decision making directly about harvesting rests with hunters and not with administrators. It is also the case that hunting activities are profoundly affected by decisions concerning other development activities, decisions that were formerly taken outside the communities and without Cree participation. Now there is frequently a Cree role in these decisions. Native communities and organizations now actively undertake some forms of land-based economic development, on their own or through various forms of joint ventures, and they play a role in decisions concerning development initiated by others. In these cases, Cree participation is often through Cree and nonnative administrators working for Cree organizations, and hunters often have a limited role (LaRusic et al. 1979). Interviews in the communities suggest that hunters are often not satisfied with this process. In this area, the Agreement has changed decision making, creating some Cree participation but without assuring the full and effective participation of the full-time hunting sector of Cree communities. This is a problem the hunters thought the Agreement would resolve, but this has not occurred.

The introduction of ISP has led to substantial increases in local bush production of housing, specialized equipment, clothing, heating, and other bush services, including bush education and probably some traditional medical practices. This increase has occurred in both total production and per hunter/family production (Scott 1977, 1979). There have also been substantial increases in the uses of goods and services imported into Cree communities from the industrial economy of Canada. The emphasis here has clearly been on goods and services that increase the efficiency or security of bush life, but consumer goods have also increased. Items that aid transportation and communication have been especially heavily used. The long-term implications of this overall growth in the use of imported goods and services are not yet clear. Although this growth was not started by ISP, it was accelerated by the program (Brelsford 1983a). It is likely that certain of the goods and services now being used are coming to be seen not only as welcome additions to a hunting way of life but also as indispensable necessities. ISP was intended to stabilize this trend and insulate it from cycles in the industrial economy and from manipulation of the markets on which Cree depend. It seems likely to have done this, because the major cash incomes needed by Cree to purchase these goods and services now come from ISP.

But, at the same time, ISP has led to additional use of industrial imports and raised the threat that if the latter increases lead to a cycle of consumerism within Cree society, this could work against any stabilization and buffering effects. The long-term outcome is not yet clear. On the basis of limited data available from some communities, it appears that recent trends have necessarily been toward a reduction in the initial rapid growth in consumer expenditures that immediately followed the introduction of ISP and toward a stabilization in the growth of consumer goods consumption. Whether this is a long-term trend or simply a response to slower growth in incomes is not entirely clear, but a decline in comments about needed increases in ISP benefits in the last several years points to the latter.

ISP has permitted and helped the hunting sector of the Cree regional economy to expand during periods of recession in its employment, enterprise, and administrative sectors and to engage a larger number of Cree in intensive hunting activities. In 1982–83, the number of ISP beneficiary units rose from 929 the previous year to 1,122, an increase of 21 percent. I understand that this number rose again somewhat in 1983–84. About half were men joining ISP, probably for the first time, and many of these were young. In several communities, people feel that the recent rapid increase in the number of young people entering the program is related to declines in alternative economic opportunities in the present recession. How many of these young people will stay on practicing intensive hunting if employment is again more readily available cannot now be predicted. What is important is that the structure of ISP has worked so as to permit a rapid increase in levels of participation. This repeats the role hunting has played in the recent history of the Cree—the stable and secure economic sector, the one able to absorb some of the underemployment created by cycles in job markets. ISP clearly cannot absorb all, or even most, of that underemployment, however. Even so, the relative stability of hunting is perceived by some hunters as another indicator of its continuing long-term viability and importance to Cree.

ISP has created an increased confidence in the viability of the hunting way of life, and this is reflected in an increased encouragement to young people to pursue it (Feit and Scott, n.d.). Statistical data on the number of children being taken out of school to spend one or more years in the bush have been extremely limited. Existing data indicate that preschool children are now more frequently in the bush, whereas those of school age are at least as frequently in the bush as before ISP. The long-term effects of this pattern cannot be precisely predicted, but it is a good indicator for a potentially positive future for recruitment to intensive hunting. Finally, ISP has not resulted in any general or widespread overutilization or depletion of game resources, and the Cree system of hunting territory management by territory "owners" has generally continued to work to regulate harvests and conserve wildlife (ibid.). In summary, to date, ISP has been an effective means of maintaining, enhancing, and securing the subsistence sector of Cree economy and society, although the social changes accompanying the implementation of the Agreement have not fully met hunters' expectations.

PROTECTION OF RENEWABLE RESOURCES FROM THE EFFECTS OF NONRENEWABLE RESOURCE DEVELOPMENT

There is clearly no long-term future for renewable resource-based economies in the Canadian North if there is not, in fact as well as in policy, a real priority given to renewable resources in decisions about how nonrenewable resources and land are to be used in the region. Unless rights to have and to use renewable resources can be given more political weight, based on recent history, the prospect for northern development is not promising. There has been an extensive series of government policy statements and regulatory regimes designed to afford protection to at least some components of northern ecosystems. We have also seen the development of and, in many cases, the adoption of a range of tools to assist with the making of decisions and choices among various development objectives such as multiple use planning, land use planning, environmental and social impact assessment, and a plethora of others. Yet the history of northern development has shown that the key considerations in decisions concerning whether, where, and how projects and explorations have been undertaken have not been environmental considerations (Usher and Beakhust 1973; Freeman and Hackman 1975). A series of investigations over the last decade has made it increasingly clear that policy statements and tools of decision making and administration have not been effective means to do more than moderate and, where possible, remedy the effects of nonrenewable resource developments. We have not yet seen the political will, or a sufficiently large lever, to alter the balance.

JBNQA uses most of these techniques in northern Quebec as well, and concerns with their effectiveness exist here too. On economic, ecological, and social grounds, I see reasons to believe that controlled development could be quite extensive and yet still be compatible with needed environmental protection as well as being of potential benefit to native peoples in the North (Salisbury et al. 1972b; Salisbury 1986). An effective way to assure the establishment of this balance has been elusive, however. Several types of provisions were negotiated in JBNQA in an attempt to help Cree hunters continue their activities and economy despite the effect of development. As I have already indicated, harvesting rights were recognized as exercisable wherever physically possible, subject to certain limited restrictions. This recognition assured that the legal taking of land for development purposes would not, in itself, preclude use of the land. The key problem was the actual physical transformation of the land and its wildlife resources by development activity and the effects of such transformations on harvesting activities (Salisbury et al. 1972*b*; SSDCC 1982). Future development was subjected to social and environmental impact assessments and to ongoing environmental quality review, but final decisions on development rested with the responsible governments.

To survive the effects of the reduction of wildlife populations that would accompany even regulated development, native peoples clearly need access to other currently underused wildlife resources. In the James Bay area of Quebec, despite the maintenance of an intensive modern hunting society, despite the fact that all land was being used on some regular and recurring basis, and despite the fact that populations of some species were harvested very intensively, there remained significant opportunities to intensify the use of some renewable resources. There were important limitations on these possibilities as well, including limited biological productivity, low harvesting efficiencies, high cash costs, and cultural acceptability. There was no clear basis for claiming that the underused resources were fully equivalent in quality to those damaged, nor was there any assurance that they were equal in quantity to those that could be made unproductive by continued development in the long term. However, the need to provide immediate access to those wildlife resources that were available and were desired by Cree was clear.

Access to alternative wildlife resources could be provided in several ways. One attempt was to establish ISP, which provides hunters with the means to maintain, modify, or expand harvesting activities in changing circumstances. The funds made available to hunters could be used to finance travel to more distant or isolated wildlife resources, to improve the efficiency of harvesting by improving equipment, and to provide an increased level of security in the bush during a time of disruption caused by development. This buffer will work only at a general level. It will not reduce the effects on individual native hunters whose traplines are adversely affected by development. To date, the general provisions appear to have worked at the community level, although some individual hunters have experienced severe disruptive impacts. Between 1974–75 and 1978–79, no downward trends in total available weights of food from harvesting occurred in the affected

Cree communities (JBNQNHRC 1982). Nevertheless, the effects of future hydroelectric and other resource developments create uncertainty for the future (SSDCC 1982; Feit 1986).

It also needs to be emphasized that the major renewable resources used by Cree are species that are either relatively localized (e.g., moose, beaver, nonanadromous fish), in which case the effects of development have also been localized, or migratory species (such as geese and smaller populations of caribou), whose patterns have been affected only marginally by developments to date. Future developments may alter this relative insularity for the Cree, just as current developments elsewhere in the North clearly and directly threaten other important renewable resources and the native peoples who depend on them. Thus, specific immediate opportunities for resource maintenance in the face of ongoing development need to be explored and used, while longer-term efforts to find effective resolutions in this area of fundamental conflict continue.

CONCLUSION: CREE AUTONOMY AND STATE LINKAGES

This case study of James Bay Cree efforts to restructure linkages to wider economic and political systems is relatively unusual in that Cree established an intensive and extended negotiation with government representatives which touched on almost all aspects of their relationships. And because the negotiations came to be directed toward a comprehensive set of agreements, the process provided a rare opportunity to examine the fundamental positions and conflicts between Cree and governments as well as the possibilities for a range of strategies for dealing with those conflicts. The implementation of the Agreement also provided an opportunity to examine the parallel implementation of dozens of specific provisions and to seek recurring patterns in the processes involved and their outcomes. A definitive account of the results of the James Bay and Northern Quebec Agreement probably cannot be made at this time. The processes of implementing the Agreement have been long and complex, and although they have already extended over a ten-year period, they are neither completed nor fully tested. Nevertheless, several general conclusions about Cree relations to wider systems can be drawn.

First, the James Bay negotiations appear to confirm the common assertion that the most fundamental conflicts between indigenous people and liberal-democratic states with a capitalist economy center around the control of land and resources, especially for development purposes, and around assertions of state sovereignty. However, it may have been less widely expected that Cree negotiators, and their legal and professional advisers, did find considerable opportunities to develop claims, rights, programs, structures, procedures, benefits, and agreements that had some promise of effectively responding to Cree interests within the context of these two fundamental conflicts. Some of these have worked; others have not.

The conflicts over sovereignty were met with a series of legal provisions. While these did not resolve competing claims, they did afford mutual recognitions of governance without resolving questions of the origins of legitimacy or authority. On the questions of practical decision-making powers, the separate existing systems were left in place, and coordination was provided. Coordination often involved, however, a recognition of governments as holding superior authority and final responsibility, although the powers of government to act unilaterally or contrary to Cree rights and interests were constrained.

The experience with these provisions has been mixed. Where Cree authority was recognized, it has continued to be exercised effectively. And in many areas where Cree authority was extended, as in the reformulation of local community governments and the formation of regional political and service oriented institutions, Cree governance and administration have been greatly enhanced. The autonomy of Cree communities has clearly been improved by increased local control over services and resources, by enhanced ability to initiate political and administrative actions, and by recognition of Cree powers accorded by external institutions and nonnatives more generally. Nevertheless, the political and administrative practices of governments, while often extensive and responsible, have also shown a consistent pattern of derogation from legal undertakings where political or economic conflicts are directly implicated. In addition, a thin veneer often covers a recurrent paternalism, as exemplified in the tendency of some departments to treat coordination as a mere formality of consultation after policy decisions have already been taken. In this respect, the coordination provisions that involved no direct sharing of government authority have repeatedly failed, whereas those based on decentralizing government authority to Cree entities have fared better.

Thus, Cree rights and legal protections have on occasion remained mere words, denied in practice especially when there are political, economic, or administrative costs to governments for implementing these legally binding but often difficult to enforce provisions of the Agreement. This is not to deny that many, indeed probably most, provisions have been implemented and are effective. Nevertheless, the pattern of government deciding when to violate its obligations has occurred frequently enough to be general within the context of respecting the less burdensome or conflicting issues. Those conflicts over sovereignty that were dealt with by mutual recognition of responsibility have been generally successful, whereas those conflicts dealt with through coordinated decision making under government authority have only been respected insofar as they are compatible with government interests. This despite the structures and provisions intended to assure responsible government fulfillment of these provisions.

With respect to fundamental conflicts over the control of economic resources, the Agreement was clearly not successful in establishing a land base or adequate control of resource development activities for Cree, but it did provide a higher degree of economic support for the hunting economy and for Cree self-governance. That is, within the Canadian liberal-democratic state, it was possible to direct public resources to the support of the Cree hunting economy in such a way as to enhance a relative degree of autonomy from market conditions for Cree products, labor, consumer goods, and services.

But the Agreement did not resolve fully the Cree need to expand opportunities for productive economic activities for the rapidly expanding population of young adults (Salisbury 1986). True, Cree takeover and expansion of administrative services and programs in their communities has considerably increased employment opportunities in the villages. The thirty or so Cree who were fully employed as administrators before the Agreement has swollen to some three hundred since. But it is also clear that the number of administrative positions is insufficient to fully employ all those Cree who do not hunt as a primary productive activity. The provision of economic enterprises in the communities and additional employment opportunities for Cree people is a critical task facing Cree leaders. And while organizations and experience gained through JBNQA facilitate the task, the limited natural and financial resources available make the task a difficult one. Similar problems occur with respect to social development, where government funding for improved health and education have not fully met Cree expectations.

The threat to the hunting economy posed by relatively unregulated industrial development of the region pinpoints the other failure of the agreement process to effectively resolve conflicts over resource control and economic development. Large-scale industrial development projects are continuing on Cree lands. Future phases of hydroelectric development have been delayed but not abandoned. And commercial cutting of the forests is continuing on a large scale and at a rapid pace in the southern portions of the region, where it is seriously depleting wildlife resources on affected hunting territories and rendering them unusable for periods of at least several decades. In the eyes of an increasing number of hunters, the failure to adequately regulate development is a major future threat to the revitalized hunting sector. These threats demonstrate again that the agreement process was unable to resolve fundamental conflicts between the interests of Cree and those of wider economic and political institutions of the capitalist economy or the liberal democratic state. Nevertheless, the evidence seems clear that there were opportunities for Cree to expand their self-governance and to enhance their long-term capacity to carry on fights for a just and responsible relationship to wider political and economic institutions. To review these changes:

1. Basic rights to wildlife resources have been recognized and are no longer changeable by unilateral government action, although as formally codified legislation they will now be subject to continuing judicial and, in some aspects, political reinterpretation.
2. Cree also now have the organizations and political institutions needed for expanded self-governance along with experienced leaders to run them; in addition, they now have a broad consensus on goals and expanded resources.
3. Cree hunters are better insulated from changes in world and national market conditions and government policies, with assured annual incomes, but it is also the case that transactions with markets are now more extensive than they were before.
4. Cree hunters continue to manage wildlife resources essentially on their own and with less substantial inputs or threats from government wildlife administration and policy, but their use of wildlife is still threatened by large-scale resource development schemes.

The process has strengthened Cree ability to confront the problems that threaten them, but it has not fundamentally resolved those problems or provided a mutually acceptable new relationship of respect between Cree and governments. The highly focused and comprehensive nature of Cree-government negotiations suggest that this case may demonstrate the present outer limits for enhancing indigenous autonomy within extended linkages to state economies which characterize the current place of indigenous peoples in developed liberal-democratic states, subject always to the longer-term processes of change and transformation in those wider institutions themselves.

NOTES

1. This study was prepared with the aid of research grants from the Social Sciences and Humanities Research Council of Canada (SSHRCC 410-84-0547 and 410-87-0715). An earlier version was presented at the American Indian Workshop of the European Association of American Studies, in Copenhagen, April 1–3, 1985. The first version was prepared while on research leave from McMaster University, with the assistance of a Leave Fellowship from SSHRCC. Attendance at the Copenhagen conference was made possible by an SSHRCC International Travel Grant. This presentation draws on several of my papers and reports touching on related issues but frequently updates and revises these where there is overlap.

In preparing this revised version, I have drawn extensively on ideas and discussion held over the course of several years with Cree administrators and colleagues extensively involved in implementing or reviewing the James Bay and Northern Quebec Agreement. At the cost of omitting many names, I would like to specially thank Michael Asch, Philip Awashish, Thomas Berger, Fikret Berkes, Taylor Brelsford, Lorraine Brooke, Brian Craik, Thomas Coon, Rick Cuciurean, Billy Diamond, Peter Hutchins, Johnny Jolly, William Kemp, Abel Kitchen, Steve Langdon, Ignatius LaRusic, James O'Reilly, Alan Penn, Richard Preston, Richard Salisbury, Colin Scott, and Paul Wilkinson.

5
Aboriginal Land Tenure and Contemporary Claims in Australia[1]

L. R. Hiatt

The Aboriginal Land Rights (Northern Territory) Act 1976 (hereafter, the Act) and subsequent hearings of land claims by the Aboriginal Land Commissioner have focused attention on the traditional basis of Aboriginal landownership as never before. Paradoxically, the legal proceedings, considered in conjunction with the work of a new generation of ethnographers, have highlighted the adaptive and dynamic character of man-land relationships rather than the formal or ideal properties enshrined in the classic work of Radcliffe-Brown. It is now fairly clear that patrifiliation has been accorded an undue preeminence in the definition of land ownership, at the expense of other cognatic links (especially matrifiliation) and criteria such as putative conception-place, birthplace, father's burial place, grandfather's burial place, mythological links, long-term residence, and so on. The relative weight traditionally accorded to various criteria continues to be a burning question, and argument as to whether distinctions between primary and secondary rights were clear-cut, incipient, or nonexistent is obviously relevant to the juridical determination of contemporary land claims. Such practical considerations, however, should not make us lose sight of the theoretical point that, in pre-European times, multiple criteria for affiliation to landowning groups may have constituted a set of credentials enabling individuals to gain access to a wider range of physical and metaphysical resources. From this perspective, the dialectic between formalism and flexibility in identifying landowners may be seen as an element in the dynamics of competition for scarce goods and social status.

POLITICAL BACKGROUND TO THE 1976 ACT

Early in 1963, the Australian government excised 363 square kilometers from the Arnhem Land Aboriginal Reserve to enable Pechiney Aluminum (France) to mine bauxite on the Gove Peninsula. In August of that year, senior Aboriginal men living nearby at the Methodist Mission of Yirrkala drew up a petition, written on bark in the Gumatj language, and presented it to the House of Representatives in Canberra. The petitioners stated that the excision was never explained beforehand and that places sacred to Aborigines, and vital to their livelihood, were in the excised area. They appealed to the Parliament to appoint a committee to hear the views of the Yirrkala people before allowing the excision to proceed.[2]

A Parliamentary Select Committee in due course recommended that the Yirrkala Aborigines be compensated for loss of traditional occupancy of the excised area and that they be granted exclusive hunting rights within its boundaries. The committee acknowledged that Aborigines have no legal tenure of tribal lands. Giving evidence in Darwin, the Crown Law Officer stated, "When Australia was settled, the Aborigines of Australia were considered at the time not to have title to the land. The whole of our system of land tenure is built on that assumption."[3]

These events took place in the context of an emerging political consciousness among Northern Territory Aborigines. Around 1960, an Aboriginal organization known as the Council for Aboriginal Rights was formed in Darwin in the face of opposition from the bureaucracy. One of its prominent members told the Select Committee in 1963 that when he attempted to make contact with the Yirrkala leaders, he was turned back at the airstrip by a missionary who said, "If you see these people now you will only stir up more trouble on the political side" (quoted in Rowley 1972:158). A few years later, in 1966, representatives of the Council for Aboriginal Rights played an important role in the strike of Gurindji stockmen over wages and conditions and in their subsequent campaign (1967–68) for an excision of 600 square miles from the Wave Hill pastoral lease (see Hardy 1968; Rowley 1972, 1978; Middleton 1977; Coombs 1978).

Meanwhile, mining operations commenced at Gove, and a mining town called Nhulunbuy was built some twenty miles distant from the Yirrkala Mission. In 1968, three Aborigines issued a writ in the Supreme Court of the Northern Territory against Nabalco (Pty.) Ltd. (which had taken over from Pechiney) and the Commonwealth of Australia, contesting the right of the Crown to negotiate with Nabalco without consent of the traditional owners and without compensation to them for the use of their land. The Commonwealth assisted the Aborigines to present their case, which was heard by Mr. Justice Blackburn in 1970 (Maddock 1980; see also Rowley 1972; Coombs 1978; Cole 1979; Maddock 1983*a*).

The plaintiffs were represented by Mr. Woodward Q.C., who asserted a doctrine of communal native title according to which the communal occupation of land by the native inhabitants of a territory acquired by the Crown is recognized by common law as a legally enforceable right that persists and must be respected until validly terminated. In his judgment, Mr. Justice Blackburn referred to a distinction articulated by Blackstone in the eighteenth century between conquest and occupation of foreign lands: "if an uninhabited country be discovered and planted by English subjects, all the English laws are there immediately in force. . . . But in conquered or ceded countries, that have already laws of their own, the king may indeed alter and change those laws; but, till he does actually change them, the ancient laws of the kingdom remain" (quoted in Maddock 1980:7).

Now, although Australia was clearly inhabited when the first British settlers arrived in 1788, from a legal viewpoint, it was treated as *terra nullius*. That is, since the Aborigines were held to be incapable of intelligent transactions with respect to land, they were deemed in law not to inhabit the land they in fact inhabited. Mr. Justice Blackburn found that in 1788 Australia was (to use Blackstone's expression) "desert and uncultivated," meaning a country occupied by uncivilized people in a primitive state of society. He cited, as binding on him, a Privy Council decision in the nineteenth century that the colony of New South Wales (of which the Gove Peninsula was then a part) was neither conquered nor ceded but simply occupied. English law thus applied from the moment of settlement, and no such communal aboriginal right to the land as claimed by the plaintiffs was ever acknowledged to exist.

Mr. Justice Blackburn's judgment was delivered in 1971. Two years later, following the election of a Labor government in 1972, Mr. Woodward (by then Mr. Justice Woodward) was commissioned by the Governor-General to conduct an inquiry into the appropriate means to recognize and establish the traditional rights and interests of the Aborigines of the Northern Territory in relation to land. The commissioner's primary recommendations were that inalienable title in fee simple to existing Aboriginal reserves (with one or two exceptions) and to certain other areas be vested in Land Trusts consisting of Aborigines chosen by the traditional owners or their representatives and that Aborigines should be given the opportunity to lodge claims for title to specified areas of unalienated Crown land. With regard to pastoral leases (the third main category of land in the Northern Territory), the commissioner recommended setting up an Aboriginal land commission to investigate and deal with existing and future Aboriginal interests.

The Woodward Report[4] formed the basis of the Aboriginal Land Rights (Northern Territory) Bill, which was introduced in Federal Parliament late in 1975 just before the Whitlam government was dismissed by the Governor-General. Following the election of the Fraser government, an amended bill was presented, and on Australia Day, January 1977, the Aboriginal Land Rights (Northern Territory) Act 1976 became law.[5]

ANTHROPOLOGICAL BACKGROUND TO THE 1976 ACT

Although numerous observers during the nineteenth century affirmed that the indigenous inhabitants of Australia had definite concepts of landownership, the identity (corporate or otherwise) of those in whom proprietorial rights were vested, and the manner in which title was transferred or inherited, remained obscure (see Thomas 1906:8). In 1913, Malinowski ([1913] 1963) reviewed the published data in his book *The Family among the Australian Aborigines* and concluded that claims to territory probably existed at three levels—the individual or individual family, the local group, and the tribe. Actual rights of roaming, hunting, fishing, and digging usually belong to the local group. Local groups forming a tribe exercise a customary right to use the whole tribal area. Individuals or individual families have special rights to particular parts of the area occupied by the local group.[6] Malinowski judged the local group to be the most important but was unable to elucidate its structure.

During the same year, Radcliffe-Brown published the first results of his field investigations among three tribes of Western Aborigines, which had been carried out two years earlier (Radcliffe-Brown 1913). His account of landownership and use among one of them, the Kariera, formed the basis of his later generalizations for Australia as a whole (see especially Radcliffe-Brown 1930–31, [1935] 1952). In due course, Radcliffe-Brown's descriptive model became established as anthropological orthodoxy and, as such, undoubtedly shaped the definition of "traditional Aboriginal owners" in the 1976 Act. His (1913:145–146) conceptualization is characterized by simplicity and orderliness:

The tribe is divided into a number of local groups, each with its own defined territory. Membership of the local group is determined by descent in the male line; that is to say, a child belongs to the local group of its father and inherits hunting rights over the territory of that group. . . . The country of a local group, with all its products, animal, vegetable, and mineral, belongs to the members of the group in common. Any member has the right to hunt over the country of his group at all times. He may not, however, hunt over the country of any other local group without the permission of the owners. . . . Hunting or collecting vegetable products in the country of another local group constitutes an act of trespass and was in former times liable to be punished by death.

Radcliffe-Brown reported (ibid., 146) that he could find no instance of individual ownership of any part of the soil or its products; in his general survey, he stated that the tribe should not be regarded as a landholding group—the area occupied by the tribe being merely the sum of the territories owned by the component local groups (1930–31:36). We see here, then, a rejection of two of the three levels of ownership mentioned by Malinowski, that is, the individual and the tribe, and an attribution of absolute primacy to the third, now characterized as a local agnatic descent group.

Radcliffe-Brown referred to the local group as a "horde." His generalizations on Australian territorial organization remained unchallenged until Elkin (1950:17–18) expressed the opinion that "the local organization in many tribes is not the clear-cut patrilineal patrilocal exogamous group occupying a definite territory which some textbooks imply" (including, I might add, his own; see Elkin 1938:39–41). Then, in 1962, Meggitt published the results of his fieldwork among the Walbiri of central Australia, submitted as a thesis in 1955. Here was the first ethnography to quarrel openly with Radcliffe-Brown, on the basis of a single case. According to Meggitt, the Walbiri were divided into four major communities, each including from six to twelve patriclans. The adult members of each clan were ritually linked with a particular sacred site, but they did not form the basis of a local group or band and did not occupy to the exclusion of others an area surrounding their sites. Nor did they feel under any obligation to seek permission before hunting in the vicinity of the sites of other patriclans belonging to their own community.

In 1962, I published a paper in *Oceania* in which I argued that local groups of the kind postulated by Radcliffe-Brown, far from being the basic unit of territorial organization throughout Australia, probably never existed anywhere (Hiatt 1962). My own field research in Arnhem Land in the late 1950s had produced results consistent with Meggitt's. Furthermore, a review of the literature showed little in the way of empirical verification of Radcliffe-Brown's hypothesis and a good deal in conflict with it. For instance, Stanner (1933:40) wrote that local organizations southwest of Darwin "differed in some ways from what we are led to believe is, or was, characteristic of most tribes." Hunting rights of a clan over this territory were not absolute, and many stretches of country belonged to two or three different clans, sometimes of different tribes. Individuals passed between their own and neighboring horde countries with great freedom and confidence. I might add (though this emerged only after the publication of my 1962 paper) that Stanner's description of territorial organization among the Warramunga, in a manuscript prepared in 1934, is remarkably similar to Meggitt's account for the neighboring Walbiri, written twenty years later. Stanner (1965:81) apparently regarded these aberrations from Radcliffe-Brown's model as the product of European colonization, though why he should have supposed that Radcliffe-Brown's observations were more privileged in this respect than his own is hard to fathom.[7]

The anthropological debate continued throughout the 1960s and into the 1970s (see, e.g., Stanner 1965; Hiatt 1965, 1968; Birdsell 1970). One of the most telling blows against the concept of the patrilocal horde, however, came from Aboriginal witnesses in the Gove case. Mr. Justice Blackburn stated:

A close examination of the Aboriginal evidence has led me to the conclusion that it does not support the proposition that the band normally contained a 'core' or significant majority, of persons of the same clan. . . . What impresses me most on this question, however, is that not one of the ten Aboriginal witnesses who were from eight different clans, said anything which indicated that the band normally had a core from one clan, or that they thought of the band in terms of their own clan, and all of them indicated that within the band it was normal to have a mixture of people of different clans. (Quoted in Gumbert 1981:109)

In needs to be emphasized that the "horde" debate was about the composition of bands and access to resources and not about the actual ownership of land. In 1966, at the "Man the Hunter" conference in Chicago, I said that there was no quarrel with Radcliffe-Brown's generalization that throughout Australia the landowning units were patriclans (Hiatt 1968:99), and I have told innumerable undergraduates over the last decade or so that Aborigines perceived the landscape as being divided into totemic estates, each owned by a patrilineal descent group (see also Hiatt 1970, 1982*a*, 1982*b*). Evidence and arguments presented to the Aboriginal Land Commissioner since 1977, together with field research of a new generation of anthropologists, have made me less confident. Like Elkin, speaking on a related matter in 1950, I now have to concede that the situation is not as clear-cut as some textbooks imply.

THE NEW EVIDENCE: LAND CLAIMS AND DOCTORAL DISSERTATIONS

In line with the recommendations of the Woodward Report, Schedule 1 of the 1976 Act listed the reserves in the Northern Territory to be granted to Aboriginal Land Trusts. The Act also made it possible for Aborigines to claim unalienated Crown land and to convert pastoral leases already held by, or on behalf of, Aborigines to freehold title. The Act established the office of Aboriginal Land Commissioner, whose main function is to hear land claims and make recommendations to the Minister for Aboriginal Affairs.

The Act defines traditional Aboriginal owners, in relation to land, as "a local descent group of Aboriginals who—(a) have common spiritual affiliations to a site on the land, being affiliations that place the group under a primary spiritual responsibility for that site and for the land; and (b) are entitled by Aboriginal tradition to forage as of right over that land." An Aboriginal is "a person who is a member of the Aboriginal race of Australia." The Act does not define site, but a sacred site is "a site that is sacred to Aboriginals or is otherwise of significance according to Aboriginal tradition, and includes any land that, under a law of the Northern Territory, is declared to be sacred to Aboriginals or of significance according to Aboriginal tradition." Aboriginal tradition is "the body of traditions, observances, customs and beliefs of Aboriginals or of a community or group of Aboriginals, and includes those traditions, observances, customs and beliefs as applied in relation to particular persons, sites, areas of land, things or relationships."

The first Aboriginal Land Commissioner (abbreviated ALC in following land claim citations) under the Act, Mr. Justice Toohey, served from April 7, 1977, until his retirement on April 6, 1982. During his term of office, he heard and submitted reports on fifteen land claims (see Hiatt 1984, fig. 2). To date, the minister has approved the commissioner's recommendations in eight cases; he has not yet acted on one, and the remaining recommendations are the subject of either court appeals or negotiations.

The definition of traditional Aboriginal owners in the Act is identical in form and substance with the definition proposed by Mr. Justice Woodward in his suggested drafting instructions for proposed legislation.[8] But whereas Mr. Justice Woodward states in the body of his report that a local descent group is based on patrifiliation and common male ancestry,[9] no such amplification occurs in the Act. Thus, while the statutory definition, as it stands, is compatible with Radcliffe-Brown's model, the absence of an adjective or some equivalent form of words specifying the mode of descent as patrilineal clearly leaves it susceptible to wider interpretation. One of the main issues debated in land claim hearings during Mr. Justice Toohey's term of office concerned the inclusion in the list of traditional Aboriginal owners of certain nonagnates, that is, individuals linked to the area through their mothers.

Although it has been known for a long time that a man has a special relationship to the country of his mother, it is only in recent years that anthropologists have begun to appreciate the complexity and importance of this institution (see, e.g., Hiatt 1965:54–57; Maddock 1972:38–42, 1980). Whereas Radcliffe-Brown represented the matter as merely a case of obligatory hospitality on the part of the owning patriclan, it is now clear that over wide areas of Australia, symbolic affirmations of landownership depend on a complementary ritual relationship between agnates and close uterine kin. In the area I am especially familiar with, the primary responsibility for executing the emblems of a patriclan lies not with its male members but with the sons of female members. I say "responsibility," but "prerogative" would accord better with the manner in which the work is carried out. Furthermore, men exercise surveillance over the emblems of their mother's clan and on occasion issue public warnings against their theft or misuse.[10] They are also credited with the ability to control supernatural forces at particular locations in their mother's country regarded as dangerous by their mother's clan.

In his first report, the commissioner noted that the children of female members of the patriclan have "rights and duties some of which fall within English concepts of ownership and management" (Borroloola, ALC 1979a, par. 40), but he judged that they do not have primary spiritual responsibility for the land in question and therefore do not come under the definition of traditional owners. In his second report, the commissioner accepted the expert opinion of Stanner that a local descent group is "a small association of persons of both sexes and any ages each of whom is kin to every other person in the group through the paternal and grandpaternal line from a common ancestor or founder" (Warlpiri, ALC 1979*b*, par. 66). The commissioner also accepted Stanner's view that common spiritual affiliation refers "to the belief that every member of a patriline is in some sense animated by the 'patrispirit' of his clan" (Warlpiri, ALC 1979*b*, par. 67). It would follow from this that matrifiliation could not be included as part of the common spiritual affiliation referred to in the Act and accordingly could not confer a primary spiritual responsibility; therefore, it could not count as a criterion for recognition as a traditional owner.

The question of the spiritual responsibilities of the children of female members reemerged four claims later when the people of Utopia station requested that such individuals be included as claimants. By this time, the commissioner was beginning to distance himself from anthropological orthodoxy. "Anthropologists have tended to describe the patriclan as the landowning group within Australia. How true this is throughout the whole of Australia I do not know" (Utopia, ALC 1980*b*, par. 79). The Act itself did not specify patrilineality, however, and after listening to the opinion of Sansom and other expert witnesses, the commissioner concluded that it would not be unreasonable to regard each patriclan, together with the children of its female members, as comprising a descent group and, by reason of their common ties to the land in question, as a local descent group. Furthermore, the commissioner was satisfied that these common ties were of a spiritual nature. The remaining question was whether the local cognatic descent group was under a primary spiritual responsibility to the land. Here the commissioner took the view that whereas this had been shown for the agnatic part of the group, it had not been established for the group as a whole. It would not, therefore, be appropriate to include the children of female members as traditional owners of their mothers' land.

In the next claim (Willowra, ALC 1980*c*), the list of claimants again included people related to the land through their mothers. This time, the commissioner was satisfied not only that the patriclan plus the children of female members constituted a local descent group whose members had common spiritual affiliations to the land but also that the spiritual affiliations were of a kind that place the whole descent group under a primary spiritual responsibility for the land. Accordingly, he deemed it appropriate that the nonagnates included among the claimants be recognized as traditional Aboriginal owners (Willowra, ALC 1980*c*, par. 105).

If matrifiliation as well as patrifiliation is acknowledged as a basis for membership of a local descent group, and if an individual's parents belong to different descent groups, then it follows that he or she normally belongs to at least two different local descent groups and accordingly shares ownership of two different estates. In the Uluru claim, however, matrifiliation was advanced not in addition to patrifiliation but as an alternative. According to evidence submitted by Robert Layton, the anthropologist appearing for the claimants, the group that holds an estate in the Ayers Rock region is made up of some people who have inherited membership through their father and some who have inherited it through their mother. At birth, individuals have rights in the landowning groups of both parents, but during their lifetimes they come to exercise these rights predominantly in one or the other group, and it will be membership of the selected group which the individual transmits to his or her children. This gives rise to ambilineal, rather than patrilineal, descent (Uluru, ALC 1980*a*, par. 32).

The commissioner faced a new problem in the Limmen Bight claim. The evidence led him to conclude that, with respect to any particular estate, the members of the relevant patriclan and the children of its female members together constitute a local descent group (Limmen Bight, ALC 1981*a*, par. 64). Furthermore, members of this composite group share common spiritual affiliation to sites on the land in question. John Bern, the anthropologist appearing on behalf of the claimants, states, "The primary spiritual responsibility of *djunggaiyi* [children of female members of the patriclan] is not questioned. . . . The evidence on Mara ownership supports the inclusion of djunggaiyi on the three grounds: primary spiritual responsibility, common spiritual affiliation and the right to forage" (ibid., par. 71). Yet the Mara people themselves took the view that the djunggaiyi should not be included in the list of owners (ibid.).

The commissioner's dilemma is clear enough. On the one hand, claimants acknowledged that children of female members of the patriclan share with members of the patriclan spiritual affiliation to the land in question, spiritual responsibility for it, and the right to forage over it. On the other hand, they did not wish them to be classified as owners, a viewpoint that for the most part the djunggaiyi themselves accepted. The commissioner resolved the matter by judging that the djunggaiyi did not, after all, share primary spiritual responsibility and accordingly did not qualify as traditional owners under the Act.

In most of the remaining seven cases heard by the first commissioner, matrifiliation as well as patrifiliation was advanced and accepted as a ground for recognition as a traditional owner. In the Roper Bar (ALC 1982*b*) claim, however, the Ngalakan people (like their neighbors in the Limmen Bight claim) maintained that the djunggaiyi should not be listed as owners, even though they acknowledged that the relationship of individuals to their mother's land was a vital one. It is not yet entirely clear why some groups have wished to include matrifiliation as a ground for ownership status while others have excluded it (see Morphy and Morphy 1984; Bern and Larbalestier, 1985).[11]

Perhaps the most radical departure from Radcliffe-Brown's model during Mr. Justice Toohey's term of office occurred when he accepted the argument in the Daly River claim that the language group as a whole should be accepted as the landowning group. As a result of European settlement dating back to the 1870s, Malak Malak speakers have suffered severe depopulation, and numerous clans have become extinct. Solidarity at the level of the tribe has increased, while the clan as a focus of social identity has correspondingly declined in importance. In acknowledging the Malak Malak collectively as the traditional owners of the land claimed, the commissioner noted that he was extending the concept of local descent group beyond the interpretations of his earlier reports. Nevertheless, he had no difficulty in accepting the Malak Malak as a descent group, since individuals belong by virtue of being born into it, and it is a local group because it is related to a specific and identifiable area of land (Daly River, ALC 1982*a*, par. 199).[12]

Let us now turn to recent research undertaken outside the context of land claims. In the decade between 1971 and 1980, some twenty scholars submitted doctoral dissertations based on field investigations of traditional Aboriginal social life.[13] Here I concentrate on two contributions that happen to be especially relevant to my theme: one from the center of the continent, the other from Cape York Peninsula.

In 1976, Fred Myers submitted a dissertation on the Pintupi, who, until recently, occupied an arid region south of Lake Mackay in the Western Desert. Landownership, in its narrowest and most profound sense, applies to a relationship between initiated men and sacred sites. To own a place is to know its transcendental significance and to hold and exercise rights in ceremonies, songs, and sculptures connected with it. There are two major grounds for admission to the status of owner in this sense: (1) conception at the site and thus incarnation of the associated Dreaming, and (2) close cognatic links to individuals of previous generations conceived at the site. Typically, men transmit their knowledge not only to their sons but to their sisters' sons as well. In consequence, the owners of a site consist primarily of men conceived there, their male cognatic descendants, or both. Other criteria are prolonged residence around the site or death of a close relative at, or near, the site. The composition of owning groups thus differs from one site to the next. Men may belong to several different site-owning groups, and the chance of any two men owning exactly the same set of sites is low.[14]

Man-land relationships are also conceived by the Pintupi in a much wider sense. The expression "my country" means an expanse with which an individual is associated through genealogical ties, residence, and mythological links but which contains numerous sites that he does not own. Within this range, movement for hunting and foraging purposes is unrestricted (though visits to sacred sites require the permission of owners). Bands are fluctuating aggregates of individuals and represent the outcome at any one time of individual decisions and affiliations. There is no evidence that bands regularly, or even sometimes, form around a patrilocal core. Rather, the data confirm Peterson's (1972, 1974) important observation that a pivotal relationship in band composition is that between a married couple and the wife's parents.

In 1978, von Sturmer submitted the results of his investigations among the Kugu-Nganychara of the Kendall-Holroyd River system. The Kugu-Nganychara distinguish between *agu kunyji* and *agu ngalagun*, which von Sturmer translates as "full country" and "company land," respectively. "Full country" refers to a site, or set of sites, over which a particular individual, or congeries of individuals, has rights of tenure, these rights having been transmitted from father to son. "Company land," in its most common sense, refers to a domain along a river or other watercourse containing the sites of a number of different full owners or congeries of full owners.

Company land constitutes the basis for the most enduring corporations in Kugu-Nganychara society. People are classified, and classify themselves, according to the river or watercourse along which their full countries are located (e.g., the "Kendall River mob," the "Holroyd mob," etc.) In pre-European times, company camps in strategic locations (e.g., at the mouth of a river) were bases from which "mobs" exploited the surrounding countryside. Such camps were not formed around patrilineal cores, nor were people excluded from sites other than their own which belonged to members of their own mob. Von Sturmer says explicitly that rights of tenure over full country did not entitle the owners to exclude their own close cognates and spouses, or even people whose estates lie along the same river, regardless of the closeness or distance of genealogical connections with them.

Among the Kugu-Nganychara, as everywhere in Australia, some sites are more important than others. Focal sites, as von Sturmer refers to them, are favored camp locations (e.g., at the mouth of a river, offering ready access to water and food resources). They are often strategically placed with regard to trade routes, and there may also be defensive considerations. Such sites are typically invested with mythical and ceremonial importance. Furthermore, they are commonly under the control of a powerful individual, a "big man" or "boss," who spends a good deal of his time there.

A man normally inherits the status of chief controller of a focal site from his father, in accordance with a rule of primogeniture. Maintaining the position, however, depends on personal qualities, and it may be lost, through attrition or seizure, to a more forceful man able to muster the necessary moral and political support. Although the boss of a site does not try to exclude others from using it, he asserts his authority in other ways. The current boss of the river mouth camp at Waalang describes his position as follows. "I am boss for that place. . . . It doesn't matter what man comes in [to that camp]. Anyone can use that well. . . . [But] the boss man comes in front . . . other people come behind. The boss man says, 'You camp here; you camp there' " (von Sturmer 1978:429).

Several strategies are available to the ambitious younger brother faced with the disabilities imposed by primogeniture; for instance, he may attempt to establish himself politically and ritually within his own full country by camping regularly at sites not favored by the senior man. Alternatively, he may seek similar opportunities outside the patrilineal estate (e.g., in the estates of matrilineal kin). As one man put it, "No one can block you from mother's country or wife's country." Von Sturmer (ibid., 284) comments, "Given that this situation applied to each individual, and that each child is born into a situation where what is accessible to his parents is also, as a matter of course, accessible to him, any individual has rights of access to his father's (and thus his father's father's) country, his father's mother's country, his mother's (and thus his mother's father's) country, and his mother's mother's country." Each right of access is potentially convertible to a right of tenure (e.g., by occupying a site whose owning patriline is approaching extinction).[15]

Von Sturmer (ibid., 415) argues that the pursuit of individual eminence, in conjunction with strong cognatic loyalties, militates against the growth and stability of unilineal corporations. Close genealogical ties traced through females probably always take precedence over more distant agnatic connections. He concedes that a patrilineal descent ideology does exist among Kugu-Nganychara and that, consequently, corporative structures must be considered incipient or potential realities (ibid., 246). But he maintains that in practice such structures are unlikely to sustain the forces tending to undermine them: the proprietary and political aspirations of individual entrepreneurs, the conflict between familial versus descent group loyalties, sibling rivalry, and instabilities based on demographic and environmental factors.

It should be noted that the Kugu-Nganychara have neither generic nor specific names for local descent groups. Genealogies in the male line normally do not go beyond a man's father's father. Primogeniture entails that the oldest son has primary rights of control over a site and its ceremonial as well as the culturally endorsed privilege of transmitting such rights to his own oldest son. The rights of junior siblings are, at best, secondary in relation to the sites and the ceremonials of their fathers, and it might be an open question whether they are, in practice, any stronger than the acknowledged secondary rights they hold in relation to the sites of their close nonagnatic kin, such as mother's father and mother's mother's brother.

In summary, then, a man may inherit and preserve a territorial niche or he may try to carve one out for himself. In either case, according to von Sturmer (1978:340), such niches are effectively the individual's personal property.[16] No doubt there is scope here for jurisprudential debate. But, in von Sturmer's (ibid., 559) opinion, to attribute land tenure among the Kugu-Nganychara to patrilineal descent groups is, at best, to mistake ideology for reality and, at worst, to perpetuate an anthropological fiction.

CONCLUSION

Field studies of Aboriginal social life during the last decade, like anthropological investigations of previous periods, were carried out among peoples whose traditional culture has been affected in various degrees by European domination. Furthermore, land claim research necessarily has a pragmatic objective and is typically conducted with a view to furthering the interests of certain parties (Morphy and Morphy 1984). Making due allowance for these factors, I nevertheless consider that recent research strongly suggests that the orthodox model of traditional Aboriginal land tenure is in error for some regions and deficient for most. The picture emerging seems more like the three-level construct Malinowski put together with bits and pieces from the last century than the elegant model tooled by Radcliffe-Brown using the genealogical method.

To concede that patriliny has been accorded an undue preeminence is not to say that it is merely one criterion on a par with all the rest. In many parts of Australia, the land is considered to be divided between patrilineal moieties in a profound and fundamental way that makes matrilineal succession ideologically impossible. Furthermore, Aboriginal men are evidently keen to transmit property and status to their sons, and the development of agnatic corporations on that base may well represent a modal tendency. Two other tendencies exist, however, which orthodoxy has for the most part ignored. One concerns the incorporation of nonagnates; the other concerns competition *between* agnates. The former leads typically in the direction of landholding by cognatic formations (e.g., male agnates, their sisters, and their sisters' children). The latter tends toward fission or dispersal of agnatic cores, giving rise in the extreme case to individual ownership.

In Radcliffe-Brown's opinion, the alleged primacy of patriliny in Aboriginal territorial organization is to be explained in terms of the control and exploitation of resources. Patrilineal, patrilocal corporations produce a solidary male core well fitted to defend an area against trespass and theft and best able to benefit from its wealth by virtue of local knowledge (Radcliffe-Brown 1930–31, 1935). In my estimation, such a strategy rarely, if ever, gained ascendancy in Australia. The concept of solidary, inward-looking cohorts of male agnates at most signifies a tendency maintained in a state of subordination by the prevalent, and presumably more successful, strategy manifest in ramifying, outward-looking, egocentric networks of reciprocity and mutual aid. Within a finite cognatic and affinal framework, corporate agnatic rights to exclude—assuming they exist—are regularly neutralized by individual obligations to share. "No one," as von Sturmer's informant insisted, "can block you from [your] mother's country or [your] wife's country." And, if one adds, "your MF's country," "your MMB's country," and so on, then the formation of "company land" and the lability of band composition can be seen as natural outcomes instead of taxonomical aberrations.

Perhaps the most radical aspect of Myers's and von Sturmer's work is their break with traditional group sociology in order to stress the interests of individuals. It is only in these terms, it seems to me, that we can begin to make sense of the rich variety of criteria used by Aborigines to legitimate access to resources or claims to the land itself.

Birthplace, conception-place, long-term residence, father's death-place, and mythological links as well as descent along various pathways can all be found in the ethnographic record. Often they coexist in some rough order of priority, but legal and scholarly attempts to codify (and thus rigidify) distinctions between primary and secondary rights and obligations should not be allowed to obscure the point that together they constitute a set of credentials probably of the same order of usefulness to the individual as his tool kit.[17]

Such considerations need not impel us toward a radical individualism. Corporations predicated on agnation undoubtedly played a vital role in competition for goods, wives, and status (Keen 1982). Furthermore, acquisition of land through succession to deceased estates often depended on explicitly defined structural relationships between unilineal descent groups (Morphy and Morphy 1981; Williams 1986).

The generalizing and codifying tendencies in classical studies of Aboriginal land tenure, as manifested especially in a desire to identify the landowning unit throughout the continent, have not only distracted attention from regional variations but have also obscured the importance of context in the formulation of man-land relationships within each individual culture. As Williams (1986) has pointed out, politeness requires that landownership should be expressed by reference to maximal, rather than minimal, groupings. Within the maximal grouping, however, there is a differentiation of rights and privileges, and politeness also requires that these be respected in the appropriate contexts. I have argued that while the ethic of generosity prevailed throughout Aboriginal Australia, its effect on behavior was always conditioned by circumstances and context (e.g., degrees of relatedness, scarcity and abundance, perishability and durability, etc.). For example, there is evidence to suggest that rare and highly prized commodities, like greenstone for ax heads and the psychoactive drug *pituri*, were subject to unusually strict proprietary access at their sources of origin (Hiatt 1982*b*).

Finally, there is the matter of landownership and ceremonial and personal eminence. It is well established that title to land is expressed symbolically through myth and rite and that ritual performances are public affirmations of ownership. They are also pathways to prestige (Bern 1974). To emerge as impresarios of any note, men in southeastern Arnhem Land must first be acknowledged as custodians of certain sacred sites and paraphernalia crucial to one or another of a small number of major secret cults. Performance of the cult ritual certainly celebrates the land of the organizers, but, conversely, possession of the land and its sacra enables the possessors to become men of eminence. Bern states, "Control of the major rites is based on the custody of the ritual estates, and both are subject to competition. Success in this competition confers prestige on the victor, a prestige whose relevance is largely restricted to ritual performances and associated activities. The competition for prestige is a major interest in the holding of ceremonies" (ibid., 217).

It is now becoming possible to comprehend the true significance of the distinction made by Stanner (1965) between "estate" and "range" (exemplified by the Kugu-Nganychara distinction between "full country" and "company land"). Stanner and others following him have given primacy to ecological considerations, and no doubt there is some value in this approach. What it fails to explain, however, is why custodians of an estate are typically relaxed about the use of its natural resources but nervous and strict about the use of its metaphysical resources. Part of the answer, perhaps, is contained in Myers's (1982:191) observation that identification with a site contributes to personal autonomy. But the documentation of competition for ceremonial status by Bern and, following him, Sutton (1978) and von Sturmer (1978) suggests an added dimension. Company land provides men with a living; full country provides them not merely with dignity but with a potential springboard to fame as well.

NOTES

1. The original version of this chapter was delivered as the Presidential Address, Section 25, A.N.Z.A.A.S; that version then appeared in *Aboriginal Landowners: Contemporary Issues in the Determination of Traditional Aboriginal Landownership*, ed. L. R. Hiatt (University of Sydney Press, 1984). I wish to thank Kenneth Maddock for helpful comments.

2. The petition, with English translation, is reproduced in Wells (1981:37). See also Rowley (1972:147ff.) and Cole (1979:151).

3. Report from the Select Committee on Grievances of Yirrkala Aborigines, Arnhem Land Reserve: Minutes of Evidence, in *Parliamentary Papers 1962–63* (Canberra: Commonwealth Government Printer), 8.

4. Actually, there were two reports of the Aboriginal Land Rights Commission, the First Report in July 1973 and the Second Report in April 1974.

5. For an account of the successful campaign against Liberal-Country Party amendments to the Labor Bill, see Eames (1983).

6. For instance, Bennelong told Collins that Goat Island in Sydney Harbour was his property (Kenny 1973:29).

7. By the time Radcliffe-Brown arrived in Australia, the Kariera people were all living on sheep stations. Their country had been occupied by Europeans for fifty years (Radcliffe-Brown 1913:165).

8. "Traditional Aboriginal owners' means in respect of an area of land, a local descent group of Aborigines who have common spiritual affiliations to a site or sites within that area of land, which affiliations place the group under a primary spiritual responsibility for that site or sites and for that land, and who are entitled by Aboriginal tradition to forage as of right over that land." *Aboriginal Land Rights Commission Second Report*, Appendix D.

9. See *Aboriginal Land Rights Commission First Report*, par. 37, 39; and *Second Report*, 143.

10. No doubt this explains why, in some areas, sisters' sons in their custodial roles are referred to in Aboriginal English as "policemen." Other designations in use are "manager," "mailman," "helper," "worker," "boss," "head-stockman," "offsider," "constable," and "guardian"; men of the mother's clan are referred to as "owners" or "bosses" (for references and discussion, see Morphy and Morphy 1984).

11. Bern and Layton (1984) argue that among the Alawa the local descent group comprises those who have inherited roles in relation to a particular estate through their father's father, mother's father, father's mother, or mother's mother. An individual may thus belong to four different local descent groups and share traditional ownership of four different estates. They also suggest that whereas men's ritual responsibilities tend to be focused on totemic estates, women's ceremonies are more concerned with Alawa country as a whole. This points to the possibility of conceiving the local descent group at an even more inclusive level, that is, the language group or tribe (see Malak Malak in the Daly River claim, ALC 1982a). The Alawa belong to the same culture area as the Mara (Limmen Bight, ALC 1981) and Ngalakan (Roper Bar, ALC 1982b).

12. In reviewing land claims heard by Mr. Justice Toohey, I have passed over evidence relevant to the "horde" debate. I merely note here that, again and again, the hearings confirmed that neighboring clans ranged over each other's territory as a matter of custom and right (see, e.g., Borroloola, ALC 1979a, par. 41; Warlpiri, ALC 1979b, par. 30; Uluru, ALC 1980a, par. 104; Willowra, ALC 1980b, par. 117; Limmen Bight, ALC 1981, par. 188).

13. See lists of dissertations received by the Australia Institute of Aboriginal Studies library, in *A.I.A.S. Newsletter* n.s., 2, 5, 7, 9, 11, 13, 15, 17 (1974–1982). Those most relevant to the concerns here are Peterson 1972; Bern 1974; Myers 1976; Morphy 1977; Keen 1978; von Sturmer 1978; Sutton 1978; Hamilton 1979; Memmott 1979; Bell 1980; Chase 1980.

14. Myers's findings are consistent with observations made by Tonkinson (1978:51–53) in the Western Desert during the 1960s. See also Hamilton's (1979:78, 1982:101) description of land tenure in the Everard Ranges of South Australia, where rights are derived not from patrifiliation but from being born at a particular place, and Palmer's (1984) account of the strongly cognatic basis of relationships between people and the land among the southern Pitjantjara of the great Victoria Desert of South Australia.

15. Sutton and Rigsby (1982:164–165) report several cases from a neigh-

boring area of Cape York Peninsula in which men stated publicly that they wished their estates to be inherited by their sisters' sons. Some nephews maintain control of their father's country as primary territory, while others take over their mother's country. See also Sutton (1978).

16. Chase (1984) has made an ecological analysis of differences in land-ownership and political relationships between the west coast of Cape York Peninsula and the east coast.

17. See Gumbert (1981:116): "Each individual was equipped not with a single patrilineal affiliation as the classical explanations suggest but rather a unique configuration of rights and obligations stemming from his relations to a complex set of sites, individuals, and groups."

6

To Negotiate into Confederation: Canadian Aboriginal Views on Their Political Rights[1]

Michael Asch

> The relation of the horde to its territory does not correspond
> exactly to what we regard as "ownership" in modern law.
> It has some of the qualities of corporate ownership but also
> partakes of the nature of the relation of a modern state to
> its territory, which we may speak of as the exercise of "do-
> minion."
> —Radcliffe-Brown (1952:34)

The Canadian concept of "aboriginal rights" (or the rights that aboriginal peoples possess because of the presence of their ancestors in
"Canada" prior to European settlement)[2] is undergoing a period of
rapid change. As late as 1969, the government of Canada clearly stated
that any special rights guaranteed for the descendants of the aboriginal population of Canada would be terminated and that aboriginal
peoples would be rapidly assimilated into mainstream Canadian society (DIAND 1969). And in 1971, an Appeals Court judge boldly
asserted with respect to the Nishga Indians that "[they] were undoubtedly at the time of settlement a very primitive people with few
of the institutions of civilized society" (British Columbia 1970:483).
As a result of such thinking, the commonly held notion in the late
1960s and early 1970s was that aboriginal peoples had no aboriginal
rights in law (Asch 1984:48).

Yet, in the Constitution Act of 1982 (Section 35), in which Canada patriated its political framework from its British origins, it is stated that "the existing aboriginal rights . . . of the aboriginal peoples of Canada are hereby recognized and affirmed." Further, the constitution called for a series of meetings between the federal and provincial governments and the national Indian, Inuit, and Metis leaders (the peoples named as "aboriginal" in the constitution) to shape its definition. In other words, the commonly held view was now that aboriginal peoples did possess something called "aboriginal rights" that could be affirmed and recognized within Canadian state policy and law.

The causes of this reversal can be traced to a number of political and legal events. One of these is the Supreme Court of Canada's ultimate decision in 1973 regarding the particular court case cited above. There, the panel of judges generally agreed that aboriginal peoples did possess certain rights at the time of contact and strongly implied that the Canadian government should have acknowledged them (Asch 1984:53ff.). It was due, as well, to a number of other factors, of which the strong and effective lobbying efforts of the aboriginal nations ranks of singular importance (Weaver 1981:198).

This change in attitude toward aboriginal rights is perhaps most clearly symbolized by comparing the following statements made by Prime Minister Trudeau. In 1969, he said, "Aboriginal rights really means saying 'we were here before you. You came and took the land from us . . . and we want you to re-open this question.' Our answer is 'no' " (Cumming and Michelberg 1972:331). Then, in a statement made at the outset of the 1983 First Ministers' Conference on Aboriginal Constitutional Matters, he said, "Canada's constitutional process cannot be held to be fulfilled if the [aboriginal] peoples, whose ancestors have been here the longest, find that their particular rights are not adequately reflected or protected in the Constitution" (Trudeau 1983:2).

This change in stance has brought with it a change in stated policy toward aboriginal rights and the settlement of outstanding claims based on aboriginal rights. This policy, as I see it (Asch 1984:55–73), has led to a current view of the federal government (as well as of some of the provincial governments) in which aboriginal rights are seen as pertaining primarily to the protection of land use activity rights, such as a right to hunt and fish and trap on traditional lands. There is also some indication that current government policy concedes that aboriginal rights may include some aspects of property rights as well as the right to participate in management of renewable and nonrenewable resources on specified lands. And in various claims that are now being negotiated, protections in such areas as these are not uncommon. One point is clear, however. Governments (both federal and provincial) do not accept that aboriginal rights are related to "special" political rights such as the right to self-government with senior legislative responsibilities.

The reasons for governmental objections to seeing aboriginal rights as political rights range far beyond what I intend to discuss here (but see Asch 1984:74–88), although one aspect of the issue will be raised in the conclusion. I limit my discussion to the definition of aboriginal organizations at the initial First Ministers' Conference on Aboriginal Constitutional Matters held in Spring 1983. This, as I hope will become apparent, focuses very much on the issue of political rights. It is my intent to indicate both the contemporaneous nature of the political views of peoples who might be described as "hunter-gatherers" (or at least living to some extent within that adaptation) and who are often considered anthropologically only from the perspective of an evolutionary past. Second, I intend to show how their ideas relate to the underlying concept of political polity within Canada as a liberal-democratic state. I will also briefly touch on the differing opinions concerning "political" rights held by government and the aboriginal nations.

A main objective, then, is to interpret the meaning that underlies the concept of aboriginal rights as expressed by aboriginal peoples. It is an end that is made difficult to attain by two important, if tangential, concerns. The first is whether it is possible for a nonnative person to understand the meaning of the term "aboriginal rights" well enough to express it accurately. The second is the question of whose views are being interpreted, for there is truly no single "official" body to whom one can point in an appeal to authority. The first concern I will deal with explicitly during the course of this chapter. The second is an issue I will address now.

The central difficulty to be faced with respect to this question of whose views are being interpreted is the large number of groups that have an independent standing to speak to the issue on behalf of a legitimate aboriginal constituency. As the Constitution specifically defined the aboriginal nations as consisting of three distinct peoples (Indian, Inuit, and Metis), this includes in the first instance the national organizations that represent each of them. There are four: the Assembly of First Nations (AFN), which represents "status" Indians (or Indians as legally defined in Canada); the Native Council of Canada (NCC), which speaks for nonstatus Indians and Metis (or people of "mixed" ancestors); the Metis National Council (MNC), which also speaks for Metis (primarily the descendants of the Red River Settlement in Manitoba); and the Inuit Committee on National Issues (ICNI), which represents the Canadian Inuit.

Each of these national groupings, in turn, is actually a coalition of smaller ones. The AFN, for instance, includes the provincial organizations that represent status Indians in each of the ten provinces and two territories. Each of these, in turn, is composed of subregional and local groupings such as tribes and bands. Each unit within the AFN, from the individual band to the national organization itself, has a legitimate right to put forward a stance on aboriginal rights that is entirely independent of any other body. When the situation within the AFN is multiplied by similar constituent elements with similar rights within the Metis and Inuit organizations, the scope of the potential difficulty in deciding which group is "representative" becomes obvious.

What is very difficult, then, under the circumstances, is to choose which groupings to define as representative. Fortunately, this does not have to be done in this case. While it is undoubtedly true that on many issues the various aboriginal peoples speak with different voices, my analysis of the documentation with respect to aboriginal rights indicates virtual unanimity concerning the basic understanding of that term in principle. Furthermore, despite comments to the contrary, especially in the popular press, a high degree of intergroup consistency exists concerning how the principle is to be carried out in practice. It is, moreover, a point of view that is not a recent adoption but rather can be found as a consistent strain within the documentary evidence that extends back at least to the postwar period. These same points are clearly and forceably put in the speeches and dialogue that took place at the First Ministers' Conference on Aboriginal Constitutional Matters.

THE ABORIGINAL NATIONS' DEFINITION OF ABORIGINAL RIGHTS

The nature of a consensus view on the subject of aboriginal rights is not hard to identify. According to John Amagoalik, cochairman of the Inuit Committee on National Issues:

Our position is that aboriginal rights, aboriginal title to land, water and sea ice flows from aboriginal rights and all rights to practice our customs and traditions, to retain and develop our customs and traditions, to retain and develop our languages and cultures, and the right to self-government, all these things, flow from the fact that we have aboriginal rights. . . . In our view, aboriginal rights can also be seen as human rights, because these are the things that we need to continue to survive as a distinct peoples in Canada. (Canada 1983b:130)

For the Metis, Clem Chartier of the Metis National Council asserted:

What we feel is that aboriginal title or aboriginal right is the right to collective ownership of land, water, resources, both renewable and nonrenewable. It is a right to self-government, a right to govern yourselves with your own institutions, whichever way you want your institutions to run; the right to language, to culture, the right to basically practice your own religion and customs, the right to hunt, trap and fish and gather are certainly part of that, but it is not all of it. (Canada 1983a)

These views are replicated in the draft proposal to amend the Constitution presented by National Chief David Ahenakew on behalf of the Assembly of First Nations. Included within this draft are specific provisions that would guarantee autonomous cultural and economic status for aboriginal peoples, protect historically acquired rights, and, most crucially, entrench the following political rights (Ahenakew 1983:5.5): (1) the right of the First Nations to their own self-identity, including the right to determine their own citizenship and forms of government; (2) the right to determine their own institutions; (3) the right of their governments to make laws and to govern their members and the affairs of their people; (4) the right to exemption from any direct or indirect taxation levied by other governments; and (5) the right to move freely within their traditional lands regardless of territorial, provincial, or international boundaries.

An examination of the content of these and other statements presented at the conference indicates that the key concepts most central in the minds of the spokespersons pertain to a political jurisdiction that includes a land base. Thus, for example, Ahenakew argues in his opening address that central to the position of the AFN is the notion of some measure of Indian "sovereignty" and "jurisdiction" (ibid., 8). Thus, he states, "We are . . . asserting that Indian governments have jurisdiction over Indians, Indian lands and resources" (ibid., 9). Echoing this sentiment, Chartier stated that "the purpose of our participation in this conference is to entrench in the Constitution the right of the Metis people to a land base and self-government" (Canada 1983a:30). It is a view that recurs in statements made by virtually every native organization from the band to the national level which has put forward a position on aboriginal rights.

A consensus view is also expressed with respect to the conceptual basis on which these assertions are justified. Singularly important are two firmly held convictions. The first is that aboriginal rights are founded on the fact of "original" sovereignty. That is, as Georges Erasmus, president of the Dene Nation, put it at the Conference on Constitutional Matters (Canada 1983*b*:43), "We are talking about the title that our people had prior to contact with the European people and obviously . . . the rights we also had at the first contact was full sovereignty."

The second conviction is the notion that the continued existence of rights founded on this original sovereignty has not been extinguished through the subsequent occupation of Canada by settlers from Europe and other parts of the world. It is a proposition explained in contrasting, but equally relevant, manners by two aboriginal spokespersons from British Columbia. For Chief James Gosnell, of the British Columbia Region of the Assembly of First Nations, the position derives from an ontological premise based on the principle of the "gift from God," which is reminiscent of the traditional basis for the assertion of sovereignty under a European feudal policy. He says:

It has always been our belief, Mr. Chairman, that when God created this whole world he gave pieces of land to all races of people throughout this world, the Chinese people, the Germans and you name them, including Indians. So at one time our land was this whole continent right from the tip of South America to the North Pole. . . . It has always been our belief that God gave us the land . . . and we say that no one can take our title away except He who gave it to us to begin with. (Canada 1983*a*:114)

For Bill Wilson of the Native Council of Canada, original sovereignty is linked to the principle of liberation that motivated Canadian involvement in the Second World War. As he stated:

When the German forces occupied France, did the French people believe they didn't own the country? I sincerely doubt that there was one French person in France during the war that ever had the belief that France belonged to Germany, which is why, of course, they struggled with our assistance to liberate their country and once again take it back for themselves. (Ibid., 122)

Thus, he goes on:

So what we say is we have title and that is why we are talking to you about aboriginal rights, but we are not talking English Common Law definitions, International law definitions that have been interpreted and reinterpreted and sometimes extinguished by conquest and ceding treaties and other agreements like that. We are talking about the feeling that is inside all of us as Metis, Indian and Inuit people that this country belongs to us. (Ibid., 124)

In sum, then, in the consensus view, aboriginal rights can be described as encompassing a broad range of economic, social, cultural, and political rights. Of these, it appears that the notion of a land base within a separate political jurisdiction is most fundamental. These rights, in this view, flow first of all from the fact that the aboriginal peoples were in sovereign occupation of Canada at the time of contact and second from the assertion that their legitimacy and continued existence have not been extinguished by the subsequent occupation of Canada by more recent immigrants.

There can be no doubt that this is the consensus view. The question is whether such a notion is comprehensible within a nonnative conceptual framework. In other words (as English law suggests with respect to the legal nature of aboriginal rights), is the idea of aboriginal rights reconcilable to any concept that exists external to a native conceptual schema?

At first blush, it would appear that it may not be possible to discover if this is the case. The concern pertains to an ability to communicate cross-culturally the understanding of the meaning of this term as it is conceptualized by aboriginal peoples within their cultures. It is a concern that was put most forcefully by Wilson when he stated:

My whole point [is] that we must stop viewing [aboriginal rights] from the point of view of the dominant society if we are ever going to understand what the Indian people, the Inuit people and the Metis want. The question, then, is whether there is a means of understanding this concept from the Native point of view. (Canada 1983*a*:128)

At some level, this is a problem that of course cannot be completely resolved, at least not without in-depth training and detailed study of a particular culture. To know the meaning of the term "aboriginal rights" as it is understood internally within a particular native society, it is clearly necessary to know how that meaning relates to other notions within that society. This matter is complicated further because the term itself may be merely an English gloss that is used for convenience in speaking English but that can encapsulate a bundle of notions that are not readily transferable from a native language into English. Thus, without knowing in some depth and breadth how a particular native culture structures its contents, the best one can do is attempt to provide an interpretation that comes close to capturing a general meaning understood within that native culture and language.

Such a task is made much easier if one can find an analogue from the conceptual schema used in one's own society. Although such an orientation cannot do justice to the full sense of the concept as it is understood by a native society, it can, I believe, provide a general framework for cross-cultural understanding. Thus, the question is whether there is a concept within our Western intellectual framework which is analogous to the notion of a peoples' right to a land base and self-government which derives from an "original sovereignty" and remains unextinguished, even in the face of the acquisition of sovereignty by a new political authority.

It is clear that within the conceptual schema of English law, there is an acknowledgment that "rights" continue to exist even after the conquest of occupation by a new sovereign (Asch 1984). In this sense, then, there is an analogue to the notion that aboriginal rights can continue to exist. Divergence from the concept as proposed by aboriginal peoples comes quickly, however. The key point in English law is that this existence continues at the pleasure of the new sovereign. That is, it exists only until the sovereign passes legislation annulling it. This is a point of view that is not compatible with the notion that the original inhabitants can retain ongoing rights in the face of the actions of the new sovereign.

There is, of course, a valid, logical basis for the firm rejection of this native viewpoint in English law which goes beyond the narrow self-interest of new rulers. It is that world history has seen so much population movement and conflict over land that, were one to accept as valid the proposition of ongoing rights based on original habitation, a general state of confusion in world affairs would be the result. It is an argument that was put most forcefully by Prime Minister Trudeau when, in a retort to Wilson and Chief Gosnell, he said:

Going back to the Creator doesn't really help very much. So He gave you title, but you know, did He draw on the land where your mountains stopped and somebody else's began? . . . God never said that the frontier of France runs along the Rhine or somewhere west of Alsace-Lorraine where the German-speaking people of France live. (Canada 1983a:127)

And he concluded:

I don't know any part of the world where history isn't constantly rewritten by migrants and immigrations and fights between countries changing frontiers and I don't think you can expect North America or the whole of the Western Hemisphere to settle things differently than they have been settled everywhere else, hopefully peacefully here. (Ibid.)

This is obviously a reasonable (though not necessarily convincing) argument, and, speaking in general terms, it is this point of view, not that of the aboriginal peoples, that has become adopted in the conceptual schema of the world community.

There is, however, at least one set of circumstances in which the world community appears to recognize, in principle, an exception to this general proposition. A situation in which this limitation arises was alluded to by Wilson in his comment about the French under German rule in World War II: the inhabitants of a previously recognized country fell under the occupation of what is perceived by the world community to be a foreign power. It is encapsulated in the proposition respecting the territorial integrity of nation-states (passed by the General Assembly of the United Nations in 1945). A second, and perhaps more appropriate circumstance, pertains to the situation of colonialism in general, particularly that aspect of colonialism that deals with the situation wherein peoples of non-European origin come under European rule.

In both kinds of circumstances, it is clearly acknowledged in the consensus view of nation-states that, despite the self-evident emergence of a new sovereign and immigration, the rights of indigenous people (whether French or African or whatever), in particular, their sovereign rights, (at least in principle) may not be completely extinguished or eliminated even by the overt act of the new sovereign. It is to this set of circumstances that one must turn if one is to comprehend, through analogy, the basis for the convictions that lie at the heart of the declarations of the aboriginal spokespersons.

The general concept within which the expression of these sentiments is legitimized within the world community's intellectual schema is "self-determination," or the "recognition of the right of all people to rule themselves" (Cranston 1966:92), especially that right as it is perceived to exist under the condition of "colonialism," or "the aggregate of various economic, political and social policies by which an imperial power maintains or extends its control over other areas or peoples" (ibid., 17). While these are not precise or completely apparent as to meaning (see, for instance, the question of the definition of "self" in self-determination),[3] it is my view that in general form, as defined in Cranston, these notions describe well the content of the position that is asserted by the use of the expression "aboriginal rights."

Further evidence that this is the case can be derived by comparing the statements of Wilson and Chief Gosnell with the wording of a number of international accords such as the Charter of the United

Nations (Chap. XI), the Covenant of the League of Nations (see Art. 26), and, in particular, Resolution 1514(XV) of the United Nations General Assembly. Entitled the Declaration on the Granting of Independence to Colonial Countries and Peoples, the latter passed without a dissenting vote in 1961. In part, it reads (United Nations General Assembly 1961):

Mindful of the determination proclaimed by the peoples of the world in the Charter of the United Nations to reaffirm faith in fundamental human rights, in the dignity and worth of the human person, in the equal rights of men and women and of nations large and small and to promote social progress and better standards of life in larger freedom.

Recognizing the passionate yearning for freedom in all dependent peoples and the decisive role of such people in the enforcement of this independence.

Recognizing that the peoples of the world ardently desire the end of colonialism in all its manifestations.

Convinced that all peoples have an inalienable right to complete freedom, the exercise of this sovereignty and the integrity of this national territory. *Solemnly* proclaims the necessity of bringing to a speedy and unconditional end colonialism in all its forms and manifestations;

And to this end

Declares that:

1. The subjugation of peoples to alien subjugation, domination and exploitation constitutes a denial of fundamental human rights, as contrary to the Charter of the United Nations and is an impediment to the promotion of world peace and cooperation.

(and)

2. All peoples have the right to self-determination; by virtue of that right they freely determine their political status and freely pursue this economic, social and cultural development.

Compare this to the Dene Declaration, which was passed unanimously by the Dene Chiefs meeting in Fort Simpson in 1975 (Dene Nation 1977:3–4):

We the Dene of the Northwest Territories insist on the right to be regarded by ourselves and the world as a nation. Our struggle is for the recognition of the Dene Nation by the Government and people of Canada and the peoples and governments of the world.

The New World like other parts of the world has suffered the experience of colonialism and imperialism. Other peoples have occupied the land—often with force—and foreign governments have imposed themselves on our people. Ancient civilizations and ways of life have been destroyed. Colonialism and imperialism is now dead or dying. Recent years have witnessed the birth of new nations or the rebirth of old nations out of the ashes of colonialism.

The Dene find themselves as part of a country. That country is Canada. But the Government of Canada is not the government of the Dene. These governments were not the choice of the Dene, they were imposed upon the Dene.

While it is not clear that the United Nations had the situation of the aboriginal peoples of Canada firmly in mind when it passed Resolution 1514 (XV) and other resolutions, there is evidence to suggest that in principle its point of view paralleled the sentiments of Canadian aboriginal peoples.[4] In my view, the sentiments expressed in these United Nations documents accord well with the perceptions of these peoples. Hence, I argue that an appropriate analogy exists between the two points of view.

In short, then, I am asserting that the notion of aboriginal rights in the perceptions of the native spokesperson is analogous to the right to "self-determination" that is acknowledged by the world community as applicable to peoples living under colonial regimes and thus offers the counterargument to Prime Minister Trudeau's position. Canada, in this view, is not a "normal" nation-state to which "normal" legal processes such as those cited by the prime minister apply. Rather, Canada is seen as a colonial manifestation that, in principle, differs little in its right to assert permanent sovereignty over the landmass of Canada and over its original inhabitants from, say, the British in Kenya or the French in IndoChina.

It is my view, therefore, that the meaning aboriginal peoples attach to the notion of aboriginal rights is closely analogous to the idea of the right of colonial peoples to political self-determination. It is a right that is said to continue even when the indigenous nations come under the sovereignty of a new colonial regime. It is a right that is perceived to parallel that held by the peoples of Africa and Asia. And it is a position that is held among virtually all the aboriginal nations of Canada, specifically, including societies such as the Dene who still utilize hunting-gathering, and institutions related to it, as important components of their way of life.

THE NOTION OF ABORIGINAL RIGHTS AND THE ISSUE OF ASSIMILATION

This leads immediately to the question of whether the assertion of notions concerning "rights" to "sovereignty" and "self-determination" reflect something indigenous or whether it is, in effect, merely an outgrowth of the assimilated position of contemporary aboriginal peoples. I will briefly discuss this issue from the perspective of the Dene.

The way this position is phrased above (and I have often heard anthropologists state it in this way) is false. It is clear that the manner in which the notions of sovereignty and self-determination are argued is too formalistic for the concepts to appear indigenous to many aboriginal ways of life, in particular, the Dene. However, and here I can speak from personal fieldwork experience, there is a valid link between the ideas of self-determination, sovereignty, decolonization, and Dene notions of who they are and the rights they believe they possess ontologically.

In aboriginal times, the Dene retained unencumbered control over their lands and their polity. Indeed, recent evidence indicates that they had created a system of alliance potentials that could link within a loose confederation (at minimum) virtually all Dene who lived in the Mackenzie Valley (Ives, n.d.). That sense of total control remained unchanged even after the coming of the European fur traders (Asch 1979, 1982b). Therefore, under these conditions, it is a moot point whether the Dene saw themselves as having a "right" to self-determination or any of the other political characteristics outlined here, for they perceived themselves to be acting in a self-determining manner.

As soon as the Canadian state attempted to assume sovereignty, Dene assertions of their continuing control began. For example, during discussions concerning treaty agreements made in the early 1920s, the Dene took the position that these arrangements could deal only with "peace and friendship," for they would not give up control over their lands. It was a position they continually reiterated at various discussions with government agents and, ultimately, took to court. They were partially successful in this litigation in that the state acknowledged, through the opinion of the judge, that *perhaps* the discussions were about peace and friendship rather than land cession. It is a position they continue to maintain today.

Further, in the 1970s, during the course of an inquiry into the possible construction of a pipeline, one Dene assertion was that it was they, not the government, who had the right to make the ultimate decision on its disposition. It is a position they continue to state today. The Dene have not been successful in getting state institutions to accede to this view, however, and they have therefore witnessed in recent years the beginnings of a massive transformation of their land base in favor of nonrenewable resource development. I have found these ideas reflected also at the community level as expressed in attitudes toward the existing political system and developments taking place on the landscape. This has led me to conclude that there is little difference in substance (although there is in rhetoric) between what is asserted by Dene and national aboriginal leaders and what is expressed by Dene people living in communities.

My response, then, to the idea that concepts about "rights" for such matters as sovereignty, self-determination, and decolonization are foreign to Dene traditions—and hence an example of assimilation—is this. Recent history has changed the Dene situation from one in which they had effective political control over their lands but did not express notions of "rights" overtly to one in which, when control is challenged, the Dene do take the overt position that they possess these rights. Hence, I find a pattern that is continuous. The only change is that the Dene of today are stating consciously what in the past they assumed to be true: they have the aboriginal right to self-determination. While this is change, I do not see it as assimilation.

THE RIGHT TO SELF-DETERMINATION

The claim to the right to political self-determination is not unique to the aboriginal peoples of Canada. Such claims are endemic within the modern world and appear to be virtually coextensive with the existence of the modern nation-state. Indeed, as Conner (1973:1) points out, "In a world consisting of thousands of distinct ethnic groups and only some one hundred and thirty-five states, the revolutionary potential inherent in self-determination is quite apparent. All but fourteen of today's states contain at least one significant minority."

Still, the claim by Canadian aboriginal nations is unique in a number of ways. First, the appeal itself is made to something called an "aboriginal right." Second, the claim is made by indigenous peoples who have a historical (and present-day) link to hunting-gathering economies. As I said above, this indicates that Canadian aboriginal peoples see themselves as part of the same world as others who have been incorporated as minorities through the process of colonialism and nation-state formation. It is a viewpoint that does not receive enough comment within our discipline or currency in our ethics (Castile 1975). The third, and most crucial, distinguishing features of the Canadian position is the direction proposed by aboriginal people for a solution to the issue of how their political rights might be entrenched within the Canadian state. In the "classical" scenario, the political rights of an indigenous population that has come under colonial rule are realized through the assertion of total sovereignty. And, in principle, one must accept that under the logic of self-determination they would be justified in demanding such an action.

What is abundantly clear, however, is that virtually all proposals thus far developed eschew such an objective. Rather, the solution they seek is to find an accommodation that can be realized within the context of the existing Canadian confederation. Thus, Chartier (Canada 1983*a*:3) of the Metis National Council said, "We believe the realization of [the right of the Metis people to a land base and self-government] is essential to the preservation and development of our aboriginal nationality within the Canadian federation." And Ahenakew (1983:5) stated on behalf of the Assembly of First Nations, "I ask . . . that no one misinterpret our positions, strongly held, or our words, no matter how strongly spoken, to mean that we are separatists—seeking to divide Canada and assert the status of foreign nations. . . . We are committed to strengthening and building Canada—not to dismantling it." It is, in short, as the Dene said in their Declaration (Dene Nation 1977:4): "What we seek . . . is independence and self-determination within the country of Canada."

To accomplish this end, the aboriginal nations are calling for the constitutional recognition of territorial jurisdictions in which aboriginal peoples, either explicitly or through some process such as majority rule within a district, would have legislative authority over matters that impinge directly on their way of life. Specific concerns they raise pertain to language, education, civil law, and some aspects of taxation and economic development (Asch 1984:89–109). Their formulations explicitly exclude such matters as the establishment of "our own armies and our own foreign relations" (Ahenakew 1983:9).

The orientation of this kind of solution conforms analytically in many respects to what M. Smith (1969:434) calls "consociation." In consociational states, as I suggest (Asch 1984:74–88), there is a compromise between a national interest in which all members of the nation-state participate on a "universalistic" basis and an ethnonational interest in which participation is organized in such a manner that the ethnonational entity gains control over matters that are vital to its preservation as a distinct society and culture. Liberal-democratic states that have such arrangements include federations such as Switzerland, in which this is accomplished indirectly through dividing sovereignty between a national and a regional level, and unitary states such as Belgium, in which this is accomplished directly through naming certain powers to be held by specific ethnonational entities.

The matters that consociational states generally organize for control by particular ethnonational entities are education, some aspects of language, some aspects of the cultural sphere, aspects of civil law, and some powers of taxation. In other words, the very matters espoused by advocates of aboriginal self-government in Canada. There are also instances of nation-states wherein an ethnonational group gains some control over subnational citizenship within its territorial jurisdiction and some powers with respect to residence in their domains. Again, this is what some aboriginal nations are calling for in the Canadian context.

The notion that an ethnonational community can obtain guarantees for such rights is not foreign to Canadian political thought for—especially under the 1867 British North America Act (now renamed the Constitution Act 1867)—Canada has created some consociational institutions with respect to "the French-fact" in Quebec (Lijphart 1977). Specifically, these arrangements concern the division of powers between a central and a provincial level of government and the entrenchment of certain controls over education, guaranteed use of the French language, and other similar matters within provincial jurisdictions (and thus within the hands of the French majority in Quebec). Canada, however, has not completed the task of consociation with respect to the rights of the French; nowhere are there explicit guarantees for their rights under the accommodation formula. Nonetheless, it is to a large extent already "consociational" in spirit and federal in form. What the aboriginal nations seek, then, is an arrangement that is similar in nature to that which already exists in Canada with respect to the French-fact but one that is much stronger in terms of constitutional guarantees.

The view that aboriginal peoples require self-government with legislative authority is slowly becoming incorporated into Canadian state policy. Most crucially, at least on the symbolic level, is the inclusion of the clause recognizing and affirming aboriginal rights in Canada's Constitution. There is even some recognition by parliamentarians of the existence of political rights that are autonomous from those aboriginal peoples have as Canadian citizens. For example, the 1983 Report of a Special Committee of the Canadian Parliament (popularly called the Penner Report after the Member of Parliament who chaired the committee), composed of members from all parties, unanimously recommended that "the right of Indian people to self-government be explicitly stated and entrenched in the Constitution of Canada" (House of Commons 1983:141). Also, at least one provincial premier, R. Hatfield of New Brunswick, has argued in favor of recognizing self-determination for aboriginal peoples. In fact, in examining in detail the positions of the various governments involved in negotiations with the aboriginal nations, not one rejects the position out of hand. This is certainly a marked advance over the position that existed as recently as 1969.

There is still significant opposition, however, to the idea that self-government should include "sovereignty," or legislative authority for governments based on ethnonational identities, for any powers, including those to protect the cultural rights of francophones now held by Quebec (and the federal government) through current constitutional arrangements. Governments would prefer a solution whereby the aboriginal nations operate on the basis of "delegated authority," a form in which the ability to have self-governing institutions is delegated from senior "sovereign" governments. The difficulty with this orientation is simple. It would allow senior governments to disallow any legislation that might conflict with their policy interests. As such, it is seemingly unacceptable to the principle of self-determination as outlined by aboriginal peoples.

Governments have put forward many arguments to support their position (Weaver 1981). One supersedes all others, for, if true, it would undermine the moral basis for the claim to self-determination. It is the argument that holds that to grant sovereignty to aboriginal nations would be to develop an apartheidlike structure within Canada. Such a situation would be anathema to the general Canadian public; unless it is overcome, there is little chance of success for the aboriginal position.

There is a simple answer to this charge. As M. Smith (1969) clearly points out, states can take three fundamental positions with respect to ethnonational rights: "universalism," "differential incorporation," and "consociation." Most commonly, they will take the position of universalism. In this case, each individual is seen as identical in the eyes of the state. Such a situation has the (perhaps unintentional) consequence of fostering the assimilation of its minorities, for as Smith (ibid., 435) states, "The regime is inherently assimilative in orientation and effect. By assimilating all its members uniformly as citizens, it fosters their assimilation in other spheres also, notably language, connubium, economy, education and recreation." The second type, "differential incorporation," gives rise to apartheid states (ibid.). In such states, institutions are structured in a manner that provides differential access to power and resources among the various ethnonational segments. Thus, these systems, while recognizing the existence of different cultural communities, entrench inequality among them: there is no attempt to create power sharing arrangements within a common parliamentary structure, no willingness to distribute power or material resources on an equitable basis, no agreement that segmental autonomy will exist for all segments. Without such guarantees, it is clear that states with differential forms of incorporation cannot be seen as adhering to liberal-democratic values.

The idea of "consociation" reconciles the institutionalization of the rights of cultural communities with the tenet of universalism essential to liberal-democratic values, for it suggests the sharing of power in a manner that tries to ensure the rights of individuals as well as collectives. The former are protected by ensuring that many aspects of governance are done by citizenry, pure and simple. The latter are protected by ensuring that there is a principle of "equality of consideration" (Pennock 1950:82), rather than differential incorporation, when the state deals with matters in the jurisdiction of the ethno-national communities. M. Smith (1969:434) rightly calls this "coordinate status."

In short, universalism and differential incorporation each create adverse circumstances for a cultural minority. The former, by asserting the supremacy of the individual over any minority collective, in effect creates a situation in which the majority controls all institutions and hence denies self-determination to a minority. This is done through majority rule. Differential systems do accept the existence of different cultural communities; however, they deny self-determination by organizing the state in a manner that ensures that certain minorities will not effectively participate in the state's governing institutions. Consociation contrasts with both types because it acknowledges both the rights of cultural communities to participate equally and the rights of individuals to equal access to state institutions. As a result, consociation does not lead to apartheid.

CONCLUSION

Despite some positive signs, the entrenchment of real power and territorial jurisdictions for aboriginal governments is a long way off. In the two years since the initial First Ministers' Conference, negotiations have not moved beyond the general statements made in 1983. The prospect for rapid development is not strong as governments are reluctant to move on the issue (when the negotiations process as defined in the Constitution expires). To force government action will probably require encouraging signs from the Canadian public: work is now being undertaken to advance that possibility. In this regard, perhaps most important is that the aboriginal nations are not calling for separation but for a consociational means to negotiate their way into Canadian confederation.

It is important to consider why the aboriginal nations of Canada are calling for a solution that dovetails with the idea of coordinate status and the approach of consociation. I am certain the answer lies, in part, in the realpolitik of the aboriginal peoples. Comprising only 4 percent of the total Canadian population, they are hardly in a position to call for the demise of the Canadian state and, perhaps, the return of the colonists to their homelands. An important component also lies in the existence of an analogy between what the aboriginal nations are calling for and some of the principles that now exist with respect to the French-fact. Another explanation is cultural and relates to the possibility that the type of solution proposed by the aboriginal nations may arise from their own traditions and hence offers a clue to the nature of precontact aboriginal polity.

The concept of consociation and coordinate status among nations suggests a mutuality, yet a separateness. It is a system that recognizes both the right to protect the common good of all and the right of each of the member collectivities within an alliance to protect its uniqueness. It is an idea that fits with the notions of reciprocity and sharing as I understand these concepts in Dene society. Here, however, they are presented not with respect to individuals within a single group but as a central political value in a system of intergroup relations. If this is the case, then it is an indication that Canadian aboriginal nations have always had the conceptual material available to create systems of alliance among member groups. It is a view that is exemplified in the political notions of the Iroquois confederacy.

Thus, it seems that the constitutional proposals advanced by the aboriginal nations today do not merely signify an echo of modern liberal-democratic principles, such as those now in place to accommodate the French-fact in Canada, or an appeal based on realpolitik considerations. These proposals instead appear to be a modern version of the notion of alliance building based on sharing and reciprocity developed to incorporate into the aboriginal world the reality of a new potential partner: the recent European settlers in the Canadian landscape.

NOTES

1. Portions of this chapter appear in Asch, *Home and Native Land* (1984), especially chapter 3. The analysis and descriptive matter taken from *Home and Native Land* are used by permission of Methuen of Canada.

2. Various authorities and political interests define aboriginal rights differently. There is a consensus, however, that they *may* include property rights, certain rights to use the land in a traditional manner, cultural rights, and political rights. In some measure, the present constitutional process, which includes both negotiations and court cases, is an attempt by the Canadian state to define its own view as to what aboriginal rights include. For an extended discussion of the question of aboriginal rights, see Asch (1984:5–8, 11ff., 76).

3. An excellent summary of competing definitions of "self" in the twentieth century is contained in Ofvatey-Kodjoe (1977:28–38). In his view, three theories have been dominant: "national determinism," in which the nation that is the self is an ethnic community; the "plebiscite," in which the self is "a group of people with a common subjective attachment to the same state"; and "national equality," which sees the self as based on a mix of "a common territory and nationalistic outlook." A fourth theory, "national-cultural autonomy," is mentioned but not developed. It is a position that was raised by the Austrian socialists but was never adopted as state policy (ibid., 36).

Ofvatey-Kodjoe suggests that of the three dominant theories, two have been seen to have serious defects that make them unpopular from the perspective of developing an international community. The problem with the national equality theory can be reduced to a concern over precision in applicability, especially in difficult cases such as those that might arise if two nations coexist within the same state. The problem with the national determinism theory is that it appears to be antidemocratic in the sense that it does not allow people to choose their sovereignty through popular will; it also suffers from its association with the conceptual basis of nationalism under the German Nazi regime. In his opinion, it is the plebiscite theory that the international community favors in defining "self." In my readings, this is a view commonly held by experts.

The primary implication of the plebiscite theory is that only the majority of the population has the right to self-determination within a national entity. As Higgins (1963: 104, 105) suggests, "Self-determination refers to the rights of the majority within a general accepted political unit to the exercise of power. In other words, it is necessary to start with stable boundaries and permit political change within them. . . . If, then, the right of self-determination is the right of the majority within an accepted political unit to exercise power, there can be no such thing as self-determination for the Nagas. The Nagas live within the political unit of India and do not constitute the majority therein."

The idea propounded by Higgins concerning majority rule could have an important consequence for Canadian aboriginal people. Some authorities would follow her interpretation and argue that, like the Naga of India, the native people of Canada, a minority of the total population within a recognized nation-state, have no special political rights under provisions of United Nations declarations.

4. The problem is that the aboriginal peoples of Canada are unlike the indigenous populations on other continents: they are a numerical minority, and they are contained within a recognized nation-state. Thus, by some interpretations, they would be considered a minority population, and as the plebiscite theory (see n. 3, above) suggests, they would not have a right to self-determination. There is evidence to suggest that at least some nation-states would prefer, on practical and political grounds, to see this interpretation adopted in principle. However, no resolution does so. Rather, the documents appease the concerns of these nation-states by relying on peripheral considerations to exclude indigenous groups from the effects of the responsibilities of the administrative powers. Thus, for example, Resolution 1514(XV), in interpreting which self-governing territories had to have their development toward self-government reported on, stated that it was a self-evident proposition only when the "colony" was ethnically and/or culturally distinct and geographically separate from the administrating power.

The issue is debatable. Clearly, the United Nations has trouble dealing with this issue, perhaps because most nation-states have minorities within their national borders which could use principles such as those contained in Resolution 1514(XV) to demand self-determination. Yet, the United Nations has not denied, in principle, that at least some of these groups could have the same right to self-determination as is proclaimed by Resolution 1514(XV). For detailed discussion on this point, see Bennett (1978a, 1978b, 1983).

7

Can Namibian San Stop Dispossession of Their Land?[1]

Robert Gordon

> A great advance for these Bushmen [will be] in their recognition of personal property. This is the basis of all civilization.
> —Claude McIntyre, First Bushman Affairs Commissioner at Tsumkwe, 1968

The issue of indigenous land rights in Namibia has not been a subject of concern for legal scholars, nor have the courts had any case in which the issue was directly raised and addressed. The closest we come to confronting the issue is in the Commission of Enquiry into the Rehoboth Baster Uprising, in which South African Appeal Court Judge Mr. Justice de Villiers briefly considered the validity of treaties made between the Rehoboth Basters and the German regime. The basic legislation that concerns us is the 1903 Crown Lands Disposal Ordinance of the Transvaal, as amended and applied to what was then South West Africa by proclamations 13 and 54 of 1920. In these, " 'Crown lands' mean all unalienated land within the Protectorate . . . however acquired, which was lately the property of the German Government, and such further land as may be acquired by the Government of the Union of South Africa." I discuss this legislation as it affects Zhu rights with respect to current Department of Nature Conservation plans to appropriate their land, now known officially as Bushmanland, for a game park. I also discuss the validity of a treaty between "Bushman" Captain Aribib, of the Heixom, and German Governor Leutwein, which was signed in 1895, guaranteeing the Heixom habitational rights and protection in an area that covers the present-day Etosha Game Park (de la Bat 1982).

In considering the argument that statutory grounds already exist for applying to the Supreme Court in Windhoek for an injunction to prevent the declaration of Bushmanland as a nature reserve and, in addition, to argue against the settlement of Angolan San-speakers there, I follow three strands: (1) the question of San land rights will be discussed; (2) the doctrine and intention underlying the Native Administration Proclamation will be briefly analyzed; and (3) a case will be made that current policy proposals are contrary to the spirit of the Mandate under which South Africa claims to administer Namibia. My conclusion is that while the courts have shown a clear reluctance to undertake juridical review, they do possess the authority to interpret legislation and particularly administrative action based on it.

DISPOSSESSION BY CONSERVATION IN SOUTH AFRICA[2]

At the 1936 Empire Exhibition held in Johannesburg, one of the star attractions, and certainly the most controversial, was an exhibit of living "Bushmen" brought there from the southern Kalahari by a big game hunter named Bain. The pamphlet accompanying the exhibit eulogized them as the "last living remnants of a fast dying race" and intimated that 50 percent of the profits from their exhibition would go toward providing them with a reserve. Bain claimed that since 1925 he had been involved in trying to get a tract of land for these San-speaking people and that the matter had become more urgent in recent years. In 1931, the 9,450-square-kilometer Gemsbok National Park had been proclaimed on land that had originally been surveyed as farms for whites but which, except for these "Bushmen," had remained unoccupied.

The Minister of Native Affairs of what was then the Union of South Africa visited the exhibit (see also Schrire 1984). He was suitably impressed, promising that those exhibited people would be able to pursue traditional hunting in the park. "We must treat the Bushman as fauna and realize he is incapable of assimilating European ideas," the Minister said (*The Cape Argus*, 25 Aug. 1936). Unfortunately, the park fell under the National Parks Board, an autonomous body, and was thus ostensibly impervious to manipulation by politicians. Despite the Minister's friendly assurances, San-speakers continued to be persecuted for hunting in the park.

To protest harassment of these people by Parks officials, Bain took a San deputation, fifty-five strong, to the Parliament in Cape Town. Smuts, the Prime Minister, expressed sympathy for these "living fossils" and also promised they would be allowed to hunt in the Gemsbok Park as long as they used "traditional weaponry" (Boydell 1948). The National Parks Board was still unsympathetic, however; it presented an argument on the following grounds: (1) these "Bushmen" were not pure Bushmen, and, moreover, many of them spoke Afrikaans or Hottentot; (2) it was useless to spend money on protecting game that these people would kill and whose skins would be sold to smugglers; (3) if a number of them were allowed to settle, they would attract other squatters, and soon the game would be "wild" again and difficult for tourists to see (*The Cape Argus*, 11 May 1937). Arguments of this kind had been raised before. In refutation, Raymond Dart (*The Star*, 24 Sept. 1936) pointed out that there was no such thing as a "pure race." Further, the fact that they spoke Afrikaans did not make them any less Bushmen than an Englishman who spoke Chinese became a Chinese. Dart's arguments, as those of his followers, have remained unconvincing in South Africa.

In 1941, a more influential politician, Denys Reitz, became Minister of Native Affairs. He ordered an immediate census of all San-speaking peoples in South Africa and set aside for their use a tract of 12,000 morgan (slightly less than 6,000 hectares) on a farm next to the Gemsbok Park. Under the hegemony of the National Parks Board, San-speakers became increasingly dependent on welfare and tourist handouts. The relationship was always an uneasy one. Kloppers (1970), who worked in the park and later wrote a laudatory book about its chief warden, probably reflected official opinion in his conclusion: "I wish I was in a position to add another to this impressive list of prestations, and that is the removal of the Bushmen out of the Gemsbokpark." He listed what he perceived to be the problems created by "Bushman" residence in the park: (1) their numbers increased because game attracted many outsiders; (2) their ideas about nature conservation differed from that of their patrons; (3) they had started to make more demands, that is, to keep dogs, to hunt freely, to move freely, to receive visitors, to have better housing (the verdict on this was "utterly untraditional"); and (4) worst of all, they did not want to be humbled by working.

These arguments are remarkably similar to those used by the National Parks Board in 1936 and to those advanced by Namibian Nature

Conservation officials with respect to why the Etosha Heixom and Topnaar Khoi should be dispossessed of their land rights in Namibian game parks. Such parallels do not bode well for Zhu should Nature Conservation expand its hold on Bushmanland. In short, "tradition"—as defined by petty bureaucrats, not by the people themselves—is compulsory if one wants to remain on land slated to become a park.

Publicly, the rationale for making 562,000 hectares of Bushmanland a game park is the "relatively scarce game species encountered there and the absence of other suitable regions" (*The Windhoek Advertiser*, 19 July 1984). The reason given by officials, however, is that any form of subsistence by San-speakers other than foraging would present a major ecological threat to the fragile Kalahari ecosystem. Ironically, the present situation is far from "natural," the region having been subject to considerable economic and ecological exploitation and change over the last 150 years (Wilmsen 1982*b*, 1983; Gordon 1985; Kinahan 1986), and Nature Conservation itself is visibly involved in creating a contrived "naturalness" by actively maintaining plant and animal species defined by them as desirable while eliminating undesirable species. An examination of the evidence leads one to concur with the conclusion reached by Galaty (1981:280):

Ecological arguments are widely used against pastoral economic activities and constitute a potent weapon. Without devaluing the benefits of careful ecological study and controlled comparisons, I suggest that many ecologically based arguments derive from ideology rather than scientific fact.

Planning for the game park has been going on for at least six years, ever since a white nature conservator was appointed to the "homeland." Suggestive of the depth of research that backs up the game park proposal is the fact that originally it was intended to make western Bushmanland, which is relatively uninhabited, the game reserve. However, when the South African army started camps and resettlement schemes there for San-speakers other than Zhu, Nature Conservation managed to get approval from the Bushman Advisory Council to change the game reserve to eastern Bushmanland where the majority of Zhu live. Zhu were persuaded to agree to this because they were led to believe they would be able to continue their subsistence pastoralism without having to accommodate many strangers.

Nature Conservation believes that a game reserve will generate cash for Zhu by attracting "tourists." It also fits into their master plan, which calls for a grand circular tour going from Grootfontein to Rundu and then along the Okavango River and coming back via the proposed Bushmanland reserve through the newly established 25,000-hectare Mahango and 380,000-hectare Khaudum reserves (*The Windhoek Observer*, 28 May 1983).

In Bushmanland, the attraction will not be game *per se* but "wild Bushmen" of the variety packaged in the popular South African movie, *The Gods Must Be Crazy*. San-speakers will thus become objects of the leisure rituals of affluent whites. Ethically, such policies of "enforced primitivism," which are typically engaged in either to promote tourism or defended as "a means of preserving the tribe's cultural identity," are untenable (World Bank 1982:21). A game park to attract tourists will inevitably affect whatever development assistance is rendered to Zhu in the area: state aid is only available insofar as it will allow Bushmanland to be fashioned more closely into its role of leisure object for the elite. Development of this kind will simply reinforce the manifest and basic inequalities in Namibian society (Overton 1979).

Western (1981), one of the most respected ecologists to have worked in Africa, reported on his work in the Amboseli ecosystem in terms equally applicable to the Kalahari. The game park is too small to survive by itself, and "whatever their value nationally and internationally, parks, far from benefiting local communities on which they depend, place enormous burdens on them" (ibid., 14). He concluded by raising the general ethical question the Administrator-General for South West Africa and the Department of Nature Conservation appear to have ignored: "Why, after all, should they, the poorest sector of the population, bear the costs of supporting wildlife when economically and aesthetically the benefits accrue nationally and internationally to others much wealthier?"[3]

IDEOLOGY AND DISPOSSESSION

Dispossession of San land in northern Namibia has been part of an ongoing systematic process since at least 1884. At first, the colonizers were strikingly unsuccessful. Indeed, on occasion, they were forced to treat with San peoples. After 1906, with the development of a railway line to Grootfontein, there began a massive influx of settlers which led to a state of open undeclared war between first the German and then the South African colonial forces and San-speakers. During this period, the image of these peoples held by colonizers, and academics, underwent a not-so-subtle transformation. As Schultze (1914,2:290) put it in the *Colonial Handbook*:

With such people the colonists cannot contend; they are allowed to live as long as they, at minimum, cause no trouble. Where they do not fulfill these requirements, they have been shot as predators.

Even liberal academics like Marquard believed that San peoples in Namibia were "unable to adapt" and thus retreated before civilization (Marquard and Standing 1939:251–252). The defining characteristic of this inability to adapt was said to be the fact that they owned no private or fixed property. Indeed, this image of "rootlessness" is arguably the single most important ideological factor leading to San dispossession—despite the fact that scholars, such as Schinz (1891), Passarge (1907), and Vedder (1937), who reported on the San-speaking peoples of this area stress their notion of territoriality. Unlike other colonized peoples, they allegedly had no fixed address. Even Vedder (1937:416–436), who recognized the validity of San territorial claims, merely offered practical advice on how to "tame the Bushmen" (itself a revealing metaphor). When he eventually came to plead for a San reserve, it was not because these people had a right to land but because "Bushmen" were important to science. The administration rejected such arguments on the grounds that as nomads, they would not stay in the reserves. Versions of this argument are still found today: black Africans have land tenure while San "Bushmen" have only territoriality. This emphasis on difference and scientific uniqueness is one of the keys to understanding how ethnocide against San-speaking peoples could be rationalized while at the same time it delayed its course.

After the Second World War, the policy of apartheid was elaborated and applied to what was then still recognized as the mandated territory of South West Africa. This reinforced administrative dismissal of San land claims. A San reserve was proposed for the NyaeNyae area, which was well isolated from white farms. Troublesome "Bushmen" from other parts of the country, and even South Africa, were to be resettled there. But even this reserve did not take shape until the administration was forced to act because so many San-speaking farm laborers were fleeing to Botswana. It was felt a Bushman reserve would stem this tide, or at least control it.

Nature Conservation's efforts can best be conceptualized as yet another in a long series of land encroachments, this time by "elephant and giraffe ranchers," as Marnham so bitingly put it. Indeed, he says "the practice of conservation through game reserves is largely irrelevant to animal survival. Even today the greater part of Africa's wildlife survives outside the reserves" (1980:12). The establishment of every game reserve in Namibia has involved interference in the rights of local people.

In light of this history, what are San aspirations? And can we decipher them adequately? I think we can. It is now well established in the literature that San peoples express an almost unanimous desire to raise cattle; this should surprise no one. As is the situation of any people in a state of oppression, they have constantly asked themselves what has caused them to be oppressed. For the San, the answer inevitably has been not skin color but lack of cattle ownership, which is the one thing that differentiates them from their neighbors (Silberbauer and Kuper 1966; see Denbow and Wilmsen 1986 and Wilmsen, n.d., for a history of San cattle keeping). As a group of Zhu told a visiting South African cabinet minister:

Times are difficult. The season is dry and game is scarce. We cannot go on living like this. Teach us to do something ourselves like the Bantu . . . so that we can live like other people . . . [Another said] we live like the wild animals of the veld. We have no home because we are harassed everywhere. (*Die Burger*, 13 Aug. 1960; van der Merwe 1960)

Zhu and donor agencies such as the World Bank agree on one issue: the urgency of legally guaranteeing Zhu rights to Bushmanland and extending title to additional land that is traditionally theirs. One of the primary reasons the Bushman Advisory Council initially accepted the game reserve proposal was because they felt that it would discourage, even prevent, the in-migration of landless San-speakers who originated either in Angola or from the white farms in the old Police Zone. The Council also believes that Zhu cattle and goats would attract other San peoples to Bushmanland.

In exploring possible legal remedies to this potentially deleterious situation, my focus will be on land rights. Various authorities have recently emphasized the importance of land in such cases; for example, Bennett says:

Without the ownership of their lands, tribes are hopelessly vulnerable to exploitation, and lack the capital upon which to build a viable future. On these grounds alone the recognition of aboriginal tenure is crucial to their effective protection; but equally important, simple justice demands that the law should acknowledge the rights of peoples who have occupied their lands since time immemorial—lands with which they have typically formed an irrevocable spiritual bond (Bennett 1978a:29).

INDIGENOUS LAND RIGHTS: THE ARIBIB TREATY

Contrary to the myth of the Bushmen being harmless people, at the onset of German colonialism in the territory, they were a power to be feared, to the extent that Leutwein, the governor, was forced to conclude a treaty with some of them. In 1895, he concluded a treaty with Heixom Captain Aribib, and in 1898, one of his subordinates unintentionally replicated the ritual. This "protection treaty" deserves to be quoted in full:

The Bushmen cede to the German government the entire territory to which they believed up to now to have claimed. It extends from the area of Outjo up to the area of Grootfontein. The northern limit is the Etosha Pan. The southern limit is formed by the northernmost werfts of the Hereros.

In return, the German government promises to provide the Bushman with security and protection from everyone. The Bushmen may not be driven away from the waterhole !Naidaus, where they are presently. They are also entitled at all times and everywhere on their former territory to collect veldkos.

In return they promise not to oppose the settlement of German farmers, but to be of assistance to them and to remain on good terms with them. In particular they promise not to set grass fires.

Captain Aribib vows to remain always loyal to the German government and to meet its requirements with good will. He receives, as long as he fulfills this obligation, an annual salary of 500 marks. For every grass-fire noted in the area described in paragraph 1, 20–50 marks will be deducted.[4]

Aribib was a captain of some influence because he had checked the northward expansion of the cattle-herding Herero. He was apparently a loyal ally of the Germans. In 1904, on the instructions of the Ovambo chief, Nehale, he was shot for killing a number of Ovaherero at Namutoni during the German-Herero war.

Undoubtedly, some contemporary commentators (see Stals 1984) would argue that by drawing up this treaty Leutwein was simply displaying his ethnological ignorance for the Bushmen were not supposed to have chiefs. Even if this were true, it is irrelevant because in his system of control, Leutwein concentrated on the personalities of men of influence. As Bley (1971:39) sums up:

He constantly attempted to put their political and social functions on to a personal level. Their plans for their tribes could thus be glossed over as personal traits of character of the chiefs' ambition, the desire for prestige and power, good living and luxury. The constitutional position of the chiefs in their tribes could be ignored by turning them into important private citizens of the state. . . . Leutwein avoided admitting the clash of interests between German and African claims. He hoped that by the cautious application of "the right treatment" one could cover up the chiefs' decisive loss of function.

Even as Leutwein was signing treaties of this nature, there was considerable debate in legal circles about whether a state could conclude a treaty with its subjects. It appears that the viewpoint represented by Snow, an international lawyer, carried the day, at least initially. In Snow's (1921:127) view, "The term 'treaty' as applied to an agreement between a civilized State and an aboriginal tribe is misleading, and such an agreement is, according to the law of nations, a legislative act on the part of the civilized State, made upon conditions which it is bound to fulfill since it insists that the aboriginal tribes shall be bound on their part."

Leutwein did try to fulfill the government's part of the agreement with Aribib and thereby arguably recognized the legitimacy of the agreement. For example, in replying to his subordinate, von Estorff, who had concluded a treaty with Aribib in 1898, Leutwein (see n. 4) pointed out that he had concluded a similar treaty in 1895 and that any changes should be made by agreement with Aribib, not through the conclusion of a new treaty. The provision under which the Bushmen ceded all their land was particularly problematic because according to the official view, "Bushmen" did not own land.[5] The area in question was to be treated as government land; von Estorff was to arrange matters accordingly. Aribib received his annual subvention until 1903, but after his death, the departure of Leutwein, and the 1907 proclamation of the Etosha Game Park, the Heixom were pushed out of the park and forced to work for white settlers. I could find no evidence, however, that the treaty was ever formally abrogated.

Interestingly, it appears that when the South Africans took over the country in 1915, they respected these treaties. For example, Johannes Kruger, a Griqua Baster who was made chief over the local Gaub Bushmen by the Germans and forced to sign a similar treaty, had the Guigab, Hiebus Nord, Chudib, and Chudib West farms reserved for him for the duration of his lifetime. Kruger's father had apparently been chief of the Waterberg "Bushmen" and Bergdama and had substantially killed off the elephants in that district. This hunting tradition was carried on by his son with the help of his "Bushmen" (Vedder 1934: 501). This example illustrates how fluid "ethnic identities" were during this time. Concurrently, after an unsettled period, Bushmen were allowed to stay and, later, even encouraged to settle in the Etosha Game Park.

INDIGENOUS SOVEREIGN RIGHTS?

The question of whether aboriginals have sovereign rights over the lands they occupy has generated a large literature among jurists. The issue appears to revolve around the definition of sovereignty. Early scholars, Acquinas and Fiesco, for example, declared in favor of rights of indigenous peoples, among whom are subsumed aboriginals as this term is used here. But it was only with European expansion in the late fifteenth century that it became a major practical issue. Perhaps the best and most authoritative source on these matters is Lindley's classic study, *The Acquisition and Government of Backward Territory in International Law* (1926). Lindley shows how arguments were split three ways on this question.

There were those sixteenth- and seventeenth-century legal scholars like Vitoria, Las Casas, Grotius, and Blackstone who agreed that indigenes had sovereignty. Grotius (cited in Lindley 1926:13), perhaps the most important source in this matter, followed Vitoria and argued that the Spaniards had no right to take American Indian territory:

Praetoria inventio nihil juris tribuit, nisi in ea quae ante inventionem nullius fuerant. Atqui Indi, cum ad eos Lusitani venerunt, etsi partim idolatrae, partim Mahumetani erant, gravbusque peccatis involuti, nihilominus publice atque privatim rerum possessionumque suarum dominum habuerunt, quod illis sine justa causa eripi non potuit. . . . Imo credere infedeles non esse rerum suarum dominos, haereticum est: et res ab illis possessas lillis ob hoc ipsum eripere furtum est, et rapina, non minus quam si fiat Christianis.

Freely translated, this is:

Discovery grants no right unless in those places which had been no one's prior to discovery. Certainly the Indians when the Spanish [Lusitani] came to them, although some were idol worshipers and others Mohammedans [Mahumetani], and lived in heavy sins, nevertheless they had, both as a public entity and as private individuals, ownership and rule of property and wealth and of their own possessions, which ownership could not be taken from them without just cause. At bottom, to believe that infidels are not owners of their own property is heretical; and to take things possessed by them away from them on account of this particular reason [i.e., that they are infidels] is robbery and pillage no less than if the same thing were done to Christians.

There were those who saw the situation in terms of indigenes having limited sovereignty. This group, a decided minority, argues that indigenes have no such rights. Their best representative, as Lindley (1926:18–29) points out, is Westlake. In essence, they conclude that where there are no states, there can be no sovereignty. The territorial rights of indigenes are thus merely moral rights, not legal ones.

The one South African judge who addressed this issue, Mr. Justice de Villiers, in his Rehoboth Commission report, argued that sovereignty of the Rehoboth Gebied (territory) was acquired by occupation since the land was *territorium nullius*[6] because the barbarians were without an organized government. In reaching this conclusion, he approvingly cited Chief Justice Marshall's classic 1831 United States Supreme Court decision in *Johnson v. MacIntosh*, in which the doctrine of "original discovery" was first clearly articulated. Mr. Justice de Villiers then cited Westlake as the most modern authority. Westlake's position, as befits a legal scholar writing in the heyday of British imperialism, not surprisingly argued that indigenous peoples did not have sovereignty. While this view had wide support in England, it found, contra Mr. Justice de Villiers, little support on the continent or among classical writers (Lindley 1926; Bennett 1978*a*).

Critical scrutiny suggests that Mr. Justice de Villiers erred in a number of critical aspects. As both Lindley and Bennett have pointed out, this doctrine rests on a fallacious assumption "that aboriginal communities who do not happen to have been the victims of either conquest or treaty are incapable of enjoying a proprietary relationship to the lands they have held since time immemorial" (Bennett 1978*b*:630). This assumption has been thoroughly discredited by anthropologists. Similarly, Lindley pointed out that even the definition of states within the "Family of Nations" was far from precise.

Justice Marshall's landmark decision, in which the notion of title through discovery was developed, also deserves to be examined further. Mr. Justice de Villiers ignores the fact that the Chief Justice (as cited in Bennett 1978*b*:621) observed that the notion of title by discovery could not

annul the previous rights of those who had not agreed to it. It regulated the right given by discovery among the European discovers; but could not affect the rights of those already in possession, either as aboriginal occupants, or as occupants by virtue of a discovery before the memory of man . . . [the original inhabitants] were admitted to be the rightful occupants of the soil, with a legal as well as a just claim to retain possession of it, and to use it according to their own discretion.

The abstract principles Chief Justice Marshall enunciated in this case were given clarity in later decisions—*Cherokee Nation v. State of Georgia* and *Worcester v. State of Georgia*. In the Cherokee Nation decision (1831), Justice Marshall developed the notion of "domestic dependent nations." He argued, inter alia:

They may, more correctly, perhaps, be denominated domestic dependent nations. They occupy a territory to which we assert a title independent of their will, which must take effect in point of possession when their right of possession ceases. Meanwhile they are in a state of pupilage. Their relation to the United States resembles that of a ward to his guardian. . . . They look to our government for protection; rely upon its kindness and its power; appeal to it for relief to their wants; and address the president as their great father. (Cited in Price 1973:59)

The next year, 1832, the Supreme Court was again forced to deal with the issue in *Worcester v. State of Georgia*. In this judgment, we see the evolution of Justice Marshall's position to the acceptance of complete sovereign rights of indigenes and the repudiation of the notion of conquest first advanced in *Johnson v. MacIntosh*. In this landmark decision, the learned justices split four ways. Their disagreement reflects the controversy that still surrounds the issue of aboriginal land rights, but at the same time, it indicates a clear direction for future reasoning. Justices Marshall and McLean held that tribes were domestic dependent nations; Justices Thompson and Story argued that tribes were sovereign nations; Justice Baldwin felt that tribes have no sovereignty; and Justice Johnson felt that while at present tribes did not have sovereignty, they had the political capacity to develop sovereignty.

In his careful reexamination of the Colonial Charters, Justice Marshall noted that while treaties supposedly provided Europeans with title to these lands, in reality indigenes' lands were occupied by

numerous and warlike nations, equally willing and able to defend their possessions. The extravagant and absurd idea, that the feeble settlements made on the sea coasts [by Europeans], or the companies under whom they were made, acquired legitimate power by them to govern the people, or occupy the lands from sea to sea, did not enter the mind of any man. (Cited in Berman 1978:661)

He continued:

The very term "nation," so generally applied to them [American Indians], means "a people distinct from others" . . . The words "treaty" and "nation" are words of our own language, selected in our diplomatic and legislative proceedings, by ourselves, having each a definite and well-understood meaning. We have applied them to Indians, as we have applied them to the other nations of the earth. They are applied to all in the same sense. . . . The very fact of repeated treaties with [Indians] recognizes [their sovereignty]; and the settled doctrine of the law of nations is that a weaker power does not surrender its independence—its right to self-government—by associating with a stronger, and taking its protection. A weak state, in order to provide for its safety, may place itself under the protection of one more powerful, without stripping itself of the right of government, and ceasing to be a state. (Cited in Price 1973:660–661)

The position taken by Westlake and Mr. Justice de Villiers is decidedly ethnocentric. Seen from a San perspective, the absurdity of this reasoning becomes manifest. For in accepting that only the state confers land rights, we reach the peculiar situation that because a petty German official reads a strange-sounding document, which even few of the Germans present could understand, and fires a volley of shots, suddenly all San peoples find their rights to land entitlement have mysteriously been removed without their even knowing.

Does possession amount to title? The Roman jurists regarded possessory title as a rule of natural law. This notion was only displaced by feudalism when royal charter replaced it, that is, the doctrine of *praescriptio longi temporis* was complemented with the idea that title to the land was conferred by the sovereign or feudal lord, but even then it did not completely do so. Vitoria (Watermeyer 1963), for example, successfully argued that American Indians owned the land they occupied, and thus the Spaniards could not claim title through discovery, and title through conquest was also difficult since it had to be done in a "just war," which was defined with canonical precision.

Bennett (1978a:29) has admirably summed up the situation:

The rights of first occupants have been widely supported by moral philosophers . . . and almost all legal systems in their early development acknowledged continuous use and occupation as the sole source of title. Later, other methods of acquisition were evolved, but acquisition by occupation remained a founding principle: indeed, it was regarded by the Roman jurists as a rule of natural law reaching back into antiquity and immune from challenge.

Roman-Dutch law includes the doctrine of sixteenth-century Spanish natural law writers such as Vitoria. Indeed, the Dutch argued for their claims to the New Netherlands and South Africa on the basis that their title had been acquired by a grant or purchase from the indigenes (Berman 1978:653). A strong case can be made that the British and the Germans de facto, and possibly also de jure, recognized the sovereign rights of tribes because they both had a policy of noninterference in the internal affairs of the people under their protection unless deemed necessary (Jennings 1963). Indeed, Lord Hailey (1956:695) claims that the basis of the German Protectorate was a series of land purchases.

Now it is a principle in Roman-Dutch law that the laws of the conquered territory remain in force until changed by the new rulers and that, moreover, Roman-Dutch authorities are superior to English authorities such as Westlake. Where the old Roman-Dutch masters are in conflict, the court will adopt the view that "appears to it most in keeping with reason, equity and modern notions of justice" (Hahlo

1960:37). I submit that this can only be interpreted to mean that the court at Windhoek should look favorably on a request for an interdict against the establishment of a game park in Bushmanland. This is especially so if we follow Lindley (1926:350):

It is improbable that today any colonial power would dispute the proposition that native tribes under its sovereignty, who have held lands in common or collective ownership, are entitled to be secured in the possession of a sufficient quantity of land to enable them to obtain an adequate subsistence in the circumstances of their condition as modified by the presence of a white population.

THE DOCTRINE OF SUPREME CHIEF

The key legislation appears to be the draconian Native Administration Proclamation (15/1928). This proclamation, which was adopted almost verbatim from the South African Native Administration Act of 1927, allows the Administrator-General of Namibia, formerly the Administrator of South West Africa, to, among other things, appoint and dismiss chiefs and headmen. In addition to various other powers, the Administrator-General may also "define the boundaries of the area of any tribe . . . and may from time to time alter the same and may divide existing tribes . . . or constitute a new tribe as necessity or the good government of the Natives may in his opinion require" (section 1:c, Native Administration Proclamation). Furthermore, he "may, whenever he deems it expedient in the general public interest, order the removal of any tribe or portion thereof or any Native from any place to any other place within the mandated Territory upon such terms and conditions and arrangements as he may determine" (section 1:d).

More ominously:

The Administrator shall not be subject to any court of law for or by reason of any order, notice, rule or regulation professed to be issued or made or of any other act whatsoever professed to be committed, ordered or done in the exercise of the powers and authority conferred by this Proclamation. (Sect 2)

The key difference between the South African legislation and its South West African counterpart is that in South Africa, according to section 1 of Act 38/1927, "The State President shall be Supreme Chief of all Bantu in the Republic." It is this critical notion of the State President as supreme chief which provides the rationalization for government's autocratic powers. This was by no means a novel approach to colonial administration. Similar views and systems were common in British Africa as well as in the United States of America, where the sovereign and the president were also seen as the supreme chief of the Indians. What makes the South African case exceptional is, as Welsh (1968) has shown, how the government saw the supreme chief as behaving in a dictatorial mold. Because the supreme chief could not be tried in any court, the minister of Bantu Administration, acting as the State President's delegate, was given immunity from the jurisdiction of any court.

The ideological notion—as opposed to the statutory status—of the Administrator (now the Administrator-General) as chief executive officer of the state being supreme chief of all the natives permeates much legislation in Namibia. For example, the Secretary for South West Africa provided this (rather fanciful) justification of land tenure to the Permanent Mandates Commission:

The position must be clearly understood. The native had no conception of the individual ownership of immovable property. All immovable property was held by the Chief and was communal. In South Africa, where the native lived in a natural state, the Chief held all land for the tribe. Nowadays, if a native reserve became too small the Chief could buy more land, which became tribal. If a native became advanced in his ideas and wished to break away from his tribe, became detribalized, there was nothing to prevent him buying land outside the tribal reserve. (PMC Minutes of Hearings, 30 June 1928, p. 67. Cited in Olivier 1961.)

In South Africa, most challenges to this legislation have collided on the juridical rock that sees this autocratic power as flowing naturally from the role of the State President as supreme chief. For Namibians, the situation is different. Except for a brief period when the South West Africa Native Administration Act 56/1954 established the State President as supreme chief, they have never had the Administrator as their great chief. The reason for this omission is hardly surprising: there were Namibian ethnic groups, like the Damara, Heixom, and Zhu, which, according South African government ethnologists, did not have chiefs. This vacillating attitude of the administration concerning whether or not the State President is supreme chief provides some potentially interesting scenarios. Would the *audi alteram partem* (hear the other side) rule be applicable? Could the legislation be declared *ultra vires* (beyond the scope of legal power)? These issues have never been raised by Namibians. It would be interesting to see how the courts would react.

THE "SPIRIT OF THE MANDATE"

While there is some dispute about who exactly has sovereignty over the Mandate, most jurists (with some notable exceptions in South Africa) agree that it does not reside in the mandatory. The notion of the "sacred trust of civilization" is so obviously paternalistic that it fits closely with the doctrine of the great white chief. In this regard, it might be worthwhile to refer to the way Chief Justice Marshall framed the state's obligations as great white father: since the indigenes did not really ask for his appointment or understand its consequences, it was the state's obligation to undertake this role seriously and with compassion. South Africa still claims to administer the Territory in "the spirit of the Mandate," and this has important implications because

guardianship of aboriginal tribes implies not merely protection, not merely benevolence towards private missionary, charitable and educational effort, but a positive duty of direct legislative, executive and judicial domination of aboriginals as minor wards of the nation, and equally direct legislative, executive and judicial tutorship of them for civilization, so that they may become in the shortest possible time civil and political adults participating on an equality in their own government under democratic and republican institutions. (Snow 1921:108)

CONCLUSION

The legal wrangling involved in the process of nudging South West Africa through the rite of passage from which Namibia will emerge is a painful and dangerous task. Going to court on behalf of San peoples could provide an important precedent that other groups in the Mandate might also wish to apply. The importance of focusing attention on the question of San land rights is more than simply a legal question, however. Xavier Herbert, the Australian novelist, saw the issue far more clearly than most lawyers and anthropologists when he wrote:

Until we give back to the black man just a bit of the land that was his, and give it back without provisos, without strings to snatch it back, without anything but complete generosity of spirit in concession for the evil that we have done to him—until we do that, we shall remain what we have always been so far: a people without integrity, not a nation, but a community of thieves. (*London Sunday Times*, 9 Oct. 1983)

In sum, then, San peoples were forced to yield their labor and land because of political weakness, and as Maybury-Lewis (1977) has reminded us, "There is no natural or historical law that militates against small societies. There are only political choices." In the final analysis, the future of San-speaking peoples will depend on political decisions taken at both the national and international levels. But do we as anthropologists, academics, and outsiders have a right to get involved in what clearly could be a messy business with no clear possibility of an equitable solution? Apart from the fact that it is now accepted that the work of all anthropologists is inherently political (Hymes 1969), "the fundamental reason why we must help other cultures survive is because, in all conscience, we have no alternative. It is a moral imperative of the sort that insists that the strong ought not to trample on the rights of the weak" (Maybury-Lewis 1977:61). It is not that we want to decide for Zhu what is good for them, or to preserve them as "living zoos." To argue for simply leaving them alone is to deny them the power to act, choose, and change in the face of oppression. The strategy ought to be geared toward optimizing Zhu ability to "control, create, reproduce, change, or adapt social and cultural patterns for their own ends" (T. Turner 1979:12). Such a stance allows us to remain critical while being sympathetic to San aspirations.

NOTES

1. This chapter was written at a National Endowment for the Humanities Summer Seminar, "Anthropological Approaches to the Study of Law." I am grateful to Larry Rosen, Monty Lindstrom, and Beverly Brown for advice and encouragement. Fieldwork was made possible by a Maryknoll Walsh-Price Fellowship.

2. An earlier version of portions of this section were published in Gordon (1985).

3. Since this chapter was first drafted, international pressure has resulted in the Namibian administration putting its Bushmanland Game Reserve development plans on hold.

4. German legal sources are obscure. A copy of this treaty was found in the Windhoek State Archives; the revelant dossiers are (1) ZBU W.11.2043 Verwaltung der Eingeborenenangelegenheiten, Begrenzung der Stammesgebiete, usw. Buschleute, 1895–1915, and (2) ZBU 1008–1010 Geographische und Ethnographische Forschungen 1885–1901.

5. This wholly erroneous view has been convincingly dispelled by anthropologists, most recently and most thoroughly by Wilmsen (1983).

6. Glossed in some legal dictionaries as "territory that is not under the jurisdiction of or subject to international law." This view is usually propounded by supporters of imperialism. The more contemporary glass is to see it simply as "empty" lands.

8
Involved Anthropologists[1]

Kenneth Maddock

In addition to making scientific studies, anthropologists in Australia have often involved themselves in the difficulties in which Aborigines find themselves. In 1891, for example, F. J. Gillen (soon to enter into his renowned collaboration with Baldwin Spencer) helped put an end to the campaign of terror that Mounted Constable Willshire had waged for ten years in central Australia. In Strehlow's (1971:xxxiv) words, "to Gillen's everlasting credit . . . he had the extraordinary courage to stand up for native rights against a confident police trooper backed by strong white sentiment in the district patrolled by him." Strehlow himself played a crucial part in saving Rupert Max Stuart, an Aranda convicted of murder in 1959 on the strength of a dubious confession. According to McNally (1981:124), "without Strehlow's expert evidence, Stuart would certain have gone to his death through the trap of the Adelaide Gaol gallows."[2]

These were sensational interventions in the affairs of Aborigines. Most involvement by anthropologists is less dramatic, and much of it seems unconnected with anthropology—as, indeed, was Gillen's part in the Willshire affair.[3] Thus, Elkin's advocacy of citizenship rights as early as the 1940s could, in theory, have come from a historian or a lawyer. The disproportionate involvement by anthropologists raises a question of the relation of science and sympathy. Is sympathy aroused or made more effective through scientific interest in its subject? Does sympathy advance understanding?

These questions are raised by implication on the last page of Rose's (1968) *Australia Revisited*:

I am proud, in the course of these three decades, in my own and, perhaps for the outsider, somewhat obscure field of research, of having been a witness and to an extent a participant in this historical process (of Aboriginal advancement). I moreover hope that I can take some further part.

Unfortunately, the 260 pages before this passage do not show how Aboriginal interests were furthered through anthropology. In the stupendous panorama Rose describes (his subtitle is *The Aborigine Story from Stone Age to Space Age*), anthropologists as scientists, or as well-wishers, could only be dwarflike figures.

Whether being an anthropologist is more then accidental to political and legal involvement is, I would argue, largely a consequence of policy and organization in the wider society. My point is illustrated by two passages from Rose's long review of *Australian Aboriginal Studies* (Shiels 1963), the proceedings of the conference from which the Australian Institute of Aboriginal Studies arose. In the first passage, he says "the demand is raised by the Aborigines that they are a people with their own cultural heritage and as such will remain distinct from the Australians of European origin" (Rose 1967:147). If policy gave effect to this demand, anthropological knowledge would be relevant to a variety of administrative problems and questions of the day.

In the other passage, Rose spoke of a time "when the Aborigines are economically fully integrated and have achieved full equality with the white section of the population" (ibid., 158). This should be read in the light of his materialism, according to which a "superstructure" is determined by the "socio-economic basis . . . how Aborigines obtain the wherewithal to live and the organizations they adopt to achieve this end" (ibid., 157). Admittedly, a superstructure may outlive its base but not indefinitely, for to do so would falsify materialism. If Aborigines were fully equal and integrated, their distinctive culture would soon disappear, and anthropologists could no longer play a special role in relation to them. That day has yet to come. Modified forms of the pre-European culture are gaining room to develop through changes in the policy and organization of the wider society. Change is most evident in the Northern Territory, mainly as a result of the Aboriginal Land Rights (Northern Territory) Act 1976, which arose from the work of the Woodward Commission of 1973–74. The Northern Territory is therefore an ideal place for studying anthropological involvement.

Anthropologists did not, of course, write the new law, and they had no power to force legislators to pass it, but especially through their writings of the 1960s and 1970s they helped create a climate of opinion in which recognition of Aboriginal land rights was more likely. Indeed, a quarter century before Mr. Justice Woodward completed his inquiry, Elkin (1949:229, original emphasis) had unequivocally insisted on aboriginal people's right to community land:

Deprivation of land, or external interference with the use of it, has religious, moral or psychological as well as economic effects. It undermines communal life and its sanctions, leaves the individual adrift, and leads to unbalanced personality development. It is clear, therefore, that a *basic right of primitive man . . . is the right to retain his land with its many-sided associations and meanings.* That is, all administering powers should guarantee their primitive peoples the permanent use of their land.

In looking into the involvement of anthropologists in land claims, I want, on one hand, to ask about their part in litigation and to see how important it is and to what difficulties it gives rise, and on the other hand, to ask whether anthropology advances through this involvement. Most of my material will come from the Gove Land Rights Case of 1970–71 and from claims under the 1976 Land Rights Act.[4]

DID ANTHROPOLOGISTS LOSE THE GOVE CASE FOR THE ABORIGINES?

Two leading anthropologists, R. M. Berndt and W. E. H. Stanner, were called to give evidence for the Aboriginal plaintiffs. Middleton (1977:156), one of Rose's students, was to explain the loss of the case in these terms:

One major ground . . . was the evidence given by liberal anthropologists that the essential association of the Aborigines with their land was religious and not a property relationship. This view provided a legal argument with which to rob the Yirrkala Aborigines of their land but it also revealed the ideological position of the anthropologists themselves. They did not understand that in Aboriginal traditional society the economic relations were primary, were the decisive factor in the society, and that religion was secondary, that it was part of the superstructure of beliefs and institutions which are based on, and reflect, the material base of the society.

The implication of these comments, which convey a view of Aboriginal society inspired by Rose, is that had "liberal anthropologists" seen it his way, the case might have been won.

Another paradoxical testimonial (anthropology is highly important, but experienced anthropologists who are keen on Aboriginal advancement get things disastrously wrong) comes from Gumbert (1981:110):

This almost unbelievable conflict of evidence (between expert and Aboriginal witnesses) came entirely from one side. Every day, of course, evidence disputing the contentions of one litigant is brought by his adversary. Here the evidentiary case for the plaintiffs collapsed within itself without the 'assistance' of the other side. . . . The learned Queen's Counsel, Mr. Woodward, had an immense legal battle on his hands. . . . Clearly he might well have assumed that the *evidentiary* aspects of his case were pretty well sewn up. He had all reasons to rely on his experts.

Gumbert, a lawyer, would have known that the Aboriginal plaintiffs lost the case on questions of law, not of fact. Of course, had the court found for them on these questions, matters of fact (including those on which anthropologists testified) would have been decisive.

Neither Berndt nor Stanner has defended himself against criticism of this kind. It seems from one of Berndt's recent papers, however, that he found it hard to communicate with lawyers. In trying to justify the Aboriginal claim anthropologically, he (Berndt 1981:11) described what he "considered to be traditional ownership . . . and how ownership was linked to land utilization." But it was foreign territory for lawyers knowing nothing of anthropology and having little understanding of Aboriginal traditional life, though they were willing to learn. To communicate Aboriginal views, Berndt had to oversimplify, and Stanner made matters worse by overgeneralizing and attempting to fit the facts into a broader abstract model.

Berndt's reflections suggest that anthropological involvement is not easy and can be painful. For example, traditional ownership and its connection with the use of land are good subjects of inquiry for anthropologists, but their findings will help claimants only if they can be included in a convincing legal argument. One argument at Gove was that clans "owned" (had property in) land. The lawyers failed to establish this, partly because anthropological generalizations about use of land conflicted with Aboriginal recollections of the social composition and territorial range of the groups in which they lived before 1935 and also (and, I think, more important) the lawyers failed to show that the relation to land of these groups or their members had significant features in common with property rights as known in English and other major legal systems.[5] This rather unfair controversy over the responsibility of anthropologists invites the question of whether there is any need for them to become involved in Aboriginal claims to land.

WHAT NEED IS THERE FOR ANTHROPOLOGISTS?

Before land rights were recognized, Eggleston (1976:302), a lawyer, was urging that anthropologists be called as expert witnesses and their writings referred to in cases concerning tribal law. She was convinced that anthropology had something useful to offer. A contrary view is that Aborigines know it all. Mr. Justice Woodward, for example, explained why so few Aborigines wrote letters or made submissions to him by suggesting that "discussion of land ownership seems to them unnecessary. They know which Aborigines own which tract of land by Aboriginal law" (Woodward 1973:7). Another lawyer, Hookey (1974:102), has said that among Aborigines "in a customary law situation . . . there would be no doubt at all what the binding rules were and no possible argument that there were different sorts of norms to choose from." More recently, an Aboriginal land rights organization told Aborigines that "in a land claim, you just say what land you want. We don't need lawyers and anthropologists to make a land claim, we can do it ourselves" (New South Wales Aboriginal Land Council 1981:3). A variant of such views is that any need for anthropology has been created by witting or unwitting legislators. Thus, Tatz (1982:12), a political scientist, feels that in the 1976 Land Rights Act, "the techniques and taxonomies of the anthropologist loom larger than the articulation and overt behaviour and social history of the Aborigines themselves."

Quite different is the argument presented by the Northern and Central Land Councils, two Aboriginal organizations charged with the administration of Aboriginal land in the Northern Territory, in their joint submission (dated 11 May 1977) to the Land Commissioner on his procedure for hearing claims.[6] They gave "good reasons" for restricting cross-examination of Aborigines:

(2) Aboriginals are at a proven disadvantage in giving evidence and that this disadvantage is not overcome by the use of interpreters. . . . (4) Aboriginal traditional law severely restricts the extent to which Aboriginals could give evidence on many matters. . . . In particular, individuals can be precluded from talking individually or in front of uninitiated people.

Evidence to support a claim should accordingly be given by informed outsiders. Thus, under the heading D. Difficulties of Obtaining Details of Claims, the land councils stated the need for "detailed anthropological evidence." Under E. Forms of Claims, they described a claim as a two-stage process. First, the relevant land council would notify the Commissioner that some Aborigines wished to claim an area and that research would be conducted to substantiate or reject their claim. Second, the land council would submit a claim book containing the results of this research by anthropologists.

Even if these points made by the two Northern Territory organizations exaggerate the problems, it would not follow from the (supposed) Aboriginal certainty about relations to land that their testimony could stand alone. A key issue is whether the claimants' relation to the land amounts to traditional ownership (the primary issue in claims under the Land Rights Act) or satisfies the common law conception of property (an issue in the Gove case). Folk opinions are legally assessed by criteria formulated in another culture. The lawyers representing the claimants would have to grasp these opinions to put the claim both honestly and persuasively—if, that is, the case for the claimants is to be presented through argument and evidence (by claimants and others) that twist folk reality as little as possible while still leaving a fair chance of legal success. Obviously, this is more likely if there are persons able to mediate between the different cultures. They would not have to be professional anthropologists, but anthropology is the only profession whose members are likely to know how to play the part. Yet their standing was strongly attacked in the Gove case.

ARE ANTHROPOLOGISTS ACCEPTABLE AS EXPERT WITNESSES?

The expert is a familiar figure in court. "At common law . . . the opinions of skilled witnesses are admissible wherever the subject is one upon which competency to form an opinion can only be acquired by . . . special study or experience" (Phipson 1976:486). But they do not decide the issue; that is the court's job. The Gove case was the first in Australia in which anthropologists testified about Aboriginal land tenure. The barrage of objections they faced were all overruled, but two are worth notice because of their relevance to later land claims or to theoretical questions in legal anthropology.

The defense contended that evidence by Berndt and Stanner about "the social organization or 'laws' of the aboriginals" should be excluded as hearsay, since it was based on what Aborigines had told them. In effect, anthropology as "a valid field of study and knowledge" was called into question. In accepting that it is, Mr. Justice Blackburn held that the hearsay rule does not block evidence expressed in anthropological propositions. So, although it would be impermissible for an anthropologist to say "Mungguruwuy told me that this was Gumatj land" (Gumatj is a clan), he could testify in such words as these:

I have studied the social organization of these Aboriginals. This study included observing their behavior; talking to them; reading the published work of other experts; applying principles of analysis and verification which are accepted as valid in the general field of anthropology. I express the opinion as an expert that proposition X is true of their social organization. (Commonwealth of Australia 1971)

This ruling could be helpful if Aboriginal land rights were again to be the subject of ordinary litigation. But for claims under the 1976 Land Rights Act, it is not so important, because the Land Commissioner stated in his practice directions dated June 8, 1977, that he would admit hearsay, the test of evidence being its relevance.

The defense at Gove also maintained that Berndt and Stanner

tended to apply unwarranted concepts of their own to the actual facts of Aboriginal behaviour and to talk in terms of such concepts, even to the extent of expressing themselves in terms which anticipated the findings of the court on the issue before it. It was maintained, for example, that questions and answers expressing the idea of the 'rights' of clans of Aboriginals to particular land were objectionable . . . the objection was not merely that the Court should not allow an expert to decide a question which it was for the Court to decide. The contention was really that the experts tended to 'conceptualize' . . . rather than to state facts objectively. (Commonwealth of Australia 1971)

Mr. Justice Blackburn's response was that an expert's function is to talk in terms of concepts that are appropriate both to his field of knowledge and to the court's understanding; to forbid him to conceptualize would be to prevent him from communicating his science. In this case, where one of the court's problems was to find out what Aborigines saw as their rights, it was convenient to let experts use words like "right," "claim," and "law." But the court had to decide, first, whether expert opinion on what Aborigines saw as their right was justified by the evidence (expert and Aboriginal) and, second, whether an expert's use of such concepts as "ownership" and "possession" was jurisprudentially sound.

In claims under the Land Rights Act, the central concept is "traditional owners," defined by section 3(1) to mean "a local descent group of Aboriginals who—(a) have common spiritual affiliations to a site on the land that place the group under a primary spiritual responsibility for that site and for the land; and (b) are entitled by Aboriginal tradition to forage as of right over that land."

Except for "Aboriginal" and "Aboriginal tradition," the terms are not defined. Three of them—"local descent group," "common spiritual affiliations," "primary spiritual responsibility"—have been much debated since 1976, both among anthropologists and during the hearing of claims. There can be few claims in which anthropologists have hesitated to identify traditional owners (who alone may claim land) or to interpret the statutory definition.

In the Yutpundji-Djindiwirritj (Roper Bar) claim, for instance, Morphy and Morphy (1981:31, 37) stated that "the landowning unit" is the patrilineal clan and that people "are quite definite that *djunggaiyi* (children of a clan's female members) do not own the land and should not be included as claimants." In the Anmatjirra and Alyawarra (Utopia) claim, Sansom (1980:3) maintained that the notion of primary spiritual responsibility is central to and "governs all else" in the definition. In the Alligator Rivers Stage 2 claim, Keen (1981:10) maintained that "knowledge or belief held by members of the descent group alone is not a sufficient condition for the existence of common spiritual affiliations."

Counsel for the defense at Gove would have sprung to his feet to denounce these examples of unwarranted conceptualization (as he would have called them). But what if traditional ownership and the terms in which it is expressed belong to anthropology? Then the position would be as Phipson (1976:505) stated: "where the words [of a statute] have a special or technical meaning," the opinion of an expert in that branch of knowledge "is of necessity admitted" in order to determine their meaning.

The relation of jargon to ordinary English became important in the Utopia claim, largely because an attempt was made to add the children of female members of patrilineal clans as traditional owners (in statutory terms) of the land associated with those clans. The Land Commissioner, Mr. Justice Toohey, commented in his report of May 30, 1980:

105. In the present claim it is open to someone to show that expressions used in the Land Rights Act have acquired some technical acceptance in the field of anthropology, that the words are used with a particular meaning. That will be expert evidence as the term is generally understood.
106. Where the words have acquired no such usage I must resolve for myself their meaning by looking at them in the context of the Act.
107. Several anthropologists gave evidence. . . . There was general agreement that, with the exception of the phrase 'local descent group', neither the term 'traditional Aboriginal owners' nor the components used in its definition were technical anthropological expressions or had any generally accepted meaning among anthropologists.

This view has been sustained in later claims, yet anthropologists have continued to interpret the definition freely when writing claim books and giving evidence. Part of the explanation for what would otherwise be their mystifying behavior is that their role in claims goes far beyond what is usually expected of experts.

THE EXTENDED ROLE OF ANTHROPOLOGISTS IN LAND CLAIMS

When anthropologists are blamed for conflicts between their evidence and that of Aborigines at Gove, the implication can only be that they did more than testify. Otherwise, it would make as much sense to blame the Aborigines or the lawyers (I am assuming that no one is suggesting that evidence should be twisted). But what else could they have been doing? Whatever may have happened at Gove, there can be no doubt that anthropologists engaged on claims under the 1976 Land Rights Act are doing work that would usually be done by lawyers.

Lawyers who prepare a case not only formulate a legal argument and draw up documents (such as a statement of claim) but also see to the evidence for their clients. This can include finding and interviewing witnesses, cross-checking their statements, and forming an opinion on the impression they are likely to make when testifying. Often (as in the Gove case), the work is divided between an instructing solicitor (commonly the lawyer to whom the client went in the first place) and a barrister briefed to appear in court. Evidence, in other words, should be "sewn up" by lawyers before the hearing starts. It is not for expert witnesses to take up needle and thread.

It is easy to understand, however, that lawyers preparing the Gove case would have been tempted to rely on their experts to do more than testify. City lawyers would have been at a loss in dealing with Aborigines from Arnhem Land. How could the grounds for complaint of these unusual clients have been sifted, or statements of their evidence elicited, or their evidence checked for inconsistencies and loose ends, if not by dealing with them through anthropologists? This might have lessened the chance of spotting discrepancies between the kind of local organization for which the lawyers argued and Aboriginal memories of the past (as revealed under cross-examination by members of the plaintiff clans).

The puzzle is that, as Hiatt (1982a) has shown, the lawyers knew that the views of local organizations on which they based their case were controversial, to say the least. So, in formulating their argument as they did, the lawyers must have "verified" the Berndt-Stanner model through interviews with their Aboriginal clients (who mysteriously resiled when in court) or left this part of the preparation of the case to the anthropologists they intended to call as expert witnesses (thereby pushing them into a lawyerlike role), presumably after having satisfied themselves that their anthropologists were probably right. Certainly, anthropologists do much of the preparation in claims under the Land Rights Act. Their work covers a lot of ground that is ordinarily left to an instructing solicitor, even though everyone knows they will appear as expert witnesses. The explanation for this lies in the nature of a claim.

The Land Rights Act enables the traditional owners of certain areas to claim them. Whether an area answers to the description of claimable land can be discovered by searching through land registry records. But that is only the beginning of a drawn-out task culminating in a hearing before the Land Commissioner. The relevant land council must find out whether a claimable area has traditional owners as defined by the Act. Because of the newness of the term, it would usually make little sense to go into an Aboriginal community and ask traditional owners to come forward. Moreover, because of population movements in this century, the whereabouts of people with traditional connections to an area is often uncertain. Most of them will live away from the land under claim, and some may even live outside the Northern Territory.

The land council therefore has to consult Aborigines who know the area and through them, if they are not its traditional owners, trace those who are. Three aspects can be distinguished in this research: (1) traditional ownership must be interpreted, (2) traditional owners, so understood, must be listed, and (3) their traditional ownership must be documented. These need not be successive steps. A preliminary list of owners, for example, may change as the claim is documented, or ownership may be reinterpreted and the list of claimants amended. The land councils, whose duty it is to act on behalf of traditional owners, usually leave the research to anthropologists.

In interpreting, listing, and documenting, an anthropologist will work with an eye to the Land Commissioner, for it is he who hears claims and recommends whether, and to whom, land should be granted. Many people (e.g., claimants, other Aborigines, anthropologists) give evidence during a hearing. The questioning of witnesses is likely to go over much of the ground already covered by the anthropologist. If there are objectors, cross-examination of witnesses will probably aim, as in the Gove case, at bringing out and exploiting any and every kind of discrepancy.

Two examples demonstrate the work that can be required in putting together and presenting a land claim. The Warlpiri and Kartangarurru-Kurintji claim, on which the commissioner reported on August 4, 1978, was to about 95,000 square kilometers. There were more than 1,200 claimants. One hundred thirty-eight persons (mostly Aboriginal) testified during a hearing lasting thirty-five days. Ten lawyers, including a Queen's Counsel, took part, of whom three represented the claimants. In addition to the oral evidence, the evidentiary record included 192 exhibits (including maps, photographs and photographic slides, written statements by experts, articles, excerpts from books, legal documents, letters, policy statements, and parliamentary papers).

In the Alligator Rivers claim, on which the commissioner reported on July 2, 1981, the claim book (written, as usual, by an anthropologist) ran to 226 pages, excluding appendixes. It included a history of the region, an interpretive discussion of traditional ownership, an account of descent groups and their members, an account of the spiritual affiliations and responsibilities of these groups and their members, a discussion of people's feelings about the country, and a list of advantages and disadvantages that could be expected to follow from a successful claim. During the hearing, which lasted thirty-nine days and included scores of visits to sites, eighty-seven persons (mostly Aboriginal) gave evidence. Twenty lawyers, including four Queen's Counsels, took part, of whom three represented the claimants. The transcript of the hearing ran to 2,861 pages, and there were 168 exhibits.

We can safely assume that the reasons for leaving so much preparation to anthropologists (instead of making lawyers do work that is rightfully theirs) include the difficulty lawyers face in communicating with Aborigines, the need to gather most of the claimants' evidence through time-consuming fieldwork in conditions that may be very uncomfortable (water is short, the temperature is a hundred degrees in the shade, and the lawyer—that is, anthropologist—may be mending ten punctures a day), and the trained capacity of anthropologists to handle traditional material. Almost inevitably, anthropologists must try to define people's legal rights (even if that was not their original intention). Some have been loath to admit it.

The anthropologists involved in the Warlpiri and Kartangarurru-Kurintji claim, for example, saw themselves not as "the authorities on . . . landownership" but as recorders on behalf of the traditional owners. The Land Commissioner (ALC 1979b, par. 58) quoted them without comment in his report on this claim but seemed more skeptical soon afterward when reporting on the Alyawarra and Kaititja claim, remarking that such a profession "may underplay the role of anthropologists."

Taking the role of a recorder might be justified if traditional ownership were thought to be so settled in meaning as to be mechanically applicable or if Aborigines were deemed capable of applying the statutory definition to themselves. The first assumption is at best an ideal for the future. As for the second, Aborigines may feel strongly about who should claim an area, but their feelings are unlikely to be rationalized by their own statutory interpretation. Thus, an anthropologist to whom Aborigines dictated a list of claimants would still have to work out whether there was a sense in which the persons listed could plausibly be put forward as traditional owners of the area. Could they, for instance, be argued to form a local descent group composed of persons with common spiritual affiliations to a site? The anthropologist's position in this example is analogous to that of a lawyer who interprets provisions of the law to give effect to a client's wishes. But depending on the sense in which traditional ownership is understood, it might be that too few or too many names were on the dictated list. It could even happen that none of the people listed were able to claim.

Is the alternative to put oneself forward as an authority? If being an authority means being able to decide an issue before a court, then anthropologists are not authorities (any more than legal practitioners are). But in another sense, authority means one who is qualified by study or experience to deal expertly with a subject. Perhaps the anthropologists in the Warlpiri and Kartangarurru-Kurintji claim were only denying being authorities in the decision-making sense. They could have regarded themselves as (and indeed were) authorities in the sense of being able to give an informed opinion. But as I have tried to show, anthropologists are ambiguously placed. On the one hand, as expert witnesses, they express opinions in the claim book and witness box on questions of ritual, social organization, land use, and the like. On the other hand, they have preceded all this with the lawyerlike activity of interpreting statutory provisions in order to further the interests or give effect to the wishes of those who are, in fact, their Aboriginal clients. How could it be disputed that such a dual role endangers intellectual integrity? It is as though an instructing solicitor, having first prepared a client's case for successful hearing, were to turn up in the guise of a witness professing to answer nothing but the whole truth to questions raised during the hearing.

ARE ANTHROPOLOGISTS RUBBER STAMPS FOR ABORIGINES?

The suspicion that anthropologists who give evidence for Aboriginal claimants are hopelessly biased is strengthened by the difficulty objectors to land claims have in getting anthropological advice. The defense lawyers in the Gove case, for example, having applied to Hiatt in vain, ended up with nothing better than a retired missionary. In the Alligator Rivers claim, the mining company Peko-EZ strongly contested parts of the claim, but the research on which they relied was carried out by a solicitor, who apparently had no training in anthropology. The issue was raised in the Borroloola land claim, the first to be heard. The Land Commissioner (ALC 1979*a*, par. 52–53) commented that

some criticism was made of both Mr. Avery and Mr. McLaughlin on the grounds of lack of experience, the way they went about their work and particularly in the case of Mr. McLaughlin what was said to be bias towards Aboriginals. No doubt both men were sympathetic to the interests of Aboriginal people and Mr. McLaughlin was inclined to wear his heart on his sleeve. Nevertheless on matters going to traditional ownership I have no reason to doubt the truth of what they told me. . . . At the same time it is true that too close an involvement of an expert witness with the party calling him is likely to lead to misunderstanding. Perhaps this would have been avoided had Mr. Avery and Mr. McLaughlin each confined his role to that of witness and not been responsible for the compilation of the claim book . . . which was in essence the applicants' written case.

The last sentence conveys the misleading impression that Avery and McLaughlin had a real say in the matter. As employees of the Northern Land Council, which financed and presented the claim, their duty was to write a claim book if asked; later, while still employees, they were scarcely able to refuse if the Land Council wanted to call them as witnesses. In view of what I have argued, one is left wondering who else could, or would, have written a claim book, since the task requires a detailed knowledge of potential claimants and the area available for claim. The commissioner's suggestion of how to avoid misunderstanding would have been better directed to the Land Council lawyers.

In all claims, the commissioner is advised by an anthropologist of his own, who normally attends while evidence is taken from Aborigines or from other anthropologists and later makes a written report on anthropological aspects of the claim. If the dual role of Land Council anthropologists reduces the likelihood that they will be impartial, will not scientific balance be restored by the commissioner's adviser?

The question is intriguing, for invariably the adviser has research experience among Aborigines—often in or near the area affected by the claim and therefore among the claimants and their relatives. Thus, the commissioner's adviser, though not caught in as acute a role conflict as the Land Council anthropologists (expert *or* advocate), undoubtedly faces a weaker form of the same dilemma. It arises from the nature of anthropological research.

Fieldwork requires fairly long-term relationships with the members of what is usually a small community. Many anthropologists feel a moral commitment to help "their" people. As material aid on any but the smallest scale is usually out of the question, the anthropological "debt" is best—and most visibly—expressed by championing the interests of the community. Less visibly, anthropologists can refrain from bringing forward embarrassing information, for example, details of land use or tenure that conflict with a claim before the Land Commissioner might never get mentioned. Such suppression, which is of course different from outright falsification, could be defended on a variety of grounds—repaying informants, preserving field access, uplifting the downtrodden, and so on. My guess, however, is that an uncalculating sympathy for Aborigines is prior to these considerations, which merely reinforce it, and that it largely explains the frequency with which anthropologists get involved in preparing claims. Outsiders may see things differently and be inclined to stress anthropological self-interest with its side effect of partial testimony.

I am not asking whether such testimony has ever been given or whether the commissioner has ever made recommendations that he might not have made had the anthropologists testified differently. It may be useful here to comment on a few claims. When Hagen and Rowell (1979:3) wrote up their research for the Utopia claim, they defined the local descent group required by the Land Rights Act as comprising members of a patrilineal clan together with children of the clan's female members, and they stated that this was what the Anmatjirra and Alyawarra wanted. In the Roper Bar claim, the Morphys, also agreeing with what they stated to be Aboriginal wishes, defined the local descent group purely patrilineally. From these examples, it might seem that anthropologists twist their concepts to please their Aboriginal clients in the way we might expect of a lawyer. But two points can be urged in defense of anthropology.

One is that anthropological usage accepts patrilineal, matrilineal, and cognatic descent groups. An Aboriginal wish for children of female members of a patrilineal clan to be treated as members of the Act's local descent group requires no departure from established usage. The second is that in some claims, the commissioner was advised by an anthropologist who argued against the claim book's interpretation: Sansom (1980) argued for a patrilineal local descent group at Utopia, and Bern (1982:1–7) argued in the Roper Bar claim that children of female members satisfied requirements about spiritual affiliations and responsibility as well as did the members of the patrilineal clan. It is unlikely that Sansom or Bern were arguing thus to curry favor with the Aborigines of the area.

It is not always the commissioner's anthropologist alone who expresses himself independently about a claim. In the Limmen Bight claim book, which Bern prepared together with Larbalestier and McLaughlin, the anthropologists listed claimants according to patrilineal criteria, which is what their clients wanted, but they maintained that children of female members of the patrilineal clan also qualified as traditional owners (Bern, Larbalestier, and McLaughlin 1980:30–31).

In some other claims also (e.g., Finnis River and Alligator Rivers), anthropologists have disagreed with one another or with Aborigines over the listing of claimants or the interpretation of the definition of traditional ownership. More generally, problems raised by the meaning of traditional ownership, by the choice of claimants, and by the relationship of statute to tradition have been widely discussed by anthropologists since 1977, the first year the Land Rights Act was in effect, as has the fact of their dual role (though the tendency has been to avoid grasping the dilemma inherent in this duality). Accordingly, there is perhaps no good reason to sweepingly impugn the evidence of anthropologists. Doubts about their veracity cannot be stilled, however, and they combine with fears that anthropological involvement leaves the discipline where it was.

IS ANTHROPOLOGY ADVANCING THROUGH INVOLVEMENT BY ANTHROPOLOGISTS?

Though land claims, in which anthropologists are playing so large a part, more than one-fourth (or about 130,000 square miles) of the Northern Territory is likely to end up under virtually inalienable Aboriginal title for the benefit of Aborigines traditionally connected with it. In addition, nearly one-fifth of the Territory—mainly reserves—was transferred to Aborigines without having to be claimed. The powers and advantages that the 1976 Land Rights Act confers on the beneficiaries (particularly if they qualify as traditional owners) give them a great deal of control over the future development of this land.

Depending on local wishes and circumstances, the result might be tradition-based life in outstations far from white people and strange Aborigines or royalty flow worth millions of dollars. Aborigines, then, are certainly gaining greatly from a process in which anthropologists loom large.

Radcliffe-Brown (1944:260) long ago observed, "The demand on social anthropologists to spend too much of their time on practical problems would inevitably reduce the amount of work that can be given to the development of the theoretical side of the science." Without a sound theoretical basis, applied anthropology would degenerate from science to mere empirical practice. We may be less optimistic than Radcliffe-Brown about the prospects of theory in anthropology, but we can still share his doubts about the scientific value of busy involvement by anthropologists in other people's practical problems.

There are different ways a branch of learning might be seen as advancing. For example, it might be contended that progress consists in accumulation of knowledge. During research in support of land claims, sustained attention is given to recording information about places and territories and about the grouping of people in relation of them. Data are gathered not at random but according to whether they are classifiable under headings provided by the Land Rights Act (e.g., local descent group, primary spiritual responsibilities). These categories, which are relevant in all land claims, are not necessarily those of anthropology, but at least they stand in identifiable relationships to concepts used by anthropologists. So a mass of information, unusual in quantity and comparability, is becoming available to our discipline. It may also be said that the information is unusually reliable, because anthropologists and their Aboriginal informants testify publicly within quite a short time (perhaps a year or two, perhaps only a few months) of the completion of research. They may be questioned at length with a view to testing both fact and concept. This forensic process can be salutary, even allowing for the ulterior motives inspiring it. More information may emerge, and it may even conflict with what is stated in the claim book.

The emergence of contradictions can be disconcerting, although it is not always clear what conclusion should be drawn. A nice example occurred in the Alligator Rivers claim during the taking of evidence about the Djindibi clan, which had been put forward as a local descent group having traditional ownership of part of the land. Counsel for the Northern Land Council was thrown off balance when one of the witnesses, a man named Joseph, affirmed his membership in the clan. According to the claim book, Djindibi had just the two members, Left-

Hand Johnny and his half-sister Hazel (Keen 1980:115–116). It turned out that two influential members of the Bunidj clan, another local descent group involved in the claim, had assigned Joseph to Djindibi about two years earlier as a way of overcoming uncertainty about his status which was created by his father being an outsider who had married a local woman. The ascription certainly had justification, for Joseph's mother was sister to Johnny's mother. Unhappily, there was no real evidence to show that Joseph was generally accepted as a Djindibi man. Johnny, for example, seemed to know nothing about it, and Hazel could not be asked for her opinion, because no one knew where she was.

Another view of the advancement of science is that it consists in an expansion of theories (verified or not yet falsified, according to philosophical taste) rather than in the mere accumulation of more and more facts. Thus, Radcliffe-Brown saw anthropology as a comparative science aiming at theoretical generalizations about the structure and function of social life. The involvement of anthropologists in land claims does not appear to have brought about any advance in this sense. We cannot be surprised. Even setting aside doubts (strong in my case) about the possibility of a "natural science of society," there remains the point that emphasis in litigation falls on facts, problems, and concepts (however distorted their presentation), not on theories as most scientists would understand them. This suggests that if anthropology has made any gain (apart from piling up material), it would consist in a clearer understanding of terms and their relations, in a larger awareness of the pitfalls of hasty conceptualization.

Better understanding (assuming it to be obtained) need not apply in any direct way to the problems of anthropology. Take, for example, the concept of a descent group. In the Alligator Rivers claim, the best evidence was that the Djindibi clan had but one member. No one knew whether Hazel was alive, and Joseph's membership by ascription was not generally accepted. Could Djindibi, with Johnny as its sole member, be treated as a local descent group as required by the definition of traditional owners? The Land Commissioner (ALC 1981c, par. 161) answered that it could not, because he took the definition to require a group in the ordinary sense of a number of persons. Anthropologically, there is no difficulty about a descent group with one surviving member, and anthropologists are unlikely to modify their use of the term because of the Land Commissioner—except, of course, when preparing claims in future. As for lawyers, they might be constrained to follow anthropological usage if the term had a clear and generally agreed meaning among anthropologists, but in the

Utopia and Alligator Rivers claims it was argued with conviction that "local descent group" did not have such agreed on meaning. In this case, then, lawyers and anthropologists were using the same term (which happens to have a history in anthropology but is newly arrived in law) for the meaning of which lawyers' reasoning had the upper hand because of the legal context but of which there was no implication for anthropological practice outside this context.[7]

A more consequential example is the concept of property. Anthropologists have often spoken of land being owned by groups of Aborigines. The most usual opinion during the 1960s and early to mid-1970s was that these groups were constituted by patrilineal descent. So it was argued at Gove that the patrilineal clans of the area had a proprietary interest in land in a sense that Australian law could recognize. The argument failed, but it would not be satisfying to explain this as another example of lawyers and anthropologists having the same word, with anthropologists being free to go their own way except in a law case. As the concept of property comes from law, and lawyers have paid the most attention to it, anthropologists ought to take the Gove lesson to heart, unless further inquiry suggests that Mr. Justice Blackburn erred in his reasoning or that crucial evidence was not put before him. To do otherwise would be to deny that anthropology is a comparative science. Anthropologists might, of course, develop their own concept of property, but even so, would it not have to comprehend the legal sense known in our society?

Different considerations apply to the concept of traditional ownership since it draws its force not from a history of use in law or anthropology but from its position in the Land Rights Act. We do not need to assume that statutory traditional owners have, independently of statute, a relationship to land that is proprietarial in the sense required at Gove. In the Finnis River claim, on which he reported on May 22, 1981, the Land Commissioner (ALC 1981*b*, par. 134) stressed the specificity of his responsibilities when discussing the possibility of changes through time in the identity of the Aborigines associated with an area:

The anthropological debate will continue. The resolution of these claims lies within the framework of a particular piece of legislation and I am concerned to range no more widely than is necessary to carry out my functions under the Act. It may be that the answer demanded by the Act is not that demanded by anthropology, if indeed anthropology is able to insist on one answer.

The distinction between owners in a statutory sense and owners in a sense that is prior to statute is not always observed, however, and so we find the commissioner referring in his next paragraph to an anthropologist who

was at some pains to distinguish between ownership of land and the right to use land. The traditional owners of land may give to others the right to use it temporarily or permanently without necessarily surrendering their own rights of ownership. She thought that tacit consent to occupation and use would not result in loss of traditional ownership, emphasizing that the right to exploit land is not the same as ownership.

My general view is that anthropologists who study Aboriginal relations to land should keep statutory criteria out of their analyses. I would admit two exceptions. One is where an anthropologist wishes to compare the local organization of an area with the pattern laid down in the Land Rights Act. The other is where the Aborigines of the area have been affected by the operations of the Act. But in each case, it will be important to distinguish, in principle, between rights originating in modern statute law and rights having some other origin. Otherwise, anthropologists will smuggle into their accounts a legal view that, intended to express a traditional reality, has been shaped in its original formulation and its subsequent development by the exigencies of legal policy and reasoning.

I am not implying that the authors of the Act made a poor job of defining traditional ownership. They wished to identify the strongest traditional relationship of a group to land, to express the essential features of this relationship in English legal language, and to enable the group so defined to exercise powers resembling those of a proprietor. Only the first of these aims is shared by anthropology, and all the aims may be legally achieved in differing (though related) ways, as may be seen by comparing traditional ownership on the Northern Territory model with the significance of the same term in the Pitjantjatjara Land Rights Act of 1981 (South Australia).[8]

Perhaps the best way of expressing the value such statutory concepts can have for anthropology is to say that they foster reflection. Their interplay, in the context of claims involvement, with more purely scientific considerations can reorient anthropological thinking. The most striking example is probably our changing perception of the children of female members of a patrilineal clan. In the early claims under the Land Rights Act, local descent groups were described patrilineally. This followed the Gove model, which, in turn, had been based on a then fairly common anthropological view (itself corresponding to a widespread Aboriginal view). But in the Utopia claim the groups were described cognatically to accommodate the children of female members. The new approach combined local Aboriginal wishes with anthropological rethinking, and it proved legally acceptable. It is now being followed often enough for the Land Commissioner to have been able to comment in his annual report for 1980–81 on a discernible trend to the broadening of an earlier, somewhat restricted approach.

I do not know that any anthropologist before 1976 attributed ownership of land to cognatic groups of quite this sort. The main stimulus to the new opinion was the elementary consideration that if the Land Rights Act controls access to and use of land, rights under it should be distributed in accordance with traditional patterns of control over access and use. The next question was whether the definition of traditional owners would allow a departure from the patrilineal model. That was really a legal argument, but anthropologists (no doubt encouraged by their lawyerlike participation in claim preparation and presentation) joined in exuberantly.

Although the need to respect concepts enshrined in an act of Parliament must sometimes act as a brake on anthropological rethinking, it brings a compensating advantage: close attention is compelled to the meaning of words and to the marshaling of evidence for or against possible constructions. This intellectual discipline tended to be absent from anthropological accounts of local organization, at least so far as they concerned the tenure or holding of land. This or that kind of group would be identified as having ownership, usually with only the most perfunctory explanation of what was meant and with little or no attempt to relate the meaning to legal senses of the word. One can hope that those days are gone, never to return. Taking part in claims has made anthropologists see that ownership does matter, whereas before, when Aborigines either had no land rights worth speaking of or had rights unrelated to their traditions, it must have seemed inconsequential.

A recognition of the importance of rights, conceptual clarification, and a great accumulation of data—these have gone hand in hand. They not only enable anthropologists to play their legal roles more effectively but also spill over into a more purely scientific domain where inquiry and analysis are free from anthropologically irrelevant legal constraints.

It is most unlikely that anthropology would be making this progress if anthropologists had held back from furthering the interests of Aborigines through land claims. Even the most frenzied involvement by anthropologists would not, however, have advanced their discipline if the land rights of Aborigines had been separated from their traditional culture. In this case at least, science and sympathy have been able to stimulate each other because of the policy and organization of the wider society.

Hanging over this apparently bright picture is the nagging and, as yet, unresolved doubt expressed by Morphy and Morphy (1984:46):

> Some people think that the vast amount of data gathered by anthropologists during the preparation of land claims in the Northern Territory will add significantly to the body of knowledge about Aboriginal social organization. However, the information is not being gathered in a neutral context; and it is becoming increasingly clear that models of Aboriginal social organization emerging from Land Rights cases are significantly influenced by ideological and pragmatic objectives.

I would like to add only two points to this comment. First, the choice of a patrilineal model, which the Morphys seem to favor, can itself reflect the pursuit of ideological and pragmatic objectives. Second, distortion in the models is an outcome of the sympathy anthropologists have for Aborigines and the dual role they are playing. Should we be more coolly objective, or should we abandon our claim to expertness and take up advocacy instead?

NOTES

1. I originally wrote this chapter for a volume David Turner and I planned in honor of Frederick Rose, one of the more important contributors to the development of Australian Aboriginal studies. The plan lapsed when it became clear that we were unlikely to find a publisher in Australia. The original version was given in 1983 to audiences at the Universities of Auckland and of Western Australia, to whom I am indebted for questions and comments. The present version has been revised to accommodate more recent developments and to allow for one or two doubts I share with, for example, Howard and Frances Morphy (1984) concerning the anthropological value of evidence given in Aboriginal land claims in the Northern Territory.

2. From McNally's (1981:123–124) account, it seems that Strehlow remained convinced until the day of his death that Stuart should have been acquitted. However, Inglis, a historian, maintains in his book on the case that Stuart was probably quilty (1961:308).

3. Gillen's intervention, however, turned out happily for anthropology. A few years after Willshire's removal, Aranda "gratitude found its expression in the ceremonial festival held at Alice Springs in 1896, where the secret totemic cycle of Imanda was revealed for the first time before the eyes of white men—to Gillen and to his friend, Baldwin Spencer" (Strehlow 1969:48–49).

4. Adjudicated claims to land have been virtually confined to the Northern

Territory. For views on the background to land rights in the Territory, see Maddock (1980, 1983a); and for Australia generally, including the Territory, see Maddock (1983b), Peterson (1981), and Peterson and Langton (1983). For Mr. Justice Blackburn's judgment in the Gove case, with which, in a way, it all began, see *Milirrpum v. Nabalco Pty. (Ltd.) and the Commonwealth of Australia* (Gove Land Rights Case), 1971, Federal Law Reports 141.

5. Many anthropologists have thought that clans own land, but one doubts if they had a lawyer's idea of property in mind. Probably what they meant was that clans have a relation to land that is stronger in significant respects than that of any other kind of group. What this strong relation has in common with proprietorship in English or European law is a question that could usefully be investigated.

6. Land councils are corporations established under the Land Rights Act; their membership is exclusively Aboriginal, although they may, and do, employ non-Aboriginal staff. The Land Commissioner is a judge appointed under the Act to hear traditional land claims. Such a claim may be made to designated classes of land in the Territory by or on behalf of the traditional Aboriginal owners (as defined in the Act) of the land concerned. For a description and discussion of the many facets of the Act, see Hiatt (1984) and Maddock (1983b, especially chaps. 3–5).

7. The term "local descent group" has necessarily been discussed in every claim under the Land Rights Act. In anthropology, it seems to have been coined by Edmund Leach (1951) for purposes unconnected with land tenure. For contrasting opinions on its anthropological use, particularly in Australia, see Berndt (1981) and Maddock (1980:117–124).

8. That Australia is a federation of states helps to explain why there can be these differences, which, moreover, are justifiable by differences in the position of Aborigines and the purposes of legislation. Differing solutions to the legal problem of giving a formulation to traditional relations to land are discussed by Maddock (1985).

References

Aboriginal Land Commissioner
  1979a   Borroloola Land Claim. Canberra: Australian Government Pub-
           lishing Service (A.G.P.S.).
  1979b   Claim by the Warlpiri and Kartangarurru-Kurintji. Canberra:
           A.G.P.S.
  1980a   Uluru (Ayers Rock) National Park and Lake Amadeus/Luritja
           Land Claim. Canberra: A.G.P.S.
  1980b   Anmatjirra and Alyawarra Land Claim to Utopia Pastoral Lease.
           Canberra: A.G.P.S.
  1980c   Lander Warlpiri Anmatjirra Land Claim to Willowra Pastoral
           Lease. Canberra: A.G.P.S.
  1981a   Limmen Bight Land Claim. Canberra: A.G.P.S.
  1981b   Finniss River Land Claim. Canberra: A.G.P.S.
  1981c   Alligator Rivers Stage II Land Claim. Canberra: A.G.P.S.
  1982a   Daly River (Malak Malak) Land Claim. Canberra: A.G.P.S.
  1982b   Yutpundji-Djindiwirritj (Roper Bar) Land Claim. Canberra:
           A.G.P.S.
Aboriginal Land Rights Commission
  1973   First Report.
  1974   Second Report.
Ahenakew, D.
  1983   Opening remarks to the Constitutional Conference of First Min-
           isters' on the Rights of Aboriginal Peoples. Ottawa, March 15,
           1983.
Almagor, U.
  1978   Locality and the regulation of grazing among the Herero of Bot-
           swana. SSRC Conference on Land Tenure in Botswana, University
           of Manchester.

1980   Pastoral identity and reluctance to change: the Mbanderu of Nga-
            miland. *Journal of African Law* 24:35–61.

Anonymous
1976   *The James Bay and Northern Quebec Agreement.* Quebec: Editeur
            officiel.

Asad, T.
1978   Equality in nomadic social systems? *Critique of Anthropology* 11:57–
            65.

Asch, M.
1979   The economics of Dene self-determination. In *Challenging anthro-
            pology*, ed. D. Turner and G. Smith, 339–352. Toronto: McGraw-
            Hill Ryerson.

1982*a*   Capital and economic development: A critical appraisal of the
            recommendations of the Mackenzie Valley Pipeline Commission.
            Culture 2:3–9.

1982*b*   Dene self-determination and the study of hunter-gatherers in the
            modern world. In *Politics and History in Band Societies*, ed. E. Lea-
            cock and R. Lee, 347–372. Cambridge: Cambridge University
            Press.

1983   Proposals for Amendments and Additions to the Constitution
            Act. Unpublished Manuscript.

1984   *Home and Native Land: Aboriginal Rights and the Canadian Consti-
            tution.* Toronto: Methuen of Canada Ltd., Assembly of First Na-
            tions.

Barnard, A.
1976   Nharo Bushman kinship and the transformation of Khoi kin cat-
            egories. Ph.D. dissertation, University College, London.

1978   Universal systems of kin categorization. *African Studies* 37:69–81.

1979   Kalahari Bushmen settlement patterns. In *Social and Ecological
            Systems*, ed. P. Burnham and R. Ellen. ASA Monographs 18:131
            –144.

de la Bat, B.
1982   Etosha 75 years. *South West Africa Annual*:11–22.

Beckett, J.
1985   Colonialism in a welfare state: The case of the Australian Abo-
            rigines. In *The Future of Former Foragers*, ed. C. Schrire and R.
            Gordon, 7–24. Cambridge: Cultural Survival.

Bell, D.
1980   Daughters of the Dreaming. Ph.D. dissertation, Australian Na-
            tional University.

Bennett, G.
1978*a*   *Aboriginal Rights in International Law.* London: Royal Anthropo-
            logical Institute of Great Britain and Northern Ireland in associ-
            ation with Survival International, Canada. First Ministers' Con-
            ference on Aboriginal Constitutional Matters. Occasional Paper
            No. 39.

1978*b* Aboriginal title in the common law: a stony path through feudal doctrine. *Buffalo Law Review* 27:617–636.

1983 Unofficial and unverified verbatim transcript. March 16, 1983, vol. 2.

Berger, T.

1977 *Northern Frontier, Northern Homeland: The Report of the Mackenzie Valley Pipeline Inquiry.* Vols. I and II. Ottawa: Minister of Supply and Services Canada.

Berkes, F.

1977 Fishing resource use in a subarctic Indian community. *Human Ecology* 5:289–307.

1979 An investigation of Cree Indian domestic fisheries in northern Quebec. *Arctic* 32:46–70.

1981*a* Fisheries of the James Bay area and northern Quebec: A case study in resource management. In *Proceedings of the First International Symposium on Renewable Resources and the Economy of the North*, ed. M. Freeman, 143–160 Ottawa: Association of Canadian Universities for Northern Studies.

1981*b* The role of self-regulation in living resources management in the North. In *Proceedings of the First International Symposium on Renewable Resources and the Economy of the North*, ed. M. Freeman, 166–178. Ottawa: Association of Canadian Universities for Northern Studies.

1982 Waterfowl management and northern native peoples with reference to Cree hunters of James Bay. *Musk-Ox* 30:23–35.

Berman, H.

1978 The concept of aboriginal rights in the early legal history of the United States. *Buffalo Law Review* 27:637–668.

Bern, J.

1974 Blackfella business, whitefella law: Political struggle and competition in a south-east Arnhem Land Aboriginal community. Ph.D. dissertation, Macquarie University.

1982 Report on the Yutpundji-Djindiwirritj (*Roper Bar*) land claim hearing. Typescript.

Bern, J., and J. Larbalestier

1985 Rival constructions of traditional Aboriginal ownership in the Limmen Bight land claim. *Oceania* 56:56–76.

Bern, J., J. Larbalestier, and D. McLaughlin

1980 *Limmen Bight Land Claim.* Northern Land Council, Darwin.

Bern, J. and R. Layton

1984 The local descent group and the division of labour in the Cox River land claim. In *Aboriginal Landowners*, ed. L. Hiatt, 67–83. Sydney: University of Sydney Press.

Berndt. R.

1981 A long view: Some personal comments on land rights. *Australian Institute for Aboriginal Studies Newsletter* 16:5–20.

Biebuyck, D.
  1963   *African Agrarian Systems*. London: Oxford University Press.
Birdsell, J.
  1970   Local group composition among the Australian Aborigines: A
            critique of the evidence from fieldwork carried out since 1930.
            Current Anthropology 11:115–131.
Bleek, D.
  1929   *Comparative Vocabularies of Bushman Languages*. Cambridge: Cam-
            bridge University Press.
Bley, H.
  1971   *South-West Africa under German Rule, 1894–1914*. Evanston: North-
            western University Press.
Bohannan, P.
  1957   *Justice and Judgment among the Tiv*. London: Oxford University
            Press.
  1965   The differing realms of the law. In The Ethnography of Law, ed.
            L. Nader. *American Anthropologist* 67.6, pt. 2:33–42.
Bosman, D., I. van der Merwe, and L. Hiemstra
  1982   *Tweetalige Woordeboek: Afrikaans-Engels*. Tafelberg: Uitgewero Be-
            perk, Kaapstaad.
Boydell, T.
  1948   *My Luck Still In*. Cape Town: Stewart.
Bourdieu, P.
  1977   *Outline of a Theory of Practice*. Cambridge: Cambridge University
            Press.
Brelsford, T.
  1980   Report on the subsistence issue in Alaska. McGill University Pro-
            gramme in the Anthropology of Development, Brief Communi-
            cation 46, Montreal.
  1982   *Equality and Science: A Thematic Analysis of Sportsmen's Opposition
            to the Alaska Subsistence Priority*. Montreal: Centre de recherche et
            d'analyse en sciences humaines.
  1983a   Hunters and workers among the Namaska Cree: The role of ide-
            ology in a dependent mode of production. M.A. thesis, McGill
            University.
  1983b   A theoretical and methodological review of the Alaska subsistence
            literature. Unpublished report from research under contract be-
            tween McMaster University and the Office of the Northern Re-
            search and Science Advisor, Department of Indian Affairs.
British Columbia
  1970   *Calder et al. v. Attorney General of British Columbia* (1970). 74 WWR
            481 (BCCA).
Brody, H.
  1981   *Maps and Dreams*. Harmondsworth: Penguin.

Campbell, A., and G. Child
    1971   The impact of man on the environment of Botswana. *Botswana Notes and Records* 3:91–110.
Canada. First Ministers' Conference on Aboriginal Constitutional Matters.
    1983*a*   Unofficial and unverified verbatim transcript. March 15, 1983, vol. 1.
    1983*b*   Unofficial and unverified verbatim transcript. March 16, 1983, vol. 2.
Cashdan, E.
    1977   Subsistence, mobility, and territorial organization among the G//anaque of the northeastern central Kalahari Game Reserve, Botswana. Report to the Ministry of Local Government and Lands, Gaborone.
    1982   The ecology of human subsistence. *Science* 216:1308–1309.
    1983   Territoriality among human foragers: Ecological models and an application to four Bushmen groups. *Current Anthropology* 24:47–66.
Castile, G.
    1975   An unethical ethic: Self-Determination and the anthropological conscience. *Human Organization* 34:35–40.
Chase, A.
    1980   Which way now? Tradition, continuity, and change in a north Queensland Aboriginal community. Ph.D. dissertation, University of Queensland.
Cole, K.
    1979   *The Aborigines of Arnhem land*. Adelaide: Rigby.
Colson, E.
    1953   Social control and vengeance in plateau Tonga society. *Africa* 23:199–212.
Comaroff, J.
    1973   Competition for office and political processes among the Barolong boo Ratshidi. Ph.D. dissertation, University of London.
    1978   Rules and rulers: Political processes in a Tswana chiefdom. *Man* 13:1–20.
    1982   Class and culture in peasant economy: The transformation of land tenure in Barolong. In *Land reform in the Making*, ed. R. Werbner, 85–116. London: Rex Collings. (Also *Journal of African Law* 24:85–116.)
Comaroff, J., and J. Comaroff
    1981   The management of marriage in a Tswana context. In *Essays on African Marriage in Southern Africa*, ed. E. Krige and J. Comaroff, 29–49. Cape Town: Juta.
Comaroff, J., and S. Roberts
    1981   *Rules and Processes: The Cultural Logic of Dispute in an African Context*. Chicago: University of Chicago Press.

Commonwealth of Australia
    1971   Gove Land Rights Case, *Federal Law Reports* 141.
Conner, W.
    1973   The politics of ethnonationalism. *Journal of International Affairs*
                27:1–21.
Coombs, H.
    1978   *Kulinma*. Canberra: Australian National University Press.
Cranston, M. (ed.)
    1966   *A Glossary of Political Terms*. London: Bodley Head.
Cumming, P., and N. Michelberg
    1972   *Native Rights in Canada*. 2d ed. Toronto: Indian-Eskimo Association
                of Canada and General Publishing.
Denbow, J., and E. Wilmsen
    1986   The advent and course of pastoralism in the Kalahari. *Science*
                234:1509–1515.
Dene Nation (Indian Brotherhood of the Northwest Territories)
    1977   The Dene declaration. In *Dene Nation: The Colony Within*, ed. M.
                Watkins, 3–4. Toronto: University of Toronto Press.
DIAND (Department of Indian Affairs and Northern Development)
    1969   *Statement of the Government of Canada on Indian Policy, 1969*. Ottawa:
                Queen's Printer.
Eames, G.
    1983   The Central Land Council: The politics of change. In *Aborigines,
                Land, and Land Rights*, ed. N. Peterson and M. Langton, 268–277.
                Canberra: Australian Institute for Aboriginal Studies.
Eggleston, E.
    1976   *Fear, Favour, or Affection*. Canberra: Australian National University
                Press.
Egner, B.
    1981   The remote area development programme: An evaluation. Eco-
                nomic Consultancies (Pty.) Ltd., Gaborone.
Elkin, A.
    1938   *The Australian Aborigines*. Sydney: Angus and Robertson.
    1949   The rights of man in primitive society. In *Human Rights: Comments
                and Interpretations*, ed. UNESCO, 226–241. London: Allan Win-
                gate.
    1950   The complexity of social organization in Arnhem Land. *South-
                western Journal of Anthropology* 6:1–20.
Engels, F.
    [1891]   *The origin of the Family, Private Property, and the State*, ed. E. Lea-
    1972   cock. New York: International Publishers.
Estermann, C.
    [1957]   *Ethnography of Southwestern Angola*, ed. G. Gibson. New York:
    1976   Africana Publishing Company.

Fabian, J.
  1965   !Kung Bushman kinship: Componential analysis and alternative interpretations. *Anthropos* 60:663–718.

Feit, H.
  1980   Negotiating recognition of aboriginal rights: History, strategies and reactions to the James Bay and Northern Quebec Agreement. *Canadian Journal of Anthropology* 1:159–172.

  1982   The future of hunters within nation-states: Anthropology and the James Bay Cree. In *Politics and History in Band Societies*, ed. E. Leacock and R. Lee, 373–411. Cambridge: Cambridge University Press.

  1983   The income security program for Cree hunters in Quebec: An experiment in increasing the autonomy of hunters in a developed nation-state. In *Aborigines, Land, and Land Rights*, ed. N. Peterson and M. Langton, 439–454. Canberra: Australian Institute for Aboriginal Studies.

  1984   Conflict arenas in the management of renewable resources in the Canadian North: Perspectives based on conflicts and responses in the James Bay region, Quebec. In *National and Regional Interests in the North: Third National Workshop on People, Resources, and the Environment North of 60°*, 435–458. Ottawa: Canadian Arctic Resources Committee.

  1985*a*   Legitimation and autonomy in James Bay Cree responses to hydroelectric development. In *Indigenous people and the nation state: fourth world politics in Canada, Australia, and Norway*, ed. N. Dyck, 27–66. St. John's: Memorial University, Institute for Social and Economic Research.

  1985*b*   Aboriginal rights in Canada: Indigenous strategies for relative autonomy within the Canadian state. In *The Canadian Constitution: Civil and Minority Rights*, 40–65. Cardiff: Canadian Studies in Wales Group.

  1986   Hunting and the quest for power: the James Bay Cree and whitemen in the twentieth century. In *Native peoples: the Canadian experience*, ed. R. Morrison and C. Wilson, 171–207. Toronto: McClelland and Stewart.

  n.d.   The power and the responsibility: Implementation of the wildlife and hunting provisions of the James Bay and Northern Quebec Agreement. In *The James Bay and Northern Quebec Agreement, Ten Years after*, ed. S. Vincent. Montreal: Reserches Améridienes au Québec. In press.

Feit, H., and C. Scott
  n.d.   *Income Security for Cree Hunters: Initial Socioeconomic Impacts and Long-term Considerations*. Montreal: McGill University Programme in the Anthropology of Development. In press.

Freeman, M., and L. Hackman
  1975   Bathurst Island, N.W.T.: A test case of Canada's northern policy. *Canadian Public Policy* 1:402–414.
Friedman, L.
  1977   *Law and Society: An Introduction.* Englewood Cliffs, N.J.: Prentice-Hall.
Galaty, J.
  1981   Organizations for pastoral development: Contexts of causality, change and assessment. In *The Future of Pastoral Peoples*, ed. J. Galaty et al., 68–88. Ottawa: International Development Research Center.
Gartrell, B.
  1983   Some notes on structural variations in colonial situations. Paper submitted to a symposium on the Fourth World and the state. International Conference of Anthropological and Ethnological Sciences, Vancouver.
Gibson, G.
  1959   Levels of residence among the Herero. Paper presented to American Anthropological Association Annual Meeting, Mexico City.
Gluckman, M.
  1955   *The Judicial Process among the Barotse of Northern Rhodesia (Zambia).* Manchester: University of Manchester Press.
  1965   *The Ideas of Barotse Jurisprudence.* New Haven: Yale University Press.
  1971   *Politics, Law, and Ritual in Tribal Society.* London: Basil Blackwell.
Godelier, M.
  1973   *Horizon, trajets marxistes en anthropologie.* Paris: Maspero.
  1975   Modes of production, kinship, and demographic structures. In *Marxist analysis and social anthropology*, ed. M. Bloch, 3–27. New York: John Wiley.
  1977   *Perspectives in Marxist Anthropology.* Cambridge: Cambridge University Press.
Gordon, R.
  1984   What future for the Ju-/wasi of NyaeNyae? *Cultural Survival Occasional Paper* 13.
  1985   Conserving the Bushmen to extinction in southern Africa. *Survival International Review* 44:28–42.
  n.d.   *The Bushmen: A Myth and the Making of a Namibian Underclass.* Johannesburg: Ravan Press. In press.
Gumbert, M.
  1981   Paradigm lost: Anthropological models and their effect on Aboriginal land rights. *Oceania* 52:103–123.
  1984   *Neither Justice nor Reason: A Legal and Anthropological Analysis of Aboriginal Land Rights.* St Lucia: Queensland University Press.

Hagen, R., and M. Rowell
  1979   *The Anmatjirra and Alyawarra land claim to Utopia pastoral lease*. Cen-
          tral Land Council, Alice Springs.
Hahlo, H.
  1960   *The Union of South Africa: The Development of Its Laws and Consti-
          tution*. Cape Town: Juta.
Hahn, T.
  1895   Who are the real owners of Ghanse? CO 16669 (23 Sept.), Public
          Records Office, London.
Lord Hailey
  1956   *An African Survey*. Rev. ed. London: Oxford University Press.
Hamilton, A.
  1979   Timeless transformation: women, men, and history in the Aus-
          tralian Western Desert. Ph.D. dissertation, University of Sydney.
  1982   Descended from father, belonging to country: Rights to land in
          the Australian Western Desert. In *Politics and History in Band So-
          cieties*, ed. E. Leacock and R. Lee, 85–108. Cambridge: Cambridge
          University Press.
Hansen, K., and L. Hansen
  1977   *Pintupi-Loritja Dictionary*. Alice Springs: Institute for Aboriginal
          Development.
Hardy, F.
  1968   *The Unlucky Australians*. Melbourne: Nelson.
Harpending, H.
  1976   Regional variation in !Kung populations. In *Kalahari Hunter-Gath-
          erers*, ed. R. Lee and I. DeVore, 152–165. Cambridge: Harvard
          University Press.
Harris, O., and K. Young
  1981   Engendered structures: Some problems in the analysis of repro-
          duction. In *The Anthropology of Precapitalist Societies*, ed. J. Kahn
          and J. Llobera, 109–147. Atlantic Highlands: Humanities Press.
Heinz, H.
  1966   Social organization of the !Ko Bushmen. M.A. thesis, University
          of South Africa.
  1972   Territoriality among the Bushmen in general and the !Ko in par-
          ticular. *Anthropos* 67:405–416.
  1979   The nexus complex among the !xo Bushmen of Botswana. *An-
          thropos* 74:465–480.
Hiatt, L.
  1962   Local organization among the Australian Aborigines. *Oceania*
          32:267–286.
  1965   *Kinship and Conflict*. Canberra: Australian National University
          Press.
  1968   Ownership and use of land among the Australian Aborigines. In

Man the Hunter, ed. R. Lee and I. DeVore, 99–102. Chicago: Aldine Press.

1970   Comment on J. Birdsell, Local group composition among the Australian Aborigines: a critique of the evidence from fieldwork conducted since 1930. *Current Anthropology* 8:134–135.

1982*a*   Letter to the editor. *Oceania* 52:264–265.

1982*b*   Traditional attitudes to land resources. In *Aboriginal Sites, Rights, and Resource Development*, ed. R. Berndt, 13–26. Perth: A.S.S.A.

1984   Introduction. In *Aboriginal Landowners: Contemporary Issues in the Determination of Traditional Aboriginal Landownership*, ed. L. Hiatt, 1–10. Sydney: University of Sydney Press.

Higgins, R.
1963   *The Development of International Law through the Political Organs of the United Nations*. Royal Institute of International Affairs. London: Oxford University Press.

Hitchcock, R.
1978   Kalahari cattle posts: A regional study of hunter-gatherers, pastoralists, and agriculturalists in the western sandveld region, Botswana. Gaborone: Government Printer.

1982   Tradition, social justice, and land reform in central Botswana. In *Land reform in the Making*, ed. R. Werbner, 1–34. London: Rex Collings. (Also, *Journal of African Law* 24:1–34.)

Hitchcock, R., and A. Campbell
1980   Settlement patterns of the Bakgalagari. In *Settlement in Botswana*, ed. R. Hitchcock and M. Smith, 148–160. Marshalltown: Heinemann.

Hitchcock, R., H. Vierich, and E. Wilmsen
1977   Basarwa mobility and migration patterns. Paper presented to First National Migration Study Workshop, Gaborone.

Hoben, A.
1986   The political economy of resource tenure in Somalia. Workshop on Land issues in Africa, Harvard University, 15 March.

Hookey, J.
1974   Comments on land rights. In *Aborigines, Human Rights, and Law*, ed. G. Nettheim, 99–103. Sydney: Australian and New Zealand Book Company.

House of Commons, Special Committee on Indian Self-Government
1983   *Indian Self-Government in Canada: Report of the Special Committee*. Ottawa: Queen's Printer.

Howard, M.
1982   Introduction. In *Aboriginal Power in Australian Society*, ed. M. Howard, 1–13. Honolulu: University of Hawaii Press.

Hunt, C.
1978   Approaches to native land settlement and implications for northern land use and resource management policies. In *Northern Tran-*

sitions. Vol. II, *Second National Workshop on People, Resources, and the Environment North of 60°*, ed. R. Keith and J. Wright, 5–41. Ottawa: Canadian Arctic Resources Committee.

Hymes, D.
 1972   *Reinventing Anthropology*. New York: Pantheon.

Inglis, K.
 1961   *The Stuart case*. Melbourne: Melbourne University Press.

Ives, J.
 n.d.   Northern Athapaskan socioeconomic variability. Ph.D. dissertation, University of Michigan.

James Bay and Northern Quebec Native Harvesting Research Committee (JBNQHR)
 1982   *The Wealth of the Land: Wildlife Harvests by the James Bay Cree, 1972–73 to 1978–79*. Quebec: JBNQHR.

Jennings, R.
 1963   *The Acquisition of Territory in International Law*. Manchester: Manchester University Press.

Joyce, I.
 1938   Report on the Masarwa in the Bamangwato Reserve, Bechuanaland Protectorate. General: League of Nations Publications (vi.B. Slavery, c. 112, M.98), Annex 6, 57–76.

Kahn, J., and J. Llobera
 1981   Towards a new Marxism or a new anthropology? In *The Anthropology of Precapitalist Societies*, ed. J. Kahn and J. Llobera, 263–329. New York: Humanities Press.

Keen, I.
 1978   One ceremony, one song: An economy of religious knowledge among the Yolngu of north-east Arnhem Land. Ph.D. dissertation, Australian National University.

 1980   *Alligator Rivers Stage II Land Claim*. Northern Land Council, Darwin.

 1981   Statement of evidence to the Land Commissioner, Alligator Rivers Stage II land claim. Typescript.

 1982   How some Murngin men marry ten wives: The marital implications of matrilateral cross-cousin structures. *Man* 17:620–642.

Keenan, J.
 1981   The concept of the mode of production in hunter-gatherer societies. In *The anthropology of precapitalist societies*, ed. J. Kahn and J. Llobera, 2–21. New York: Humanities Press.

Kenny, J.
 1973   *Bennelong: The First Notable Aboriginal*. Sydney: Royal Australian Historical Society.

Kerven, C. (ed.)
 1982   *Migration in Botswana: Patterns, Causes, and Consequences*. Gaborone: Central Statistics Office.

Kinahan, J.
   1986   Settlement patterns and regional exchange: Evidence from recent
             Iron Age sites on the Kavango River, northeastern Namibia. *Cim-
             bebasia* 3:110–116.
Kiyaga-Mulindwa, D. (ed.)
   1980   Politics and society in Letswapo. *Tswapong Historical Texts* 2. Ga-
             borone: University College of Botswana.
Kloppers, J.
   1970   *Gee My -n Man*. Johannesburg: Afrikaanse Press.
LaRusic, I.
   1979   *The Income Security Program for Cree Hunters and Trappers: A Study
             of the Design, Operation, and Initial Impacts of the Guaranteed Annual
             Income Programme Established under the James Bay and Northern Que-
             bec Agreement*. Montreal: McGill University Programme in the An-
             thropology of Development.
LaRusic, I., et al.
   1979   *Negotiating a Way of Life: Initial Cree Experience with the Administra-
             tive Structure Arising from the James Bay Agreement*. Montreal: Centre
             de recherche et d'analyse en sciences humaines.
Leach, E.
   1951   The structural implications of matrilateral cross-cousin marriage.
             Journal of the Royal Anthropological Institute 81:23–55.
Leacock, E., and R. Lee
   1982   *Politics and History in Band Societies*. Cambridge: Cambridge Uni-
             versity Press.
Lee, R.
   1965   Subsistence ecology of !Kung Bushmen. Ph.D. dissertation, Uni-
             versity of California, Berkeley.
   1972   !Kung spatial organization: An ecological and historical perspec-
             tive. *Human Ecology* 1:125–147.
   1979   *The !Kung San: Men, Women, and Work in a Forager Society*. Cam-
             bridge: Cambridge University Press.
   1982   Politics, sexual and nonsexual, in an egalitarian society. In *Politics
             and History in Band Societies*, ed. E. Leacock and R. Lee, 37–59.
             Cambridge: Cambridge University Press.
Lee, R., and I. DeVore (eds.)
   1968   *Man the Hunter*. Chicago: Aldine.
Lévi-Strauss, C.
   1966   *The Savage Mind*. Chicago: University of Chicago Press.
Lijphart, A.
   1977   *Democracy in Plural Societies: A Comparative Examination*. New Ha-
             ven: Yale University Press.
Lindley, M.
   1926   *The Acquisition and Government of Backward Territory in International
             Law*. London: Longman.

Lohe, M., F. Albrecht, and L. Leske
    1977   *Hermannsburg: A Vision and a Mission*. Adelaide: Lutheran Publishing House.
Luttig, H.
    1933   *The Religious System and Social Organization of the Herero*. Utrecht: Kemink en Zoon N.V.
MacCormack, G.
    1983   Problems in the description of African landholding. *Journal of Legal Pluralism and Unofficial Law* 21:1–14.
McIntyre, C.
    1968   SWA: Information for visitors, official and otherwise. *The Cape Argus*, April 15.
McNally, W.
    1981   *Aborigines, Artifacts, and Anguish*. Adelaide: Lutheran Publishing House.
Maddock, K.
    1972   *The Australian Aborigines: A Portrait of Their Society*. Harmondsworth: Penguin.
    1980   *Anthropology, Law, and the Definition of Australian Aboriginal Rights to Land*. Nijmegen: Instituut voor Volksrecht, Publikaties over Volksrecht.
    1982   Aboriginal land rights traditionally and in legislation: A case study. In *Aboriginal Power in Australian Society*, ed. M. Howard, 55–78. Honolulu: University of Hawaii.
    1983a   "Owners," "managers" and the choice of statutory traditional owners by anthropologists and lawyers. In *Aborigines, Land, and Land Rights*, ed. N. Peterson and M. Langton, 211–225. Canberra: Australian Institute for Aboriginal Studies.
    1983b   *Your Land is Our Land: Aboriginal Land Rights*. Ringwood: Penguin Books Australia.
    1985   How to do legal definitions of Aboriginal rights. *Anthropological Forum* 5:295–308.
Malinowski, B.
    1926   *Crime and custom in savage society*. London: Routledge and Kegan Paul.
    [1913] *The Family among the Australian Aborigines*. New York: Schocken
    1963   Books.
Malouf, A.
    1973   *La Baie James indienne: Texte integral du jugement du juge Albert Malouf*. Montreal: Editions du Jour.
Marnham, P.
    1980   *Fantastic Invasion*. London: Johnathan Cape.
Marquard, L., and J. Standing
    1939   *The Southern Bantu*. London: Oxford University Press.

Marshall, L.
1957   The kin terminology system of the !Kung Bushmen. *Africa* 27:1–25.
1960   !Kung Bushmen bands. *Africa* 30:325–355.
1961   Sharing, talking, and giving: Relief of social tensions among the !Kung Bushmen. *Africa* 31:231–249.
1976   *The !Kung of NyaeNyae.* Cambridge: Harvard University Press.
Marx, K.
[1867] *Capital.* New York: International Publishers.
1967
Mauss, M.
1954   *The Gift.* London: Cohen and West.
Maybury-Lewis, D.
1977   Societies on the brink. *Harvard Magazine,* January-February, 56–61.
Meggitt, M.
1962   *Desert People.* Sydney: Angus and Robertson.
Meillassoux, C.
1967   Recherche d'un niveau de determination dans la societe cynegetique. *L'Homme et la Société* 1:93–105.
1972   From reproduction to production: A Marxist approach to economic anthropology. *Economy and Society* 1:93–105.
1973   On the mode of production of the hunting band. In *French Perspectives in African Studies,* ed. P. Alexandre, 187–203. London: Oxford University Press.
1980   From reproduction to production: A Marxist approach to economic anthropology. In *The Articulation of Modes of Production,* ed. H. Wolpe, 189–201. London: Routledge and Kegan Paul. (Reprint of 1972 article.)
van der Merwe, S.
1960   Die Boesmans van Suidwes-Afrika. *Die Staatsanotebaard,* November, 32–34.
Memmott, P.
1979   Larkil properties of place: An ethnological study in man-environment relations. Ph.D. dissertation, University of Queensland.
Middleton, H.
1977   *But Now We Want the Land Back.* Sydney: New Age Publishers.
Morgan, L.
[1887] *Ancient Society,* ed. E. Leacock. New York: World Publishing Company.
1963
Morphy, H.
1977   Too many meanings: An analysis of the artistic system of the Yolngu of North East Arnhem Land. Ph.D. dissertation, Australian National University.

Morphy, H., and F. Morphy
    1981   *Yutpundji-Djindiwirritj (Roper Bar) Land Claim*. Northern Land Council, Darwin.
    1984   Owners, managers, and ideology: A comparative analysis. In *Aboriginal Landowners*, ed. L. Hiatt, 46–66. Sydney: University of Sydney Press.

Munn, N.
    1970   The transformation of subjects into objects in Walbiri and Pitjantjara myth. In *Australian Aboriginal Anthropology*, ed. R. Berndt, 141–163. Nedlands: University of Western Australia Press.

Myers, F.
    1976   'To have and to hold': A study of persistence and change in Pintupi social life. Ph.D. dissertation, Bryn Mawr.
    1979   Emotions and the self: A theory of personhood and political order among Pintupi Aborigines. *Ethos* 7:343–370.
    1982   Always ask: Resource use and landownership among Pintupi Aborigines. In *Resource Managers*, ed. N. Williams and E. Hunn, 173–195. Boulder: Westview Press.
    1986a   The politics of representation: Anthropological discourse and Australian Aborigines. *American Ethnologist* 13:430–447.
    1986b   *Pintupi Country, Pintupi Self: Sentiment, Place, and Politics among Western Desert Aborigines*. Washington: Smithsonian Institution Press.

New South Wales Aboriginal Land Council
    1981   *Land Claims in NSW*. Kings Cross.

Ofvatey-Kodjoe, W.
    1977   *The Principle of Self-Determination in International Law*. New York: Nellon.

Olivier, M.
    1961   Inboorlingbeleid en administrasie in diemandaatgebied van Suidwes-Africa. Ph.D. dissertation, Stellenbosch University.

Overton, J.
    1979   A critical examination of the establishment of national parks and tourism in underdeveloped areas: Gros Marne National Park in Newfoundland. *Antipode* 11(2):34–47.

Palmer, K.
    1984   Aboriginal landownership among the southern Pitjantjara of the Great Victoria Desert. In *Aboriginal Landowners*, ed. L. Hiatt, 123–133. Sydney: University of Sydney Press.

Parson, J.
    1981   Cattle, class, and state in rural Botswana. *Journal of Southern African Studies* 7:236–255.

Parsons, Q.
    1982   *A New History of Southern Africa*. London: Macmillan.

Partridge, E.
1983   *Origins: A Short Etymological Dictionary of Modern English.* New York: Greenwhich House.
Passarge, S.
1907   *Die Buschmänner der Kalahari.* Berlin: Dietrich Reimer.
Pennock, J.
1950   *Liberal Democracy: Its Merits and Prospects.* New York: Rinehart.
Perper, T., and C. Schrire
1977   The Nimrod connection: Myth and science in the hunting model. In *The Chemical Senses and Nutrition,* ed. M. Kare and O. Maller, 447–459. Orlando: Academic Press.
Peterson, N.
1972   The structure of two Australian Aboriginal ecosystems. Ph.D. dissertation, University of Sydney. Australian Institute for Aboriginal Studies.
1974   The importance of women in determining the composition of residential groups in Aboriginal Australia. In *Women's Role in Aboriginal Society* ed. F. Gale, 16–27. Canberra: Australian Institute of Aboriginal Studies.
Peterson, N. (ed.)
1981   *Aboriginal Land Rights: A Handbook.* Canberra: Australian Institute of Aboriginal Studies.
Peterson, N., and M. Langton (eds.)
1983   *Aborigines, Land, and Land Rights.* Canberra: Australian Institute of Aboriginal Studies.
Phipson, S.
1976   *Evidence.* 12th ed. London: Sweet and Maxwell.
Price, E. (ed.)
1973   *Law and the American Indian.* Indianapolis: Bobbs-Merrill.
Radcliffe-Brown, A.
1913   Three tribes of western Australia. *Journal of the Royal Anthropological Institute* 43:143–194.
1930–31 The social organization of Australian tribes. *Oceania Monograph* 1.
1944   Meaning and scope of social anthropology. *Nature* 154:257–260.
1952   Patrilineal and matrilineal succession. In *Structure and Function in Primitive Society,* ed. A. Radcliffe-Brown, 32–48. New York: Free Press. (Reprint of 1935 original.)
Richardson, B.
1975   *Strangers Devour the Land.* Toronto: Macmillan.
Roberts, S.
1979   *Order and Dispute: An Introduction to Legal Anthropology.* London: Penguin Books.
Rose, F.
1967   Review of H. Shiels, ed., *Australian Aboriginal Studies. Bijdragen tot de Tall-, Land- en Volkenkunde* 123:145–160.

1968 *Australia Revisited: The Aborigine Story from Stone Age to Space Age.* Berlin: Seven Seas Publishers.

Rowley, C.

 1972 *The Remote Aborigines.* Harmondsworth: Pelican Books.

 1978 *A Matter of Justice.* Canberra: Australian National University Press.

Sahlins, M.

 1965 On the sociology of primitive exchange. In *The Relevance of Models for Social Anthropology*, ed. M. Banton, 139–236. London: Tavistock.

 1968 Notes on the original affluent society. In *Man the Hunter*, ed. R. Lee and I. DeVore, 85–89. Aldine Press.

Salisbury, R.

 1986 *A Homeland for the Cree: Regional Development in James Bay 1971–1981.* Montreal: McGill-Queen's University Press.

Salisbury, R., et al.

 1972*a* *Not by Bread Alone: The Subsistence Economies of the People of Fort George, Paint Hills, Eastmain, Great Whale, Fort Chimo, and the Nitchequon Band from Mistassini.* Montreal: Indians of Quebec Association, James Bay Task Force.

 1972*b* *Development and James Bay: Social Implications of the Hydroelectric Scheme.* Montreal: McGill University Programme in the Anthropology of Development.

Sansom, B.

 1980 Statement on the Utopia land claim. Typescript.

Schapera, I.

 1938 *Handbook of Tswana Law and Custom.* London: Oxford University Press.

 1943 *Native Land Tenure in the Bechuanaland Protectorate.* Alice: Lovedale Press.

 1963 Kinship and politics in Tswana history. *Journal of the Royal Anthropological Society* 9:159–173.

 1970 *Tribal Innovators: Tswana Chiefs and Social Change: 1875–1940.* London: University of London Press.

Schinz, H.

 1891 *Deutsch-Südwest-Afrika.* Leipzig: Schulzesche Hofbuchhandlung.

Schrire, C.

 1980 An enquiry into the evolutionary status and apparent identity of San hunter-gatherers. *Human Ecology* 8:9–32.

 1984 Wild surmises on savage thoughts. In *Past and Present in Hunter-Gatherer Studies*, ed. C. Schrire, 1–25. Orlando: Academic Press.

Schultze, L.

 1914 Südwestafrika. In *Das Deutsche Kolonialreich*, ed. H. Meyer, 270–295. Vol. 2. Leipzig: Verlag des Bibliographisches Instituts.

Scott, C.

 1977 The income security program for Cree hunters, fishermen, and trappers: An initial field report on impacts and reactions in four James Bay coastal settlements. Montreal: Grand Council of the Crees (of Quebec). Unpublished.

1979   *Modes of Production and Guaranteed Annual Income in James Bay Cree Society*. Montreal: McGill University Programme in the Anthropology of Development.

1983   The semiotics of material life among Wemindji Cree hunters. Ph.D. dissertation, McGill University.

Shiels, H. (ed.)

1963   *Australian Aboriginal Studies: A Symposium of Papers presented at the 1961 Research Conference*. Melbourne: Oxford University Press.

Silberbauer, G.

1965   *Bushman Survey Report*. Gaborone: Bechuanaland Government.

1981   *Hunter and Habitat in the Central Kalahari Desert*. Cambridge: Cambridge University Press.

1982   Political process in G/wi bands. In *Politics and History in Band Societies*, ed. E. Leacock and R. Lee, 22–35. Cambridge: Cambridge University Press.

Silberbauer, G., and A. Kuper

1966   Kgalgadi masters and Bushmen serfs. *African Studies* 25:171–179.

Smith, D.

1984   "That Register business": The role of the Land Councils in determining traditional Aboriginal owners. In *Aboriginal Landowners*, ed. L. Hiatt, 84–103. Sydney: University of Sydney Press.

Smith, M.

1969   Some development in the analytic framework of pluralism. In *Pluralis*, ed. L. Kuper and M. Smith, 27–66. Berkeley, Los Angeles: University of California Press.

Snow, A.

1921   *The question of Aborigines*. New York: Putnam.

Snyman, J.

1970   *An Introduction to the !Xū Language*. Cape Town: Balkema.

1975   *Zhu/'hōasi Phonologie en Woordeboek*. Cape Town: Balkema.

SSDCC   (Centre de recherche et d'analyse en sciences humaines)

1982   *Etude des retombes sociales et economiques sur les communauts autochtones du territoire NBR (Complexe hydrolectrique Nottaway-Broadback-Rupert)*. Montreal: Rapport produit par la Socit d'nergie de la Baie James, Direction de l'Environnement.

Stals, E.

1984   *Duits-Suidwes-Afrika na die Groot Opstande*. Pretoria: Archives Yearbook Series No. 46(11).

Stanner, W.

1933   The Daly River tribes: A report on fieldwork in North Australia. *Oceania* 3:377–405.

1965   Aboriginal society, territory, and language at Cape Keerweer, Cape York Peninsula, Australia. Ph.D. dissertation, University of Queensland.

1979   The Dreaming. In *White Man Ain't Got No Dreaming*, ed. W. Stanner, 23–40. Canberra: Australian National University Press.

Steward, J.

1955   *Theory of Culture Change*. Urbana: University of Illinois Press.

Strehlow, T.

1947   *Aranda Traditions*. Melbourne: Melbourne University Press.

1969   *Journey to Horseshoe Bend*. Sydney: Angus and Robertson.

1971   *Songs of Central Australia*. Sydney: Angus and Robertson.

Sturmer, J. von

1978   The Wik region: Economy, territoriality, and totemism in western Cape York Peninsula, North Queensland. Ph.D. dissertation, University of Queensland.

Sutton, P.

1978   Wik: Aboriginal society, territory, and language at Cape Keerweer, Cape York Peninsula, Australia. Ph.D. dissertation, University of Queensland.

Sutton, P., and Rigsby, B.

1982   People with 'politicks': Management of land and personnel on Australia's Cape York Peninsula. In *Resource Managers: North American and Australian hunter-gatherers*, ed. N. Williams and E. Hann, 155–173. Boulder: Westview Press.

Tagart, E.

1933   Report on the conditions existing among the Masarwa in the Bamangwato Reserve. London Missionary Society.

Tanaka, J.

1969   The ecology and social structure of central Kalahari Bushmen: A preliminary report. *Kyoto University African Studies* 3:1–26.

1980   *The San: Hunter-Gatherers of the Kalahari*. Tokyo: University of Tokyo Press.

Tanner, A.

1979   *Bringing Home Animals: Religious Ideology and Mode of Production of the Mistassini Cree Hunters*. St. John's: Memorial University of Newfoundland, Institute of Social and Economic Research.

Tatz, C.

1982   *Aborigines and Uranium and Other Essays*. Richmond: Heinemann Educational Books.

Taylor, J.

1979   *From Modernization to Modes of Production*. London: Macmillan.

Terray, E.

1972   *Marxism and "primitive" societies*. New York: Monthly Review Press.

Thomas, N.
1906   *Kinship and Organisations and Group Marriage in Australia*. London: Frank Cass.

Tlou, T.
1972   A political history of northwestern Botswana to 1906. Ph.D. dissertation, University of Wisconsin, Madison.
1976   The peopling of the Okavango Delta: ca. 1750–1906. *Proceedings of the Symposium on the Okavango Delta and Its Future Utilization*, Botswana Society, 49–53.
1977   Servility and political control: Bathlanka among the Batawana of northwestern Botswana, ca. 1750–1906. In *Slavery in Africa: Historical and Anthropological Perspectives*, ed. S. Miers and I. Kopytoff, 367–390. Madison: University of Wisconsin Press.

Tonkinson, R.
1978   *The Mardudjara Aborigines*. New York: Holt, Rinehart and Winston.

Trudeau, P.
1983   Opening statement to the Constitutional Conference of First Ministers on the Rights of Aboriginal Peoples. Ottawa: United Nations.

Turner, T.
1979   Anthropology and the politics of indigenous peoples' struggles. *Cambridge Anthropology* 5:1–43.

Turner, V.
1957   *Schism and Continuity in an African Society: A Study of Ndembu Village Life*. Manchester: Manchester University Press.

Tyack, D., T. James, and A. Benavot
1987   *Law and the Shaping of Public Schools, 1785–1954*. Cambridge: Harvard University Press.

United Nations General Assembly
1961   *Declaration on the Granting of Independence to Colonial Countries*.

Usher, P.
1981   Sustenance or recreation? The future of native wildlife harvesting in northern Canada. In *Proceedings of the First International Symposium on Renewable Resources and the Economy of the North*, ed. M. Freeman, 56–71. Ottawa: Association of Canadian Universities for Northern Studies.
1984   Property rights: The basis of wildlife management. In *National and Regional Interests in the North. Third National Workshop on People, Resources, and the Environment North of 60°*, 389–414. Ottawa: Canadian Arctic Resources Committee.

Usher, P., and G. Beakhust
1973   *Land Regulation in the Canadian North*. Ottawa: Canadian Arctic Resources Committee.

Vedder, H.
1910   Grundriss einer Grammatik der Bushmann Sprache vom Stamm der Buschmänner. *Zeitschrift für Kolonial-Sprachen* 1.
1934   *Das alte Südwestafrika.* Windhoek: South West Africa Scientific Society. (1981 facsimile reprint.)
1937   Die Buschmänner südwestafrikas und ihre Weltanschauung. *South African Journal of Science* 34:416–436.
1938   *Southwest Africa in Early Times.* London: Frank Cass.

Vierich-Esch, H.
1982   Adaptive flexibility in a multi-ethnic setting: The Basarwa of the southern Kalahari. In *Politics and History in Band Societies*, ed. E. Leacock and R. Lee, 213–222. Cambridge: Cambridge University Press.

Watermeyer, E.
1963   The Roman-Dutch law in South Africa. In *The Cambridge History of the British Empire*, ed. E. Walker, 858–873. Vol. 8. London: Cambridge University Press.

Weaver, S.
1981   *Making Canadian Indian Policy: The Hidden Agenda 1968–1970.* Toronto: University of Toronto Press.

Weiner, A.
1985   Inalienable Wealth. *American Ethnologist* 12:210–227.

Wells, E.
1981   Some events at Yirrkala during 1962 and 1963. *Australian Institute for Aboriginal Studies Newsletter* 15:31–40.

Welsh, D.
1968   The State President's powers under the Bantu Administration Act. *Acta Juridica* 81–100.

Western, D.
1981   A challenge for conservation. *L. S. B. Leakey Foundation News* (Winter): 1–14.

Westphal, E.
1963   On classifying Bushmen and Hottentot languages. *African Language Studies* 3:30–48.

White, C.
1963   Terminological confusion in African land tenure. *Journal of African Administration* 10:124–130.

White, L.
1943   Energy and the evolution of culture. *American Anthropologist* 35:335–356.

Wiessner, P.
1977   Hxaro: A regional system of reciprocity for reducing risk in the !Kung Bushmen. Ph.D. dissertation, University of Michigan.
1982   Risk, reciprocity, and social influences on !Kung San economics.

In *Politics and History in Band Societies*, ed. E. Leacock and R. Lee, 61–84. Cambridge: Cambridge University Press.

Williams, N.
1986   *The Yolngu and Their Land*. Canberra: Australian Institute of Aboriginal Studies.

Williams, R.
1977   *Marxism and Literature*. London: Oxford University Press.

Wilmsen, E.
1976   Report to the Ministry of Local Government and Lands on research in western Ngamiland. National Archives, Gaborone.

1982*a*   Migration of Remote Area Dwellers. In *Migration in Botswana: Patterns, Causes, and Consequently*, ed. C. Kerven, 337–376. Gaborone: Central Statistics Office.

1982*b*   Exchange, interaction, and settlement in northwestern Botswana: Past and present perspectives. In *Settlement in Botswana*, ed. R. Hitchcock and M. Smith, 98–109. Marshalltown: Heinemann Educational Books.

1983   The ecology of illusion: Anthropological foraging in the Kalahari. *Reviews in Anthropology* 10:9–20.

n.d.   *Land Filled with Flies: A Political Economy of the Kalahari*. Chicago: University of Chicago Press. In press.

Wolf, E.
1982   *Europe and the People without History*. Berkeley, Los Angeles, London: University of California Press.

Woodburn, J.
1980   Hunters and gatherers today and reconstruction of the past. In *Soviet and Western Anthropology*, ed. E. Gellner, 95–117. London: Duckworth.

Woodward, A. (Mr. Justice)
1973   *First Report of the Aboriginal Land Rights Commission*. Melbourne: Office of the Aboriginal Land Rights Commissioner.

World Bank
1982   *Tribal Peoples and Economic Development*. Washington, D.C.: World Bank.

Yellen, J.
1976   Settlement patterns of the !Kung. In *Kalahari Hunter-Gatherers*, ed. R. Lee and I. DeVore, 47–72. Cambridge: Harvard University Press.

Yellen, J., and H. Harpending.
1972   Hunter-gatherer populations and archaeological inference. *World Archaeology* 4:244–253.

Contributors

Michael Asch is Professor and Head of the Department of Anthropology at the University of Alberta. He received his Ph.D. in anthropology from Columbia University in 1972: his dissertation field research was carried out with the Athapaskan-speaking Dene of the Mackenzie River. He was invited to undertake extensive research for the Dene Nation, including the preparation of testimony on their economic history and land use institutions as well as socioeconomic impact assessments, most notably, for the Mackenzie Valley Pipeline Inquiry. More recently, he has been engaged in the preparation of position papers relating to land claims for the Dene Nation and government policy with respect to those claims negotiations.

Harvey A. Feit is Associate Professor of Anthropology at McMaster University. He received his Ph.D. in anthropology from McGill University in 1979. During the course of his doctoral research among the Waswanipi Cree, he was asked to give evidence on behalf of James Bay Cree people in the case they brought against the James Bay Hydroelectric Project. He subsequently served as senior social science adviser to the Cree, in which capacity he was appointed to the combined native and government committees mandated to review social and economic impacts of development in the James Bay region and to implement income security and coordinate wildlife management programs. In 1979–80, he was Canada Council Killam Postdoctoral Research Scholar; during this tenure, he reviewed the initial implementation of the James Bay and Northern Quebec Agreement. He has recently begun research on social movements for change in Canada and Europe.

Robert Gordon is Associate Professor of Anthropology at the University of Vermont. A native of Namibia, he first read law at Stellenbosch University and later served as personnel officer with Johannesburg Consolidated Investments at their Otjihase mine. He received his Ph.D. in anthropology from the University of Illinois, Champaign-Urbana, in 1977. The subject of his dissertation was the relations between employers and migrant laborers at the mine. Subsequent fieldwork, concerned with the resurgence of clan warfare in Highland Papua New Guinea, was undertaken while he was teaching at the University of Papua New Guinea. He is currently involved in research on the creation of the colonial state and its mode of internal pacification, focusing especially on minorities and vagrancy laws.

L. R. Hiatt is Reader in Anthropology at the University of Sydney and a Fellow of the Australian Academy of the Social Sciences. After studying philosophy and anthropology at the University of Sydney, he received his Ph.D. in anthropology from the Australian National University in 1963 on the basis of field research among the Gidjingarli of Arnhem Land. He has written extensively on Aboriginal culture, and his film *Waiting for Harry* vividly portrays the tensions between the demands of that culture and the necessities of contemporary Australian life. From 1974 to 1982, he was president of the Australian Institute of Aboriginal Studies, a period when the institute played a vital role in mobilizing academic resources in support of Aboriginal land claims in the Northern Territory.

Kenneth Maddock is Associate Professor of Anthropology and Head of the School of Behavioural Sciences at Macquarie University. He graduated in law and anthropology from the University of Auckland and was admitted as a barrister and solicitor of the Supreme Court of New Zealand. He was awarded a Ph.D. in anthropology by the University of Sydney in 1969 on the basis of field research in southern Arnhem Land. He was anthropological adviser to the Aboriginal Land Commissioner in the Alligator Rivers claim. In addition, he gave evidence for the claimants in the Utopia claim and conducted research in support of the Nicholson River and Wakaya-Alyawarra claims. He was a consultant to the Australian Law Reform Commission in its enquiry into the recognition of Aboriginal customary law. He is currently working on questions of the "Fourth World," traditional law and legal pluralism in Indonesia during the Dutch colonial period, and Australian involvement in the Vietnam War and its effects on Australian thought and society.

Fred Myers is Associate Professor of Anthropology at New York University. He received his Ph.D. in anthropology from Bryn Mawr

College in 1976 after completing fieldwork with the Pintupi of the Western Desert in Australia. His dissertation concerned individual conceptions of self and politics with regard to land; since then, he has investigated the changing political economy of gender among Pintupi peoples. Under the auspices of the Central Land Council, he was involved in the preparation of land claims brought by Walpiri, Ngartji, and Kukatja peoples; these claims were awarded in 1983 under the Aboriginal Land Rights Act. In 1984, on behalf of Pintupi peoples, he mediated claims arising from the unexpected reappearance of a group who had been living separately for many years. He plans to begin research into indigenously produced forms of Christianity among Pintupi.

Edwin N. Wilmsen is Research Associate in the African Studies Center, Boston University. He received his Ph.D. in anthropology from the University of Arizona in 1967 after teaching and practicing architecture subsequent to receiving a Master of Architecture degree from MIT in 1959. His master's thesis was on community development at Shiprock on the Navaho Reservation. Since 1973, he has worked with the Zhu, Herero, and Tswana peoples of Ngamiland in Botswana and has represented them in petitions to District and Ministry agencies. In 1975–76, he served as consultant to the Rural Income Distribution Survey and, in 1981, wrote an analysis of "Remote Area" peoples for the National Migration Study which served as a source for the subsequent sixth National Development Plan for Botswana. He plans research on the rhetorical use of ethnography by Western societies, the ways in which this use contributes to the formation of public attitudes toward the "Third World," and consequent influences on policy. At the same time, he is assisting the Zhu and Herero in their aspirations to write their own histories.

Index

Designer	U.C. Press Staff
Compositor:	Auto-Graphics, Inc.
Text:	10/12 Palatino
Display:	Palatino
Printer:	Braun-Brumfield, Inc.
Binder:	Braun-Brumfield, Inc.